TYING

ROCKS

TO

CLOUDS

For those who need to know

Meetings and
conversations with:

Mother Teresa
Norman Vincent Peale
H. H. the Dalai Lama
B. F. Skinner
Elisabeth Kübler-Ross
Ram Dass
Stephen Levine
Jean Houston
Albert Ellis
Harold Kushner
Frances Vaughan
Robert Schuller
Jack Kornfield
Laura Huxley
Brother David Steindl-Rast
Swami Satchidananda
Pir Vilayat Khan
Rabbi Zalman Schachter-Shalomi
Jagir Singh
Toni Packer

TYING ROCKS TO CLOUDS

Meetings and Conversations with Wise and Spiritual People

WILLIAM ELLIOTT

QUEST BOOKS
The Theosophical Publishing House
Wheaton, IL U.S.A./Madras, India/London, England

The Theosophical Publishing House
P.O. Box 270
Wheaton, IL 60189-0270

A publication of the Theosophical Publishing House,
a department of the Theosophical Society in America.

*This publication made possible with
the assistance of the Kern Foundation*

Library of Congress Cataloging-in-Publication Data

Elliott, William, 1959–
    Tying rocks to clouds : meetings and conversations with
wise and spiritual people / William Elliott.
        p.   cm.
    Includes index.
    ISBN 0-8356-0708-9 (hardcover)
    ISBN 0-8356-0733-X (trade paperback)
    1. Spiritual life. 2. Interviews. 3. Elliott, William,
1959–   I. Title.
BL624.E45   1994   94-30371
2008.9282—dc20   CIP

9   8   7   6   5   4   3   2   1   *   95   96   97   98   99

ACKNOWLEDGMENTS

I would first like to thank Bonnie Milgrim, who always believed in me, who continues to teach me about relationship, and whose heart is as loving as any I have encountered.

I am indebted to my sister Diane who took me in after our parents died, and Mary, Liz, Jim, and Bopie, who are the greatest brothers and sisters in the world.

I am grateful to Roger Peasley, Mike Bernarde, Dave Durose, and Mark Sweet, who read my manuscript and gave compassionate criticism during our coffee house talks; my friends Andy Moore, Robin Daley, Kak Dorgan, Francis Wiebel, Henry Brockman, David Haskin, Rich Beilfuss, Jim Kramlinger, Libby Lunning, Jeff Kassel, Alison Einbender, Karen Kunz, Michelle Prentice, Steve Stein, Richard Ramsbotham, Mary Laird, Mickey Milgrim, Michelle Prentice, Atum O'Kane, Aziza Scott, Julie Genovese, Vince Kavaloski, Julie Alexander, and Shahabuddin Less, who helped my spirits in many ways these past years; and to the late Len Nagler, who had that spark of life in him and who said, "Bill, I see crap everyday, but what you are doing isn't crap."

Don Shmauz, a friend and therapist, and the Wednesday night group who nurtured my journey.

The S. N. Goenka Minnesota Vipassana group, Kopan Monastery, and the Sufi Order of the West.

My editor Brenda Rosen and John White who recognized the potential of this book together with my line editor Pamela White, assistant publications manager Jody Piro, and assistant editor Vija Bremanis.

Special thanks to Sharon Harbeck who helped edit my book in the beginning when it was still a dream and I didn't have a dime in my pocket.

George Cramer, an art teacher beyond the beyond.

Marilyn Ferguson gave me her time, support, and experience even though I have still never met her in person.

All the people in this book, who didn't have to give their time to me, but did, and thus my dream came true.

I accomplished this book because of what I was given. My mother gave me faith, vision, and the friendship of God. My father gave me the strength and ability to ruthlessly pursue truth. My brother Bopie gave me confidence when he xeroxed the first thing I ever wrote and handed it out to his officemates and proudly said, "My brother wrote this!"

CONTENTS

To tie a rock to a cloud—
is this possible?

And if it is,
does the cloud descend to meet the rock
or does the rock rise to meet the cloud?

INTRODUCTION

"It was God's will..."

That's what he said. That's what the priest said after my parents died: "It was God's will..." I was twelve years old, and I couldn't believe what I was hearing. And what I was hearing wasn't good enough.

That day I split in half, like an amoeba with two jobs to do: one to live life like any other kid; the other to find the meaning behind the death of those whom I loved. Pictures of Hiroshima after the bomb was dropped give an idea of the state of my soul at the time. Only there wasn't anyone left behind to take pictures.

I was the only one home when my mom died, so I did what I had seen the prayer groups do. I put my hands on her head and prayed. But there was no miracle in my hands that day, and they fell to my sides.

Six months before, my father had died. One minute he was talking. The next, he had a strange look on his face, he gurgled, and he walked back to his room. When my sister and I peeked into his room, he was already dead and blue. She and I argued over who was to get a neighbor. Realizing the absurdity of this, we did something even more absurd: We laughed. Hysterically. After squelching the horrible laughter with our hands, I realized something. My father was a tough Chicago cop, and this had been the first time I had ever seen him afraid.

My mother brought me up to look behind the appearances of things. When I was a small boy, she would take me to church early, very early, even before the priest arrived. She would take me behind the altar and into the darkly lit back room where the priest prepared for the mass. I remember the sense of wonder even now. I remember the shadows of those early mornings together and the feeling that we were somewhere we weren't supposed to be. I couldn't help feeling that I was seeing something I shouldn't see. Wide-eyed and open-mouthed, I looked around the room at every holy crevice, noticing the

1

organ pipes rising dramatically to the ceiling, as if to touch heaven with their majesty. My profound awe was interrupted by a sense of fear when I spotted the golden fringed robes framed by the morning's darkness. Oh no! I thought. I'm seeing the home of God before He put on his robes! As I emerged from that room, holding my mother's hand, I was filled with sacred, intimate wonder.

I never forgot the feeling my mother instilled in me that day—that, above all, God was our friend. I guess that's what made things so difficult later: How could a friend allow life to be so cruel?

I began a search for the meaning behind the workings of the world. I didn't understand why there should be such pain and suffering. Wherever I looked, no one had the answers I needed. I was angry, confused by what I saw around me. How could people live in a world with death and not ask about death and about life? I asked whomever I could about it. Often, this drew strange looks from the people I approached, as if they couldn't—or wouldn't—quite hear what I was asking. I could almost see their minds working to no effect, like a hand trying to grasp a cloud.

For years, I continued to look for answers. My search has culminated in this book. I began the book by making a list of people who I thought had answers. When I showed this list to my friends, two things happened.

First, most people told me that no one would answer my letters, that these famous people would never agree to meet with a "nobody" like me. One friend put it succinctly: "Bill," he said, "you live in a mobile home." When I told my professor about my idea, he tried to discourage me by saying that this was a project for an older man and that I should be working on my career.

Second, my friends reacted by recommending their own choices, their own heroes. Anybody who looked at my list saw someone who didn't belong. To make matters worse, they often suggested their uncle Harry or Cousin Norm. "Oh," they'd say, "my uncle Harry—he's really wise—interview him!"

After my list was made out, I borrowed a typewriter and composed, as sincerely as possible, a letter. Looking back on it, I'm amazed that anyone replied or accepted because I took that letter and copied it a few hundred times, typing in the names later. It looked terrible. It looked like one of those chain letters you get in the mail with your name pitifully typed in at the top. You usually don't even finish reading the thing before it's in the garbage.

Still, the replies trickled in, and they always started the same way.

Dear Mr. Elliott,
   Your project sounds fascinating . . . I want to read it when it's done . . . but I'm sorry . . . I don't have time. Sincerely, blah, blah, blah.

I wrote Leo Buscaglia twice. Nothing doing. I was desperate, so when I wrote him a third time I figured I would try "psychology" on him.

"The purpose of this book," I wrote, "is to help people, and as a *caring person* I would think that *you* would want to help people by being in it."

"There is not enough time," Leo Buscaglia replied. "As *you* are a *caring person*, I know you will accept my decision."

"I am not involved in spiritual pursuits," replied Isaac Asimov.

"It's more *truth* pursuits than *spiritual* pursuits," I countered.

"I wish I had time to share," he said, "but the *truth* is I don't."

When I wrote Richard Pryor, the comedian, for an interview on the meaning of life, he sent me an autographed picture of himself.

I received a reply from Virginia Satir's assistant saying Virginia had died a month before. A few days before she died she wrote, "To all my friends, colleagues, and family, I send you love. Please support me in my passage to a new life. I have no other way to thank you than this. You have all played a significant part in my development of loving. As a result, my life has been rich and full, so I leave feeling very grateful."

Marie-Louise von Franz, the famous Jungian analyst, sent a short and sad reply. "I am too old," she scrawled on a small sheet of paper, "and too ill to give interviews any longer."

I couldn't blame them. I was a nobody who couldn't even afford a decent typewriter . . . which brings up the question people often asked me: What were my credentials? My credentials were the wounds that had caused me to search in the first place.

At some time or other, everyone asks, "Why am I here?" often in the midst of a difficult time. When I asked this question, I felt as if there was no place to look. No one seemed to be able to tell me, and I didn't know where to start. Through persistence and luck, I began to find some answers. I thought that there should be a book with these answers so that others could benefit.

With this in mind, I organized my life around doing this book. I needed money in order to travel, so I sold my blood for lab experiments. I took a job working as a counselor with the chronically mentally ill, most of whom have schizophrenia, in order to work in a helping profession, but also because the graveyard shift allowed me time to work on my book. I bought a mobile home and have lived as inexpensively as possible for the last six years in order to pay for my travel expenses. Even so, I am still paying off the debt incurred from doing this book. I am telling you this, not because I think I made a great sacrifice for a noble cause, but to tell you the extent of the desperation that fueled this book. My friend Eight-finger Eddy said it best: "If you're searching, you mustn't be happy." And I wasn't. I had to do this book in order to go on living. These were my real credentials. This, in turn, will tell you the "how" of how I was able to do the book: All along, I have been motivated and inspired.

Although the letter I sent out requesting interviews looked unprofessional, the sincerity of the request came through. People replied positively, and I went. Occasionally, they were a little surprised that they had made an appointment with someone who had no credentials.

After I waited in Robert Schuller's office for thirty minutes, he came out and asked, "Who are you?"

"Bill Elliott."

"No, who are you with?"

"I'm by myself."

"No," he said, frustrated, "what magazine or publisher are you with?"

"I'm doing this by myself."

He then scrunched up his face, and I got the impression he was a little upset about setting up time with a nobody.

This happened several times. Still, people ask, how did you get in to meet these people? Perhaps I was naive. I thought it was a good idea, and I couldn't see why they wouldn't do it.

Joseph Campbell said, "If you follow your bliss, doors will open for you that wouldn't have opened for anyone else." That is the how.

Talking about the meaning of life is difficult. Some of the people I contacted declined interviews because words fall short of the true experience of life. Those interviewed deserve respect. They took the risk of being wrong, but it is worth taking this risk because it is possible to convey an important understanding when words are used well.

4

Words are symbols, and these symbols have the power to convey the meaning behind them. And meaning changes lives.

Rabbi Zalman Schachter-Shalomi explained it this way: "Where the infinite exists, there is nothing else. We are absorbed in that, and we don't quite exist. Where we exist, our connection with the infinite is made by a root metaphor or a name, a word. That is the interface that connects us beings caught in time and space with the infinite.

"We no longer have the Holy Temple in Jerusalem, but when we had the temple in Jerusalem, the holiest person on the holiest day at the holiest time in the holiest place would pronounce the holiest word—and this is the connection..."

Perhaps a few holy words are spoken within these pages. If they are read at the right time and on the holiest of days (which may just be today), each of us may become, for a moment, a holy man or woman, connected to the infinite.

This book originally was designed to be a compilation of interviews and nothing else. I wanted to involve myself as little as possible—to get in and get out. I told Ram Dass over a year ago that the book would be easy because all I had to do were a few interviews and transcribe them, and then it would be done.

"That's what you think!" he answered.

Pir Vilayat Khan's secretary had warned me, "You don't know what you've gotten yourself into by interviewing Pir Vilayat."

"Well," I said in jest, "Pir Vilayat doesn't know what he has gotten himself into by letting me interview him."

"Oh yes, he does," she said with a wry smile.

Well, maybe he did, but I didn't. I expected the book to be a neat little experience—doing the interviews and transcribing. There also was an inner experience, however, which engaged me, and I had to engage it.

This book welled up inside of me from my deepest soul, from my blood and bone, as though, by its creation, it was actually taking something that was essential to me, and from me. Signing an agreement with Pir Vilayat Khan, I remarked on the red ink, that it was like signing in my own blood.

"If you have sinned," he said, "you have to make your absolutions in your own blood." And then he giggled—probably because it was my blood and not his.

As I proceeded, I knew what he meant. My feelings were the blood, giving life and warmth to the book, and my deep determination gave it structure and strength. Together they expressed my innermost heart and wishes. I thought I was creating a book to give to other people, to help other people, but it was more than that. Under the pretense of benefiting others, I was tricked into facing my innermost self, into healing myself. My friend George had warned me: "Sounds like you're on a white horse, but remember, the white horse shits, too." It wasn't just other people who needed this book—it was me.

On my way to Nepal in 1985, I stopped in California and went to a party. There, I met an older man whom I recognized as Bill Macy, the actor who was Maude's husband on the television show "Maude." He looked older than I remembered from the show, but he also looked wiser. I walked up to him and asked him something in a way that I thought he could take seriously or not. "So, you've been around a little longer than I," I said. "What have you learned in life?"

He looked at me closely, an eternity it seemed, while he decided where I was coming from. Then he grabbed my arm. "Come over here," he said. "Follow me." He led me into the kitchen, where he promptly told me everything he had ever learned in life for the next few hours. He also told me about myself.

"Wherever you go," he said, "you will never have any problem."

"Why is that?"

"Because you're nonthreatening." Years before, I would have taken that as an insult. Now, I accepted it. "You're very inquisitive," he said. "If you look closely, you will see that the *answer* is in the *question*."

Now I realize that I was the question. These answers gave me the courage to step back into a life I had found terrifying and painful. When a certain answer felt right, it accomplished its aim: it made me feel. This gave me the companion I had so dearly needed—feeling. Feeling the sincerity and love in the answers I got allowed me to feel those answers inside myself, in my heart. Now I had a framework of understanding that gradually would allow me to accept my whole self. *I could face the worst in myself, knowing the best.*

The book branched into two experiences: the actual compilation of the questions and answers, and what was happening to me while I made the compilation. My friend George told me, "Finish what you start." I'm glad he told me that, because the person who started the quest and the book is no longer around. He's changed.

When I was seventeen years old, I beat my big brother in arm wrestling for the first time. Afterward, I walked back to my room, shut the door, and cried. While writing this book, I became disillusioned.

The people I met had been my heroes. They weren't like me; they were something more.

After I returned from one interview, someone said, "You interviewed her! I think she's the wisest person I ever met!" Although this may be true, what I remembered most about the interview was that this person had done a very ordinary thing. She enjoyed gossiping about the love lives of her friends. "Oh, really! That's whom she's seeing? . . . Whatever happened to so-and-so? . . . Oh, *really*."

So, I've seen a different side of these "spiritual heroes," but I want to make it clear that any stories about their ordinariness are not meant to ridicule them at all. To the contrary, if there is one thing I have learned, it is that they *are* ordinary. That's what makes them so extraordinary. In the beginning I was awestruck that such people exist. Then I realized they are human, just like me—with faults and everything else—I mean, each one of them has a toilet at their house. Elisabeth Kübler-Ross even has a sign in her bathroom that reads, "If it's yellow, let it mellow. If it's brown, flush it down." You can never look at your heroes the same way after you read something like that. One person even had a document shredder in his bathroom. I didn't know—was I was supposed to put the toilet paper in there, or what?

When I realized they weren't gods incarnate, or fundamentally different from me, I felt let down. I was disillusioned. Then two things dawned on me. First of all, disillusionment is a good thing. Because of it, I can see what is real in me and around me. Second, even though the people I interviewed are just human beings, they are exceptional human beings. Since I am a human being, I can be like them. They are extraordinary people, *extra*-ordinary. It's ironic. People think of something extraordinary as being bigger than normal—greater, somehow. But *extra*-ordinary is just that: very, very ordinary—so ordinary that if they lived next door, you wouldn't notice them.

About a year ago I went to see Teresa, an old friend of my mother's. I hadn't seen her since my mother died eighteen years ago. I asked Teresa to tell me about my mother. What was she like? Was she a good friend? I wanted to know my mother as a real person, not as some shadowy mythological figure.

"I remember when I first met your mother," she said. "At one time she had a nervous breakdown. After she recovered, she became a counselor at a center for people who had nervous breakdowns. That's where I met her. She really helped me. She was also a beautician, you know—and she had very bad eyes. One time she didn't have her glasses on and she sprayed spray paint on someone's hair instead of hair spray!" She laughed. "Another time she put corn flakes in the bathtub instead of soap flakes! But your mother was a good soul. The one thing I will always remember her saying is, 'Stay small.' No matter who you are, you have to stay small. Not in an insecure kind of way, but in a humble way."

In the process of believing that my heroes were better than I was, I had done violence to myself. Ram Dass told me, "Don't do violent spiritual practices." That's what I had done. I had been exalting my heroes while trashing myself. They were on a pedestal while I unconsciously thought of myself as not good enough.

I sincerely believe, however, that my heroes want me to come up on the pedestal with them—to exalt what a human can be—then to toss that pedestal aside so that we can walk on the earth side by side, as equals. Norman Vincent Peale gave me such a lift after our interview. "You're a good interviewer!" he said. Then he turned to his wife. "Isn't he a good interviewer?"

"Yes. I heard him—he's a good interviewer!"

That's positive thinking.

I traveled a lot while writing *Tying Rocks to Clouds* because I wanted to meet each interviewee personally. I wanted to take advantage of the meeting of minds or souls that happens when two people meet. I anticipated learning a tremendous amount from those meetings, but I hadn't counted on being taught by the journey that connected them all. The experiences and stories that coincided with these meetings often taught me more than the meetings themselves. These stories and events reinforced the notion that reality is stranger and more powerful than any fiction. They're stories of insight, experiences of the ridiculous and absurd, that made me want to look around in the middle of their happening and ask, Is this for real, or what?

When I was in Oregon to interview one person, I was stopped for speeding by a state trooper. As he approached my car, his overall demeanor and walk reminded me of John Wayne's. He kind of leaned on my door, rubbed his chin for a second, and said, "You were speeding. Do you know how fast you were going?"

"No, I have no idea. I was just, you know, watching for my turnoff."

"Well, you were bombin' away goin' seventy-four!"

"I really didn't realize—I was just trying to get my turnoff."

"Well, can I see your license?" he said, as he tugged at his belt.

"Sure." I gave it to him.

"So, Mr. Elliott, what're you doin' in Oregon? Are you traveling? Vacationing?"

(Then I had an idea ... maybe if I mentioned I was doing a book on the meaning of life, he'd let me go.)

"Sort of," I said with a little hesitancy. "I'm writing a book on, well, you know ... the meaning of life ..."

He just looked at me, no reaction. Nothing. Then he walked back to his car. He was back there for awhile, and I thought he was writing me a ticket. If I couldn't get out of the ticket, maybe I could get it lowered, somehow, because nineteen miles over the speed limit— that was going to cost a lot. Or maybe if I told him that my dad was a cop, that my brother is one, maybe ...

"Mr. Elliott," he said.

"Yeah?" I said, expecting the worst.

"Mr. Elliott, the purpose of life is to survive it!" He burst out laughing, and laughing, and laughing. While he laughed, he slapped his knee. He stopped long enough to hand me my license, and he laughed some more. He was half-doubled over from laughter—barely able to walk away. He wasn't giving me a ticket. I leaned out my window and called to him, "You're gonna be in my book!" That just about killed him. So this book is more than just interviews—it's the journey.

I tried to ask the questions we all ask, questions that would, I hoped, fill in some of the blank spaces about the whys. Perhaps more importantly, I also asked questions that would reveal to each of us the hows. How do I eventually find the answers I need within myself? How do I find meaning for myself, instead of having to be told what the meaning is? Ultimately, I hoped to give spiritual seekers a greater independence through asking questions, and not unwittingly encourage people's dependence on another for answers.

I began the interviewing process a few years ago. I had only fifteen questions then. As I grew and realized some of the problems posed by these questions, the number of questions increased.

My own spiritual search included many presumptions and fantasies I had about wise and spiritual people. When I realized they aren't above getting angry or sad, or that they aren't fundamentally different from me, I added some simpler and more down-to-earth questions, such as "What makes you angry or sad?" I asked about relationships because not many people want to be a monk like Buddha or an unmarried messiah like Jesus. Life is relationship, so what are the benefits and wisdom that can be gained from being in a relationship? Increasingly, spiritual growth seems to call the individual to social action, social justice, and nonviolent change. Consequently, I asked, "What are the three greatest problems in life?"

I tried to ask the same set of questions to each person interviewed in order to compare responses, except that I added a few questions after having completed some interviews. I've edited the interviews as little as possible but have made some adjustments to the continual question-answer format so that the interviews are more readable.

On what main beliefs (or truths) do you base your life?
Do you believe in a God or Ultimate Reality? What is It like?
What is the purpose of life?
What is the highest ideal that a person can reach?
How is this ideal attained?
What is the greatest obstacle to obtaining this ideal?
Will all people eventually reach this ideal?
What do you think of death? What is it? What continues after death?
Why is there suffering? Why is there evil? What is its cause?
Do all religions lead to the same place?
If you could change anything in life, what would you change?
If you were on your deathbed, what advice would you give to your son or daughter?
If you could meet anyone throughout history, whom would you meet and what would you ask that person?
What was the most significant thing that ever happened to you and that affected your life the most? What did it teach you?
Some people think personal relationships interfere with spiritual growth. What do you think?
What is important to you?
What makes you happy? sad? angry?
What do you feel is something life still has to teach you?
What is the most important thing you have learned in life?
What are the three greatest problems in life?
Why are you doing what you are doing?
Do you feel there is a basic difference between maleness and femaleness, besides the body?
What is your core practice?
What made you approach life in this way?

1

MY GRANDMA TOLD STORIES

When I was seven years old, my mother was going to Florida to visit my grandmother. I begged her to take me with her. "I'll take you, but remember," my mother warned me, "Grandma is sick."

I had seen plenty of sick people before, so I figured it wouldn't be a big deal. Besides, by the time we got to Florida, my grandma would probably be okay. Then we would have fun just as we used to. I remembered how important I had felt the summer before when my grandma carried me on her shoulders down the streets of St. Petersburg.

My mother and I took the train to Florida. She brought a bag of cherries along with us. It was a huge bag, but instead of giving me a handful to eat, she gave me the whole bag to hold. After I ate my first handful, I looked at her, but she didn't say anything. Although she sat next to me, she seemed faraway, immersed in her own thoughts, as she vaguely looked out the window. I took another handful, and still she didn't say anything. She didn't even notice. My mom let me eat all the cherries I wanted, but when I looked down at my new shirt and discovered cherry stains on it, I was afraid I'd get in trouble. When I told my mom, she said it was okay, and she patiently wiped at the stains with a cold, wet rag.

We took a cab from the train station to my grandma's house. I got more and more excited as we approached. Grandma was a great storyteller, and her stories made me feel special whenever she told them.

"Grandma, tell me a story," I'd ask, and she would always begin the story, "Once upon a time there was a boy named Billy..." Every story started with a boy named after me. When I arrived at her house, my first words were going to be, "Grandma, tell me a story."

When I got to Grandma's house, she didn't come out to meet me. Even after I ran up the steps, she still didn't come to meet me. I went into her bedroom. In a moment, I was changed forever, because what I saw in that room wasn't my happy-go-lucky grandmother. It was a crumpled body, thin and drawn.

That night as I lay in bed, I heard my grandma moaning in pain. It had the same effect on me as someone running fingernails across the blackboard. I just wanted it to stop. It continued all night.

The next morning, I asked my mom if I could leave because it hurt too much to see Grandma that sick. She sent me home that afternoon on the plane. A few weeks later, my mother came home and asked me if it was all right if Grandma came to live with us. I said yes, but in reality I never wanted to see my grandmother again.

Although my grandma lived with us for the next few months, I never went into her room. She couldn't get out of bed. I didn't have to see her. Every so often, when I walked past her room, I could see her with her back turned toward me. Sometimes her backside showed from under her nightgown, and I saw how wrinkled it looked, with her back and bony pelvis showing through her hanging skin. I felt ashamed because I didn't think I should see this side of my grandmother.

One day, my grandma called to me as I walked by her room. I didn't want to go. Her voice struck an intimate and familiar cord inside me. It was a voice I couldn't disappoint. I followed the voice as though in a daze. In her room, I didn't look at her. I just looked at the floor and told myself that this wasn't my grandmother—it just couldn't be.

I was about to run out of the room and leave it forever when she spoke: "Once upon a time there was a boy named Billy..." I followed her words to that place beyond words and crumpled bodies, to that place of recognition and recollection: "...and little Billy loved his grandma very much..." I raised my head and looked at my grandmother. Although her crumpled and dying body hadn't changed, I could now see behind her appearance. I went into her room every day after that until she died, and every day she told me another story about a boy named Billy.

2

GOING EAST

My brother Jim is a Chicago cop. On the day I left for Nepal, he said, "You know, Bill, people ask me what you're doing with your life. They want to know why you're going to Nepal." Jim seemed confused and shrugged his shoulders.

"Well," I asked, "what do you tell them?"

"I tell them I don't know what the hell you're doing," Jim answered.

I went to Nepal in 1985 to find the meaning of life. I was told there are answers in the East that are unknown in the West.

Years before when I was depressed and life seemed meaningless, my brother said, "Bill, just find a woman and get her pregnant. You'll be fine."

My questions became a fieldwork project for the University of Wisconsin-Madison, in which I asked the "eleven wisest people" in the Katmandu Valley of Nepal philosophical questions about the meaning of life.

One day, while patrolling the streets of Chicago with my brother, I turned to him in the car and asked if he ever thought about the meaning of life.

"Bill, I'm not that deep." Then he continued: "When I come home from work and open the door, my kid is standing there, and he says, 'Daddy!' I'm not sure what it means, but that's all I need."

"But," I asked incredulously, "don't you ever think about dying? Or what happens after?"

He turned to me, hands animated, as taken aback by my thinking as I was by his. "Listen, I've seen lots of dead bodies. One moment they're talking about their family and how their wife is gonna kill them for getting in a knife fight or shot, and the next moment they're nothing but a piece of meat!" To emphasize his point, he repeated, "One moment they're alive; the next moment they're nothing but a piece of meat!"

It was easy finding the wisest people in Katmandu: I just asked at the local temple. One of these "wise" people was a Sikh named Jagir Singh.

Each morning when I arrived with my list of questions, Jagir Singh said, "Tomorrow, Mr. Bill. I will answer your questions tomorrow. Today, we will have some tea." This went on for months, but I didn't mind the delay because I was growing fond of Jagir Singh. Besides, he had the best tea in town.

Jagir Singh liked me to visit in the morning. It was also at this time that the townspeople made their visits. They came before ten o'clock because they believed Jagir Singh was no longer psychic after ten o'clock. He was considered to be a great mystic who healed people with magic mantras and herbal concoctions. Jagir Singh was, as they say, a Guru.

He enjoyed my visits, and whenever a visitor dropped by, Jagir Singh fondly referred to me as "Mr. Bill, who is writing a book." I told him my correct name and told him I wasn't writing a book, but he insisted. I didn't mind because I liked the way he said "Mr. Bill."

One day he turned to me and said, "Mr. Bill, did you notice anything different about me yesterday?"

"No, I didn't."

"Mr. Bill," he whispered, as he leaned over closer and looked into my eyes, "you could have asked me anything yesterday and I could have told you the answer."

"What do you mean?"

"Every once in a while something happens to me, something comes into me, and I can answer any question," he said. "Yesterday was like that."

Every few years in Nepal, there is a special spiritual celebration called the Kumbamela. All the yogis who have been meditating in caves and hiding out in the mountains come to this festival. I figured there might be someone there who would know something.

As I approached the main temple, a yogi stopped me. "What do you expect to find here?" he asked.

I told him I didn't know, but then I mumbled something about the Truth. We smiled at each other, and he walked off.

The gathering took place outside a Hindu temple. Off to the left, there were a bunch of naked yogis purifying themselves in a river. When a friend of mine stepped into this same river, his feet swelled, doubling in size, because the water was so polluted.

I heard that the famous "milk yogi" had come to the celebration. He had lived on nothing but milk for twenty years. Another yogi, whom I almost stepped on, had no arms and lay on his back. He had only one leg, which he used to push himself around the streets of Nepal. The funniest thing was that he had a bright green parrot sitting on his chest. This made him one of the most popular attractions to Westerners.

The "Agari babas" were also there. *Agari* means "eat anything," and their spiritual practice is to eat anything—even the insides of fish, cow dung, and parts of dead people. A yogi I regularly saw around town was there as well. He wore long orange robes, carried a staff and metal pot, and had a three-foot-long rosary around his neck that was made of seeds the size of walnuts. He was always asking me for money—but I stopped contributing when I realized he was always drunk.

In one area where a crowd was gathering, I pushed through in order to get a closer look. It was "yogi alley." There were about a dozen of the most intense-looking guys I've ever seen. One was standing on one leg; his other leg was terribly withered and bent at such an angle that the foot rested against the standing leg. I was told he had been standing like this for twelve years as an "austerity" spiritual practice. The logic is that the body or flesh tends to rule one's soul and is partly responsible for our separation from the divine. Therefore, a yogi takes on this uncomfortable pose and welcomes the physical pain, hoping to overcome any attachment to physical pain and thereby overcome the body's hold over the soul.

Another yogi had both legs wrapped around his head. They, too, were so withered from disuse, he couldn't stand on them if he wanted to. As I said, these yogis had really intense eyes, but who wouldn't look intense with legs wrapped around the head? It was ironic: When people are spiritually lost, their psyches are mangled and tied up in knots, so to speak, so then they mangle and tie their bodies into knots in order to straighten out their psyches.

I pulled out my camera when I got to the most intense yogi. He had no legs and one arm, he was covered with ashes, and there was a trident next to him. He was a Shiva devotee. Shiva is the God of destruction. I asked him if I could take a picture. He agreed. Then he looked at me with those intense eyes and said, "Bombay." That was interesting because I was leaving for Bombay the next day. I took a few more pictures that day and some more on my way to Bombay. I finished off the roll of film in Bombay and had the negatives developed. The only pictures that turned out were the few I took before I saw that yogi in Nepal and the pictures I took after arriving in Bombay. When I looked at the negatives, it looked as if they had been burned.

While I was in Nepal, I stayed at a Tibetan Buddhist monastery. The founder of the monastery, Lama Yeshe, died before I could meet him, but I was curious about him because he had a gap between his front teeth—as I did.

I first came across Tibetan Buddhism at the University of Wisconsin. To my surprise, there was a real Tibetan lama who taught in the Buddhist Studies department there. His name was Geshe Sopa. I took a few of his courses, and although he was nice enough, I never thought he was that wise or that special. There are stories about yogis who live in the cold temperatures of the Himalayas and need no clothes because they are adept at something called the yoga of inner heat, or Tummo. Since Geshe Sopa always wore a hat and a coat in the winter, I figured he didn't know that much.

In one of Geshe Sopa's classes, I sat next to a guy who was a strict vegetarian. Once when he saw the lama drinking coffee, he said, "You would think he'd be enlightened enough not to drink that stuff!" During class the vegetarian would chew wheatgrass, just like a cow. On the last class day, we had a potluck. When the lama brought something that looked like little hamburgers, the vegetarian just about died.

So when I went to Nepal and ended up in this monastery halfway around the world, I looked up on the wall in the monastery library one day and what did I see? A portrait of Geshe Sopa. "Hey, I know that guy," I said to a monk standing next to me.

"Geshe Sopa," replied the monk reverently, "was the teacher of the lamas who started this monastery."

Later that day, I was reading a book by Thomas Merton, the famous Christian monk. In the book, he asked the Dalai Lama to teach him the highest meditation practice. I paid close attention, because since it was the highest practice, of course I wanted to learn it—that's what I came to Nepal for. But the Dalai Lama told Thomas Merton that he didn't have time, so he recommended another lama—Geshe Sopa.

At dinner, I sat across from an older monk. "You know," I said, "there was this old guy named Geshe Sopa where I went to school..."

"Geshe Sopa!" the monk exclaimed, looking up from his bowl. "Geshe Sopa is a Buddha! Everybody knows that!"

At the monastery, I was taught "the graduated path to enlightenment," which we were told could take thousands of lifetimes. A German monk later told us, however, that if a person studies Tantric Buddhism, he or she can get enlightened in only three years. It didn't take a genius to figure out that the Tantric stuff was a better deal. Since I was only twenty-six years old, I figured that if I practiced for three, maybe four years, I'd be enlightened and still be only thirty years old. That would beat Jesus (who was pretty enlightened by age thirty-three) by three years and the Buddha by five years.

After I found out that Tantra was the "accelerated path," I was hooked. I was told a person had to be initiated into Tantric Buddhism by a teacher. Two days later, I was informed that a high lama would be giving initiations in two weeks, but I was also told that I was too new to the Tibetan practices to be allowed access. After all, some of the monks had been practicing Buddhism for years and still had not attended Tantric initiations. Then a woman told me I should ask the lama myself. "After all," she said, "no one but the lama knows what is really in your heart."

The next day I found myself climbing the stairs to his residence. I tried to anticipate the lama's response. Would he berate me for being pretentious and egotistical? Maybe he would just laugh at me.

With eyes closed, the lama meditated to himself. "Yes, I think it is okay," he finally said, "but you need to deepen your compassion for other people." As he said this, he pointed at me, and his finger moved in a circular fashion. The room began to move slightly, and I entered into an altered state as I watched the rhythmic motion of his hand. He stopped when a young monk entered with two cups of tea. I left his quarters with a big smile and an intoxicated feeling.

I was a newcomer to the Tibetan scene. I would sit for hours and listen to mystical stories. "One time," a woman began, "a lady tried to tell the lama her problem, and she thought he didn't understand her. 'Don't worry, dear,' said the lama, 'I can read your mind.'"

"In his last lifetime," one monk said, "the lama of this monastery meditated in a cave for twenty years."

"There was a lama who had intestinal worms," one ex-movie director said, "but he refused medicine because he didn't want to harm the worms."

Whenever we ate meals outdoors at the monastery, we had to watch for hawks. Residents at the monastery were taught nonviolence to all creatures. The hawks seemed to know this because they would swoop down out of the sky and grab the food off our plates.

Buddhists teach reincarnation, the notion of living many lifetimes. If one accumulates good karma, one will be born into a better situation next life. When I told the man next to me that I wanted to be enlightened in this lifetime, he looked at me with despair and said, "I'm just hoping for a better rebirth."

One day a monk named Pende motioned to me to come to his room. He was trying not to be conspicuous. Pende was born in Chicago and had gone to the same college in Whitewater, Wisconsin, that I had. He was a senior monk and was being trained to be a lama. Once I was inside his room, he shut the door and then reached under his mattress. He pulled out three magazines. They were *Sports Illustrated*. They all had articles about the Chicago Bears, who would go on to win the Super Bowl that year.

"The Bears are killing everybody," the monk said excitedly. "Here, read this," he said, handing me a magazine, "about where Steve McMichael pinned his football award to his bare chest!"

"He stuck the pin into his chest?" I asked, rubbing my chest and feeling the imaginary sting of the pin.

"Right through the skin!" Pende said, admiring the sheer audacity of such an act. Pende had played football while he was in college, and he still had arms the size of my legs. He also showed me a stack of newspapers that contained the NFL box scores.

"Every Monday," he said mischievously, "I send one of the young monks into the village in order to get me the *International Herald*. That way I can see if the Bears won."

After that day, I paid Pende a visit every Monday, and we'd read the highlights from Sunday's game and talk football until it was time for the afternoon meditations.

The initiations went on for a few days. After they were finished, we began the spiritual practice connected with the initiation. A couple of days into the practice, I experienced a tremendous amount of energy. My whole body felt extra-alive. My surroundings took on a brighter and more distinctive look. Trees and bushes had a halolike light emanating from them. I was ecstatic, which increased my intensity in doing my spiritual practice. I was sure I was on to something.

The next day, however, my stomach exploded, and I became horribly ill. I was sore from head to toe. I was too weak to get out of bed, and even lying down was painful for my body. I was nauseous and had diarrhea for ten days. I'd wake up in the middle of the night and realize I was still saying my mantra or repetitive prayers even while I slept. Finally, I had to force myself to stop saying the mantras because they seemed to be making me weaker. By the time my sickness left me, I weighed only 135 pounds at a height of five feet eleven inches. Even today, my stomach is still distended.

After two weeks, I attended more initiations and then went to India. The Dalai Lama was giving an important initiation in Bodhgaya, India. Bodhgaya is famous because the Buddha got enlightened there.

I traveled by bus to Bodhgaya and slept while we sped along a dirt road from one village to the next. I was awakened from my slumber by a loud thump on the side of the bus. As the bus continued, the passengers looked out the windows and quietly commented among themselves. When I inquired about what took place, I was told that the bus had hit a pedestrian and probably killed him. The bus driver didn't stop, though, because the local people would have pulled him out of the bus and beat him to death.

On the bus to Bodhgaya, I met an attractive Tibetan woman named Tsella and her friend, a New Zealand Tibetan nun. Whenever Tsella and I talked, the New Zealand Tibetan nun looked out the window and kept muttering something about lust.

One dry, dusty morning a few days later, Tsella and I set out for a holy cave that was up on a hill north of Bodhgaya. After we rode in a rickshaw to the base of the hill, we had a three-mile walk up the hill to the cave where a magical Tibetan lama had once lived. For the last mile and a half, there were beggars along the side of the path, and most of them were horribly mutilated. I was told that some of the beggars had even cut off their own limbs so that they would be more successful beggars. There were so many of them I had to get coins in order to give money to each person. The oddest thing was that there was a man who sold change. He gave you ninety pisa in coins for each rupee, which is ninety cents on the dollar. I didn't have any choice in the matter, and the glint in his eye let me know that he knew I had no choice.

We made it to the cave, which was less spectacular than I expected, but there was an experience worth noting. Off to the side of the cave was a stone slab. In India, the bodies of the dead are sometimes cut up and the pieces left for animals and birds to eat. This was the stone slab on which they did the dismemberment. When business was slow, the man who did the cutting would perform a special ritual. For one rupee, I lay down on the stone slab, and while he stood over me, he made ritual cutting motions across my torso and limbs as though I were a dead body. Then he motioned for me to sit up, and he explained that I would live a long life. When I asked him how he knew that, he said that the gods saw him slicing me up, and now the gods thought I was dead, so they crossed me off their list, and because of that, death will never come looking for me.

There were 250,000 Tibetans and a handful of Westerners present at the initiation in Bodhgaya. The Dalai Lama is known for his compassion, so it was ironic to see Westerners fighting among themselves as to who would sit closest to him. "I want to get some of his energy," one zealot screamed. One woman refused to move from a seat that was very close to the Dalai Lama, so another woman sat on her until she did. Even the Italian monks were bickering. "These rows in front are for the Western monks," they said, implying that monks had some kind of spiritual priority. Although all the Western monks wore the same-colored robes, one could always tell which were Italian: they were the ones with the designer sunglasses.

On New Year's Eve, the Westerners threw a party. A little before midnight, I left the party and walked to a Buddhist temple. Outside the temple was a bodhi tree that grew out of a cutting from the original bodhi tree, under which the Buddha got enlightened. The original bodhi tree died because devotees had stripped it of leaves in their desire to have religious souvenirs. The monks at this temple took no chances. The bodhi tree was surrounded by an eight-foot fence, and the gate was padlocked.

It was dark, and there were few people out. I climbed the fence with what I thought to be an original idea—to welcome the new year by meditating under the Buddha's bodhi tree—but I found that two other Westerners were already there. I meditated under the tree with dreams of grandeur. Sometime after midnight, I opened my eyes and accepted the fact that that night would not be the night I got enlightened. It was cold, and I walked home in the dark.

The Dalai Lama is considered by some people to be a manifestation of the quality of compassion. Another lama there was considered the manifestation of wisdom. I was told he was giving initiations that were critical to attaining enlightenment in a short time. After he initiated our group into Tantric practice, he asked us to take a vow. This vow consisted in saying a mantra, a short prayer, a number of times each day for the rest of our lives. The sound of the mantra, along with the motivation behind the recitation of the mantra, changes the consciousness of the person who repeats it.

The lama approached the members of the group and asked them to make a commitment as to how many mantras a day they would say. As he came nearer to me, I heard the pledges of others. One woman said, "Two hundred mantras a day." The man behind her said, "One hundred mantras." The bliss-filled woman seated in front of me said, "Five hundred mantras." As each person said their number, the lama gently smiled.

"One mantra," I said softly. Some people laughed; others just looked disgusted.

"One?" asked the lama.

I paused and thought to myself. "One mantra," I repeated.

The lama looked at me with a big smile. It has been seven years since I made that promise, and I've kept it ever since.

After two weeks, all the initiations were over. I packed up and walked to my bus. On the way, Tibetan children stopped me in order to feel the hair on my forearms—which apparently is something they hadn't seen before.

A Tibetan man approached me as I boarded the bus back to Nepal. "See," he said, pointing to the occupants of the bus. "They are all mountain people and do not know the ways of the world. Will you look after them on your way back to Nepal?"

The bus was filled, and they were mountain people all right. They looked dirty and dusty, but they were the sweetest-looking people I had ever seen. They looked exactly like the pictures of American Indians from a hundred years ago. I agreed to watch over the Tibetans during the bus ride but declined their offers of sampa, which is a mixture of barley flour and butter beaten to a hard, flat consistency. I couldn't speak Tibetan, so the Tibetans and I just smiled at each other for the next thirty-six hours.

During the bus ride, I wrote friends back home and told them I planned to go up north into the Himalayas and perfect my meditative ability. I'd had enough with this regular living stuff. I wanted to be enlightened, and this meant finding a path and a teacher.

At the monastery in Nepal, with a group of Westerners I was taught different kinds of Tibetan meditation. Once, a German monk named Dieter was telling us to visualize breathing in white light and breathing out black smoke. The room was quiet, and I had my eyes closed in concentration. Suddenly, a voice broke the silence. "Dieter!" said a cockney in an angry tone. "How am I supposed to imagine inhaling white light through my nostrils, when all I smell is some bloke in the back row here expelling gas?"

Giggles erupted from my fellow meditators at the blunt choice of words, compounded by a ridiculous cockney accent. "I'm serious," Chris Carney continued. "Somebody back here is a foul-smelling pig!"

I turned and looked back at Chris. He was an intimidating, muscular fellow with a shaved head. I recognized the man sitting next to Chris as the guy who had had stomach disorders since coming to the monastery. His head was bent forward, and he stared blankly at the floor with a mixture of fear and embarrassment. If he didn't find a way to deal with his gas problem—I'm sure he thought Chris would pummel it out of him.

I respected Chris after this. He was a breath of fresh air in the monastery. The monastery was a place where emotions and passion were judged as inferior states of mind. If a Westerner showed anger, well then, he was obviously very unevolved and unenlightened. But if a lama showed anger, he was expressing a "wrathful" aspect of an enlightened nature. His anger was all right, while ours was a manifestation of ignorance. Chris's vitality and realness were a relief.

Chris took to monastic life like a drowning man to a life preserver. After a month, he quickly decided to become a monk.

"Bill, come here," Chris yelled to me across the monastery courtyard one sunny afternoon. "I have to show you something."

I followed him to his room, which was on the side of the monastery that didn't get much light. In the corner of his room, to the right of his desk and chair, was a trunk. My eyes struggled to see in the dim light as Chris knelt down and opened the trunk.

"Aren't they beautiful," Chris said, admiring his new burgundy and gold Buddhist robes. He stood transfixed, seeing something more than simple monk robes.

"Yes, they're beautiful," I agreed, but I don't think he heard me.

"They're beautiful," he repeated to himself.

Chris was still staring at his robes when I left his room and the shadows cast by the monastery.

Chris and I had a routine that we followed every week. Before lunch, we'd sneak away from the monastery and hike down the hill into a small village, where we stuffed ourselves with pancakes, eggs, and coffee. We were both rapidly losing weight at the monastery, so before we left the restaurant, we'd fill our backpacks with enough food to last us till it was time to make another trip the following week.

Eventually, I traveled with Chris to Bodhgaya, where he took his ordination with the Dalai Lama. The last night Chris and I were together, we ate at an Indian-Chinese restaurant. Restaurants in Bodhgaya bear no resemblance to anything in the States. The restaurant was just a large, old, dusty tent with dirt floors. The kitchen was separated from where we were seated by a hanging blanket. I suppose if I were to give it some thought, I would feel grateful toward that blanket for not allowing us to see the conditions in which the food was prepared.

Chris and I were seated across from each other in two old and creaking chairs. Chris was solemn, and it was apparent that he was somewhere else, remembering a different time and place. The glow of the candle that stood between us enveloped us with its womblike intimacy. Chris momentarily snapped out of his recollecting trance and slapped his hand on the table. "This is the life for me," he said, assuring me that he was without those doubting demons that pursue us all. "I've had all that *that* life can give," he announced, dismissing it with a wave of his hand. But the sadness and despair he tried to push away at that moment still hovered around him. Slowly, before my eyes, Chris was again pulled back into the past.

"I was working on an oil rig in the North Sea," Chris recounted gravely. "I'd be away for a month, or more, at a time. I had a wife, two little girls, and a nice house. I had everything a man could want... One day, I returned after a month at sea. My wife, my kids, and the furniture were all gone. She'd found another man..." Holding back the sobs, Chris repeated, "I've had enough of *that* life, Bill—being a monk is the life for me."

Chris and I parted company in India. A few months later, I heard that he had given up his Tibetan robes and was back out in the North Sea, drilling for oil.

One day, while I walked the streets of Kathmandu, Nepal, I saw an old man wearing a long flowing white robe and carrying a staff. He had a long white beard and a balding head. He looked wise, the kind of wise man you see in movies—peaceful and holy. When I saw him, I figured this guy just had to know what was going on. But before I could talk to him, he disappeared into the crowd.

Every so often, I saw him again. I was told his name was Baba. He would suddenly appear out of nowhere, and then just as quickly, he would merge back into the crowded streets of Nepal.

Late one afternoon, I walked into an outdoor cafe and spotted the old man seated way in the back. I looked over at him, and as his eyes met mine, he motioned to me to come and sit next to him. I was excited. Somehow he knew I had been seeking him. Perhaps, he was the teacher who was going to tell me what life was all about.

I went back to his table and sat next to him. He didn't acknowledge me; he just gazed at the blur of people who walked past. I didn't know what to do, so I looked at them also and waited.

But he said nothing.

After some time, without turning to look at him, I spoke.

"So, what's going on *here?*" with *here* meaning the *big picture*.

"I no speak," he said, "till you buy me soda pop."

I didn't know how to reply. So I pretended I didn't hear what he said.

"I no fool! I no ask twice!" he said angrily.

I was in a dilemma. He only asked for a soda pop, though it felt like much more. But I didn't want to blow it, if this was one those mythic tests that you read about, where God or a guru asks something of a person in order to test his sincerity and devotion. I had read about a

Tibetan named Milarepa, who, in order to prove himself to the guru, had to build several stone buildings by hand. He carried the stones on his back, until he was covered with blisters and oozing sores. Then, because his guru demanded it, he took the buildings down and returned the stones to where they had come from. Then there was the biblical Abraham, who was willing to kill his own son because God asked him. Or the guru Tilopa, who made a student give him gold dust as an offering. Tilopa took the golden gift and dumped it on the ground saying, "What use have I of gold? The whole world is gold to me!"

So maybe this guy wasn't actually going to drink the soda pop. Maybe he would pour it into the potted plant next to him and say, "What use have I of soda pop? To me, the whole world is soda pop!"

I got up and walked slowly to the counter, my mind wildly searching for an answer. Compared to an offering of gold or building towers with my bare hands, a bottle of soda pop was nothing. But when I got to the counter, I didn't feel right about the whole thing.

While the battle for a solution raged in my mind, a strange sensation arose in my chest. My heart pounded deeply, as though something struggled to be born through it. I suddenly realized that my heart was trying to communicate with me and, like a compass, it was telling me which way to go. I had my answer, and it was accompanied by great sadness.

"Can I help you?" asked the man behind the counter.

"Yes," I replied handing the man some money, "see that old man back there? Bring him a soda pop." Then, I turned towards the doorway and walked through. I never saw or talked to Baba again.

3

DR. ELISABETH KÜBLER-ROSS

Elisabeth Kübler-Ross is famous for her work with death and dying. Because of her work, I volunteered at a hospice. I figured with my experiences of death, maybe I could help people. I also thought that by being around death, I would learn something very important.

My first client was a man named Harry. I visited him every Friday. He told me he had been a lard packer for twenty years. He was a stoic sort of fellow and never talked much. When he died, the hospice nurse called me on the phone: "I have Harry's last words for you."

I quickly fantasized that maybe his last words were about me. Maybe he said, "Bring me Bill" or "I need Bill" and then gasped his last.

"Harry's last words," said the nurse, "were 'I want corn nibblets.'"

Another person I worked with was Lilly, a sixty-seven-year-old Englishwoman who was dying of cancer, even though she denied it. Every week when I visited, we had the same routine. We played cards or dominos, and then she would ask me if I liked french fries.

"Sure," I would reply.

"Well, sometime we'll make french fries. They're my favorite."

Elderly people, especially dying people, appear old and lined. I can almost feel and see the dying process unfold in front of my eyes. Lilly had smoked for fifty years, and her face showed the grayness of skin that comes from that way of life.

One day in an early spring, Lilly was teaching me a new card game. The air in the house was stale from the winter's hibernation, so I opened up a window to let in the fresh air.

Lilly looked tired. As a young woman, she had lived through the bombing of London and the unexpected death of her husband. The scratchy tone of her voice seemed to be imbued by these traumas.

Listening and looking at Lilly, I could see death and sense its growing presence in the house—her old and tired face, the broken and pained body, the stale air confined to the house over those winter months—all this, together with my love for Lilly and the knowing inevitableness of my own death, began to overwhelm me.

Then, like an angelic whisper, the breeze came through the open window and caressed my skin and face, bringing my dormant senses alive. My being stood still as a paradoxical realization came forth. I wanted to beam with joy and cry at the same time. Spring was coming—the beauty and life of spring. Its newness was in our midst, and yet the presence of death could still be felt. It was only now, only after seeing the darkness of death and the coldness of winter, that I could see the full contrasting beauty of life and spring, coexisting in this moment, like two lovers, each adding value to the other.

The stillness of that moment changed into the next. Lilly's great-grandchildren came running in, their faces bright and new, hers old and lined, mine full of wonder. So, life is a cycle: Around and around and through us it goes. Promising life, promising death . . . bringing each in its time, not ours. So wonderful, so simple . . . so life.

A week later, Lilly died, and her daughter told me a secret. "Whenever Lilly knew you were coming over," her daughter said, "she put on makeup. She didn't do that for anyone else. During her whole life, I can count the number of people that my mother got along with on one hand."

"One other thing," she added, handing me a package, "Lilly wanted you to have this."

At home, I opened the package. Inside was Lilly's french-fry maker. I cried, then wrote about her.

> Death takes the things I love most.
> That is why I love them more.

> Death takes the things I love most,
> so I don't waste time.

Death takes the things I love most,
so I don't worry about bills or clean socks.

Death takes the things I love most.
Here's a toast to death.

Death took my loves and my friends,
and still
it is not done.

Death took all this and more,
and it will take,
even after it has taken me.

But in this world,
nothing takes without also giving,
and death has given a richness of life
to be valued, and cherished,
until the moment is over.
So recognize the supreme secret:
Death will one day take life from you,
so while you are able,
take the death from your life.

I arrived at Elisabeth Kübler-Ross's farm around suppertime. I walked into her house with my usual interview face on, only to find myself feeling out of place when I discovered several people sitting around the kitchen table—eating. A short, older woman, whom I recognized as Elisabeth, came over to me. Again I felt awkward when I reached out to shake her hand—because I realized she had intended to hug me. She immediately asked me if I was hungry. Soon, I was sitting also, eating homemade bread and other goodies she had made herself.

Later, she showed me around her farm. One of the most beautiful things she showed me was a log cabin she had brought piece by piece to the farm and had had reconstructed. It was for her sister, who ended up never living in it.

It was after she showed me her vast canning exploits that we began the interview. During the interview, she constantly knitted. "I'm making a scarf," she said. "I sell them to raise money for AIDS babies."

After the interview, Elisabeth Kübler-Ross drove me around in her pickup truck. Her small size behind the wheel of a large pickup truck kept me chuckling to myself. For some reason, I had not expected Elisabeth Kübler-Ross to drive a pickup truck. She also showed me her small zoo, which had llamas, horses, and peacocks. At one point, she bent down and picked up a peacock feather. "Here," she said, "take this with you."

I was delighted when she asked me to stay the night at her farm along with four other guests. Although it was late, Elisabeth, four other people, and I sat around and beat on Native American drums and sang songs. In between songs (most of which were gospels), we ate chocolate bars. After I'd finish one, Elisabeth would hand me another. It must have been the chocolate that made me remember a song from childhood. It was a silly song, but I thought it would bring a childlike, joyful quality out in Elisabeth Kübler-Ross—something she said was hard for her to feel. When I mentioned the song to Elisabeth, she was all for it.

I started out by singing the words, with the group repeating each line after me.

> Boom boom, I see your fanny.
> Boom boom, it's bright and shiny.
> Boom boom, you'd better hide it.
> Boom boom, before I bite it.

When we finished, I laughed—but I was the only one. The momentary silence was an eternity. I was embarrassed, and I realized it was probably a big mistake teaching them the "Boom boom" song.

Elisabeth spoke, breaking the silence. "Let's sing it again!" she said with glee. As we finished it a second time, Elisabeth chimed, "Now, let's do it in harmony!" As we sang, her smile could be seen and her voice could be heard above everyone else's.

Elisabeth Kübler-Ross is a medical doctor, psychiatrist, and internationally renowned authority on death and dying. She has been instrumental in the development throughout the world of hospices, which counsel the terminally ill and help them to cope with death. Her books include *On Death and Dying, Questions and Answers on Death and Dying*, and *On Children and Death*.

On what beliefs do you base your life?

I base my beliefs on my life experiences and my mystical experiences. I have always had teachers along the way. They've changed, naturally, every decade. My first real teachers were my patients, especially dying patients. When people are dying, they don't use the baloney that most "grownups" use. When we're dying, we get rid of the baloney; we throw all the baloney overboard. All the things that used to be important—like "Do I get the mink coat?" or "Can I get the vacation month in Florida?" or "Can we purchase a condominium or pay for the car?"—all these things disappear when we know we have limited time. Sometimes, my patients get well again, but they've changed their values and their whole philosophy of life.

I always watch people who have been wishy-washy Protestants or wishy-washy Catholics or wishy-washy Jews. I've found that they have terrible trouble dying. People who were *solidly* something or *solidly* nothing died with more peace. So it's better to be all *something* (in religious terms) or nothing at all. If a person is a little bit something, those basic beliefs that he or she hasn't nourished become less solid. They're just intellectual beliefs, and those intellectual defenses fall apart first.

I've found that whatever we are, we have to be genuine, authentic. We have to be all of it; if we are wishy-washy, it's not going to help. So, we can't just go to church and think we feel solid and good about it! In psychiatric language, a belief has to be really internalized to become part of our lives. In this society, there are very few genuine, authentic people. That's why many people have such trouble dying!

Gradually I've developed my work on myself. I did my own growth work. I tried to get rid of whatever was negative in my life, because I realized, in my workshops, that unless people resolve grief and get rid of hate, rage, and impotent rage—they're never whole. If they're not whole, their spiritual quadrant cannot blossom; they have to nurture it, and they cannot nurture it if they're full of hate. The more I worked on my unfinished business, the more my spiritual quadrant evolved, blossomed, began really to take off.

I was always stunned at how dying children have a spiritual quadrant that is much more evolved than that of grownups! The reason is we compensate. When our physical, emotional, or intellectual quadrant is shot through with tragedy—shot through with a birth defect, incest in childhood, or cancer in childhood—whatever quadrant is diminished, it will always get compensated. The pie always remains whole, but it may not contain the same size quadrants. If a child has cancer at age three and dies at age nine, that means two-thirds of his life he has suffered. He has had chemotherapy, he has been in and out of hospitals, he has lost his school friends because he could never go regularly to school. There were lots of traumas and a very hard life for this nine-year-old, so his spiritual quadrant was like THIS! [She gestures broadly.] Huge! I've discovered that children know everything, inside, not up here. [She points to her head.] A nine-year-old child can make a drawing, which is the language of the spiritual quadrant, that says he will die around age nine, and all the issues are in the drawing. That's what we call a symbolic language. That's how dying children became my teachers. If a nine-year-old child who has suffered so much can know all that, this knowledge must be inside all of us. How do I get to this knowledge—without having to *have* cancer or AIDS or M.S. or whatever?

One of my shortcomings is that I can't sit still, and I'm a typical Swiss workaholic, so I'm not good at meditating and sitting. I'm not really a good Californian because I can't stand wheat germ and bean sprouts! I smoke and drink coffee and still eat some beef (not much, but a little). I can't stand macrobiotic food. All the things that the New Age people say we're supposed to do to become spiritual—I just can't stand them!

Since I've been preaching all my life, the most important thing in my life is to be honest. Not just honest to others; one has to be true to oneself. I can't stand this "must have certain food" stuff because I like a cigarette and coffee, so I go have a cigarette and coffee! I know it's not healthy, but that's me, and I have to be true to myself. So, I kept my cigarettes and coffee, cup of tea or whatever, black tea, with sugar, not honey! That was the part of me I had to be in touch with. Eventually I'll get rid of it, slowly and gradually, but very much at my own pace. As soon as somebody says, "You have to stop smoking!" you'll smoke twice as much! I'm getting in touch with a lot of things I need to work on.

In spite of smoking and eating everything I like (I'm growing my own homegrown vegetables, enough for a hundred people), I have a very healthy life, relatively speaking. In spite of things like coffee, cigarettes, and Swiss chocolate, I've had lots of mystical experiences. I know that people have gone to the Himalayas for ten years, sat in a nice position and meditated, searched and sought, praying and hoping for a cosmic consciousness experience . . . while I didn't even know what one was! Yet I have had one experience after another until, many years ago, I had a cosmic consciousness experience. It blew my mind, but at the time I didn't know what to call it. I was in love with everything, every leaf, every blade of grass, every bird, even the pebbles. I walked about this high [she gestures] above the path. I talked to the pebbles. I said, "I can't step on you; I can't hurt you." I swear I was not hallucinating. I did not touch the ground, because I didn't want to hurt them.

I couldn't tell that experience to anybody, not even my husband, who would have thought I'd flipped! Some time later, about thirteen years ago, I had to go to a transpersonal psychology meeting in Berkeley, and I saw there monks and people with bald heads—a huge audience. I looked at them, and they looked very peaceful and accepting. There was love, compassion, and understanding in that room. I said to myself, This is a place where I can talk about all these things that happened to me.

Very automatically, I went up on the stage. I always talk extemporaneously, because when I prepare, it becomes really stiff and stupid. I said, "I want to share my own journey with you. I have two questions I want to ask you, and then you can ask me as many questions as you want." My main point was, "You can drink coffee, smoke cigarettes, eat Swiss chocolate. You don't have to be holier than the holy. You can be a normal, average human being, and yet, *when the time is right*, even *you* can have experiences that have no name, no words for them." I emphasized that I'd never meditated in my life, that I've ants in my pants, and that I cannot recall my dreams, so I can't ask my dreams for guidance.

Then I shared one experience after another. I shared my cosmic consciousness experience. I said I did not know what to call it, but it was such bliss that I went home, cleaned house, cooked, and washed dishes. I was in a state of bliss for three days and three nights, and all I have to do is think back to know that is possible. This is possible, to exist that way! One aspect of our lives is that we'll eventually *be* that way. That may be an end goal, the end of life or after death. Then, all the struggles, pain, and hardships are worth it. This is my idea: Mankind has to become, again, all love. The only thing that counts in life is love—not just how much love we can *give*, but we must learn how to receive it, because we can give only as much as we allow ourselves to receive. Everything has to be in balance.

The lecture was the most profound sharing I've ever done in my life. One of the monks bowed with great reverence. He said I had experienced "cosmic consciousness" and that I had merged with light and had become one with it, which was *Shanti Nilaya*, a Sanskrit term meaning the Ultimate, Final Home of Peace.

The monks said the only objection they had was that I made such a point I'd never meditated, and that this was not true, for they thought I was a very good meditator because of the way I work with dying children. I'm so tuned into them that an alarm could go off and I would not hear it. I'm so totally focused on the children that we are one soul, mind, and heart. I've done that for hundreds of hours, but as a straight, square Swiss hillbilly, I would never call that meditation, because I'm in conversation with somebody. The monk said it was a form of meditation—I think he called it a Dharma meditation. I thanked him. I was very grateful to have a label for what I'd experienced.

All my learning has involved crossing the paths of people who became my teachers. My best teacher in the world was a black cleaning woman at the University of Chicago. She was my first teacher. If not for her, I would not be, today, where I am. I would not have written a book on death and dying; I would not have been able to stick it out with my dying patients. After the black cleaning woman, other people came, and they were usually not big shots in academia. They were just special, very special human beings who crossed my path at the right time and the right things happened and I made one step further or stuck with something that I wouldn't have dared to stick out.

Those were my teachers. I really know that when we're open and request it, we grow spiritually, which is my own great effort. This is not just *my* philosophy of life. At the right time, the right teacher will appear; then, whenever a person has found what he needs to do, he moves on. The in-between periods are difficult.

I never had a guru. I never had one person I could go to. Life brought certain people to me, we crossed paths, and they stayed for awhile. I don't even know the name of that black cleaning woman, but she changed my life. As a result, she has reached millions of people, dying patients, whom I've worked with. I tell my students,

It's not who you are—you can be a cleaning woman. When you make the transition after death, you will know only then how many lives you've touched. It doesn't matter how high you are on the totem pole. You may be down here, but if you have given people something to keep them going, as they grow, you grow. The same is true of lives that have touched yours: they will get the credit on the balance sheet. When that black cleaning woman dies (if she hasn't died yet), she will get credit for the fifteen thousand lives I've touched every week. I like that. I love it.

The death of my parents destroyed all my beliefs. When I looked to see what was left, nothing was left. That's why I had to go out and search...

See! You never would have searched, and you never would have found answers yourself.

Before you were born, you made an agreement with your mom and dad: When you were very young, they would leave you in order to give you the momentum to find your own path. Otherwise, you would have been a spoiled kid, and everything would have been dandy. You would have had a few sports cars and maybe run into a nice girl at the right time and married and had a boring life.

Your parents had a love for you. They're behind you all the way. You have more of parents now than you would have if they were alive, because they can be behind you all the time, directing. There are no coincidences; there are only grand manipulations.

Remember, there is nothing stable in life. Everything is here to change. Look at trees. Look at flowers. Look at anything in nature. We have to adapt to change. There was never a time in the history of mankind when adapting to change was more important than right now, because planet Earth also has AIDS, because we have destroyed planet Earth to the point that its immune system is destroyed. It's polluted; it's almost dying. The water, air, land, everything is near death. But it's not terminal. All this is going to change in the next two decades—drastically.

I don't know if you're aware of the 1987 Harmonic Convergence. That was a big turning point. From now on, changes will happen at an exponential rate. I travel around the world every year, usually, to give workshops in New Zealand, Australia, Europe, all over. The first twenty years I did that everything changed very slowly; there was barely a difference. *Now*, there are so many changes I'm totally speechless. I can go to fundamentalist churches, where I *was* persona non grata, and ask people in the audience, "How many of you have had a death experience or out-of-body experience?" and hands go up! People are willing to go to the pulpit and share their experiences. In Australia, AIDS patients were once treated much worse than leprosy patients; now, Australians are starting support groups all over the place! Fifteen years ago, we started the first hospice in the United States; now, we have about twenty-five hundred hospices.

Change just happened—*BOOM!* Once it gets going, it just explodes. Now is the time of the separation of wheat from the chaff. We have relatively little time; that's why things are happening at such an accelerated rate. In the old days, forty, fifty years ago, one had to go to Tibet or Nepal for twenty years to become enlightened or to have any glimpse of what capacities existed within. Two thousand years ago, Jesus said, "Find the kingdom within." Nobody knew what that meant!

Now, one million, two million, five million Americans, if they are really honest, will admit that they know all the answers are there, within themselves. We don't have to go to gurus, mediums, or fortunetellers. If we really want to know, ask; it will be given— not easily, and perhaps not when we want it, but when the time is right. We have to learn patience, tolerance, and love of our *self*, which is the hardest lesson in the world. When we were growing up, we were told, If you love yourself, you are egotistical, selfish, no good. We have to change this belief.

We have the first AIDS patients who have healed themselves. Healed! Totally well. It's fantastic! I have two AIDS babies who have tested negative now. They were born with AIDS, totally full of symptoms, and now they're testing negative. Love heals my AIDS babies. They are marinated in love.

If we are ready for change and can let go, not hanging on to the past, and can accept things, then maybe everything will be different tomorrow. It's nonattached compassion. Don't be attached to the way things are, or were. Welcome change with open arms, and don't hang on to things like "I have to have a microwave" or "I have to have a relationship." Everything is in flux. Times are changing for the better, and we have to be ready by letting go of the past.

You know, while I've been talking to you, Bill, I keep thinking you look like a Buddhist monk! You have the eyes of a Buddhist monk and the forehead of a Buddhist monk, the whole facial expression! Maybe you were one in a previous existence.

I stayed in a monastery for awhile in Nepal, and I liked it, but it just didn't feel right for me to be a monk.

You got what you needed, then you left. That's how God works. I believe in God. Absolutely! No question about it, but one cannot describe God! One would be the biggest phony-baloney if one tried to describe God. We can come close to it, but words can never describe it.

I had a cosmic consciousness experience once in which I went through absolute agony and hell—thousands and thousands of deaths with pain, anguish, and agony beyond any description. Then a voice came, and I asked for a shoulder to lean on. I just could not stand it anymore. The voice said, "You shall not be given it." I didn't even have time to ask, "Why not? I've been a shoulder to thousands of patients. Why can't I have one shoulder to lean on?" The answer was, loudly and clearly, "You shall not be given it."

When one gets into more agony, one becomes less choosy. I asked only for a hand to hold. When a woman is in labor, she needs to hold a hand. Just a hand. I expected a hand to come that I could hold, but the voice said, "You shall not be given it." I wondered if I could ask for a fingertip, just to know that there was the presence of another human being. Typical of me, I said, "No. If God can't give me one hand to hold, I don't want a finger."

Then it came to me, for the first time in my life. I absolutely, totally, completely knew that God gives none of us more than we can bear, but we have to go to the total end of endurance. If we can say yes! to it, we pass the test.

Finally, I didn't want the fingertip; that was beneath my dignity. I said, "To heck with it, give me everything I have to go through." That was it. I said yes to it. The second, the absolute second of my thought, when I said yes to it, the agony stopped. I was able to breathe again. My pain went; everything left.

Then I had the most incredible vision any human being has ever seen. I went through something that looked like a lotus flower. As I got farther and farther into it, there was a tiny little light behind.

I moved, very slowly, toward that light. Then, my whole body and everything around me started to vibrate. I looked at the wall and the wood. Everything vibrated. Through the window, I saw trees, but I didn't see leaves. Everything was in molecular structural form. Everything was vibrating at high speed.

I'm a physician, so I said to myself, my skin cannot do that. It's impossible. I cannot see my skin's molecular structure. But everywhere I looked, I saw the molecular structure of everything— the whole world! I didn't have three-dimensional vision. I saw differently. As I moved through to the light, I went into that light. It was like falling into a waterbed of love. That's the best description I can give. The light was all love. I knew everything, and I became part of it. That's what God is like: It's all love, all wisdom, all understanding, all compassion, for every living thing.

This is a lousy description, because one has to experience it to understand how dense we are, how stupid, how limited, how unloving, how judgmental. We're billions of light years away from what we could be. I believe our soul is one tiny snowflake of God that descends down to planet Earth and to other planets, if we are inhabitants of other planets. We're given this physical body and a very limited recall or memory, because we cannot know what we knew before. If we knew all that, we wouldn't learn, wouldn't grow. If a schoolteacher gave us all the answers to our exam questions, we would never bother learning. We'd get the answers anyway, so why work? Gradually, as we evolve, the memories come back and we get a little wiser, more loving, more compassionate, less violent, and less destructive. It's a very slow process of climbing a ladder until we are worth it to return to the Source where all life comes from. To me, that is God—the Source of all life, of every living thing.

What is the highest ideal a person can reach?

The highest ideal we can reach is the original state in which we were created as children of God, with all the love, compassion, and creativity we used to have before we thought, "We can do it without God."

Eventually, everybody will reach this ideal. The difference between present and past generations is that now there's an accelerated time clock (though time does not exist), with a huge separation happening between the wheat and the chaff. Anybody who is loving, forgiving, compassionate serves mankind and also respects planet Earth. These people will make it much faster than any generation before us—much, much faster.

The others, who've been very negative, used their religion for their own greed, playing holiest of the holy, meanwhile having their own sex life and negativity, knocking everybody who didn't belong to their religious group. They will be the last ones. The first will be the last, the last first.

Number three task in our workshops is to get rid of the big negativity, the hate within. Each time we get rid of a little of the hate within, we become a bit closer to Mother Teresa, symbolically speaking. Anytime we get rid of negativity, the vacuum is filled with more compassion, love, and understanding. It's a slow process.

We are all our own worst enemy and biggest obstacle. I'm the world's worst enemy. I'm the worst judge when it comes to me. That's true for almost everybody.

We're not taught right. If people were taught right when they were young, they would be taught what natural emotions are. Cry when you're sad! Stamp your foot! Beat something up, but not a living thing! Take a piece of rubber hose and shred a telephone book to pieces. Then, you won't have to beat your kids; you won't have to kick your dog, bash up your wife or husband. Anger is a natural emotion. It gets destructive only when it's like a pressure cooker that erupts.

If you let children express their natural jealousy, they're not so angry, so aggrieved. They will become healthy, gorgeous kids. Then as teenagers, they'll love and respect their physical bodies. They won't destroy them with alcohol, drugs, or cigarettes. They will act naturally emotional, instead of becoming Hitlers before they're nineteen. They will respect their intellectual quadrant, and they'll love to learn because learning will be an adventure. Their spiritual quadrant will open up naturally. They will get their own answers and won't have to go from a guru to a baba, to mediums, to channelers, to everybody except themselves. They won't have to shop around for love either. They will have learned from a very young age that love is love only when it's unconditional, like a grandma's love. Not "I love you, providing you bring good grades home," not "I'll love you if you cut your hair," not "I'll love you if you bring a girl home who belongs to our congregation and economic level" . . . and all that crap.

If you know someone who's dying and is afraid, what do you tell that person? How would you help him or her?

I do not give cookbook recipes. I have to listen to each individual. There are different stages in the school of life, different spiritual evolutionary stages. Some people are just petrified of the devil and of ending up in hell. Other people are afraid to be buried because they can't stand worms. Others are afraid they will be isolated and left alone to die unattended in a hospital, hooked up to machines and suffering, their lives artificially prolonged. Others are afraid of physical pain. Others are afraid that they never had a decent relationship and can't make peace before they die. One has to listen very individually to what their biggest concerns are; then one works with that to help them.

In Vietnam, I've rarely seen people die when the son was not at home. They waited until the son arrived; then they died in peace. They couldn't die a week or ten days before he arrived. There are different issues with each person.

Death is a graduation. When we've taught all the things we came to teach, learned all the things we came to learn, then we're allowed to graduate. Some children die and graduate very early. Their sole reason to come was to be a teacher for moms and dads, usually, or for a brother or sister. Then they're allowed to go back home.

Why is there suffering? evil?

Most of our suffering is self-imposed. Some people have to suffer because they made somebody else suffer before. They want to have a clean slate. They want to make up for some boo-boos they've made earlier.

To me, suffering is—I hate to say, since I don't want to be taken out of context . . . suffering provides very little growth for most people.

One of my guides said to me, "When I'm born again to a human body, I want to die of starvation as a child."

I'm very blunt, very outspoken, and I said, "You're really a jerk! I've never met a jerk like you. You would choose to be born to die of starvation! What kind of an idiot are you?"—almost that rudely.

He said with incredible love, "Elisabeth, it would enhance my compassion." I got goose pimples! That taught me a lesson. Suffering has many faces. I'm sure many, many millions of people who suffer have chosen suffering in order to grow.

Man was given the greatest, most difficult gift: free choice. Of all the beings I know, we are the only ones who have been given such a controversial gift. We have to choose. We're the master of our destiny. We can turn anything or everything into bad or good, into black or white, into evil or a blessing. It's yin-yang; it has to be. We cannot have the whole world positive without negative; we have to have both. Our goal is to get rid of the negative as much as we can.

Evil appears as evil from a certain perspective, but from another, evil turns into the biggest blessing around. We have to look at it from a distance, however; otherwise, we'd never see it that way.

Religions do a miserable job. Miserable—at least in Western culture. All religions have the same basic truth—Islam, Buddhism, Judaism, Christianity, Hinduism—but how they teach those truths and practice them is very different. Whether it's a blessing or a curse depends on how it's practiced, and we Westerners are probably the worst in the world.

If you were on your deathbed, what advice would you give to your son or daughter?

I have no illusions that a few words on a deathbed would make any impact. I might tell them, "I love you," but I wouldn't have to tell them that because they know it. I don't believe in big last-minute statements. I'd probably just gasp my last breath.

Before I die, however, I would love to bring more love into this shitty world! There are moms who adopt AIDS babies and raise them and give nothing but love. I gave them a break for two-and-a-half days to come to my farm, just to be spoiled, nurtured, pampered, taken care of, but people here were hostile to my connection with AIDS babies and their parents, so they shot bullets through the windows! To me, that's incomprehensible. They said, "You should know, we are born-again Christians, but if you should ever call for an ambulance, we will not respond." The ambulance drivers! They always use the sentence, "We are born-again Christians," but if we ever sent one of these AIDS kids to their school, the school doors would be locked.

I told them, "I don't understand you born-again Christians. If Jesus were here on planet Earth, he would call all the AIDS patients to him and would take care of them. You call yourselves Christians! He would take care of leprosy patients, AIDS babies. Where is your real, genuine faith?"

They got up, furious, with their arms at their sides, very close to me, and said, "But you're not Jesus!"

How in the world can one get it through their heads, which are filled with fear? We now have a lynch mob on our hands: we need to get police protection just to drive back to the farm! This world is filled with fear and greed. Those are the two biggest enemies. If I had one wish, it would be to get rid of fear and greed, but there's nothing I can do about it, except, perhaps, do my own thing and be an example of no fear and no greed.

What do you think is something life still has to teach you?

Oh, there are still a lot of things—God! I'm a long way from being happy with myself. I've just learned in the last four weeks how to meditate, and in the last month, for the first time in my life, at age sixty-three, I've learned to listen to and record my dreams. Now I'm really making progress.

God, for ten years, I tried. Now I'm even trying to stop smoking, doing it less and less. It's hard. I'm still a long way from where I need to be, but I have to be patient with myself, much less judgmental about myself. I have to start with me. That's the toughie. Self-love, self-forgiveness, and self-trust are the hardest lessons to learn.

Being happy is something I have to work on. I have moments when I'm totally content, but joy and happiness have evaded me. I'm happy when I can work with dying children, can help a family. It's not really happy; it just feels good. But really happy, joyfully happy—I don't have much of that.

I don't have that joy because I've never been a little kid. Sometimes I would just love to put the music on and be able to dance, but I'd feel like an idiot, standing in my living room and dancing. I hope that comes before I die. I don't play enough; I know that. I'm a workaholic. That's very hard to give up, but I'm trying. In the past I couldn't even have been sitting here talking to you.

I give scholarships to AIDS patients for my workshops, so every scarf I make helps an AIDS patient get a scholarship. The real reason I make scarves is that I have ants in my pants. I can't sit still like this for hours and hours without doing something with my hands. Gandhi did it with his spinning. It's marvelous—another form of meditation, I'm sure.

What makes you happy? sad? angry?

I love to can, bake, cook, feed people, work with dying patients and with AIDS babies . . . but *joy* is not the right word. I've not had enough joy in my life, but I'm beginning.

Sadness comes when I look at the world, at how people kill each other, destroy each other in the name of God . . . it's just a pity. They're destroying Mother Earth with such things as nuclear testing underground. They shouldn't mess with the universe. They're destroying outer space, now, too. They aren't satisfied with destroying Earth; they have to go into outer regions. That makes me sad and sick.

I get angry when I hear about all the weapons, S.D.I. and all that stuff. Violence is the biggest problem in life. No question about it. Our general negativity. Total lack of unconditional love. Not understanding that we are all brothers and sisters, from the same source. That's the biggest problem, because if we knew that, there would be peace on earth. There would be love, not war. We would respect each other on planet Earth. The world would be the way it's supposed to be, the way it was created.

If you could meet anyone throughout history, whom would you meet and what would you ask that person?

I would like to meet Jesus in person. I would like to meet Buddha. I have a feeling I wouldn't be able to understand Buddha's language, that it would be over my head, but I would just like to be in that presence. Jesus, Jeremiah, Buddha, and Mary—I'd like just to sit in their love, in their presence. I'd be so dumbfounded, I couldn't open my mouth. I'd just want a little bit of their love.

Some spiritual teachers feel that relationships like marriage get in the way of spiritual growth . . .

Not if you meet the right person and you marry out of love, and not "I'll marry you if you buy me a mink coat, a sable coat, a big house." That's not love. If people would really love each other unconditionally and would grow together in a spiritual path, that's different. Some grow very slowly; others make rapid progress. When one person in a marriage grows very slowly or is negative—not just skeptical but totally negative—and knocks the other, it's hard for the partner to continue to grow.

People get into such relationships to find out if they can practice unconditional love. If they can, they'll love their partners as they are and not criticize them because they grow at a different speed. That is very difficult to do, but it can be done. I've done it. It's a terrific commitment. Ideally, people grow together. They don't have to use the same means or tools, but they can share with each other, encourage each other, and not criticize the other if one grows faster. *Then* marriage can work. There are very, very few marriages that work. Many spouses don't care a hoot about each other.

There's no difference between men and women. People emphasize the caring and nurturing of the female and the logic of the male, but there are both traits in both sexes. To me, a woman is 49 percent male, 51 percent female, and the male, the converse, so the difference is two percent. Literally.

What would you describe as your basic practice to help your spiritual growth?

That depends on when you ask me. Right now, I'm trying to get in touch with my soul by many means. I'm trying to meditate, trying to recall my dreams. I'm trying to do this fabulous thing where one writes the question with one's right hand and the answer with the left. Boy, does it work! I can't believe my eyes. I ask questions of my soul, and—BOOM! BOOM! BOOM!—the most poetic language comes. Fantastic language comes out, stuff I could never write or think of. I use any means and tools to get in touch and grow.

I do only the things I love to do. If I have a choice between doing A or B, I do what I love the most. I couldn't be a regular psychiatrist in a regular practice, making money, taking notes—it would drive me crazy! I couldn't work in academic life anymore because of the baloney and academic nonsense. I love to do my brand of medicine, just as I used to as a country doctor. I still make house calls, here in the valley, and visit old, dying, and sick people. I love that. I'll always be a country doctor in my heart.

I created a small zoo for my AIDS babies, but now I can't have my AIDS babies. They turned me down; they were afraid I'd be importing AIDS into the county. We can't even get AIDS babies out of the hospital. They're used for greed, moneymaking, research. There are 154 families who are eager to adopt AIDS babies. Social service agencies get a thousand a day for each baby. Make fortunes! Doctors get millions of dollars for research grants, and they experiment with AZT on two-year-olds. The babies have no bonding and no love. They have fifteen or twenty people patting them on the back, but it's not bonding.

That makes me angry, too. You can't get those children into private homes. The ones we've kidnapped out of hospitals have done fantastically; they've blossomed like flowers. That makes me happy.

What was the most significant thing that ever happened to you?

My cosmic consciousness was my most mind-blowing experience. For the first time I experienced the total, absolute, unconditional love that one cannot experience in a physical body here on earth. I was told that if I can get a moment like this, then it is possible for anybody and everybody. That is my hope: eventually all of us will become that way, and then our lives will be paradise on earth. It's not far away! My children live in this age when they will experience total love on earth. Planet Earth will be healed. To me, it's great that I live in this crazy time. Though I've gone through a thousand deaths, in many symbolic and real ways, it has been worthwhile. If I'm really blessed, I'll live long enough to see unconditional love on this earth. Then, I can dance on the galaxies and die! I'll feel I've done my share.

I don't have to worry about my children. That's a good feeling. I almost envy the children born now. They don't have to go through all the crap. They are really on a journey that will be much less painful and hard than what all of us in our generation had to go through. It will be a much better place in the next few decades. I've had a glimpse of what it's like—I can barely wait. Hurry up and get going! I don't know if I can hang around long enough. I guess I'll have to stop smoking. I'm apt to get another stroke, and then I'll be so senile, I won't know when it happens. *That* I wouldn't like. But, one always gets what one needs, so . . .

4

NORMAN VINCENT

P E A L E

When I arrived in New York, I stayed at a YMCA. It was cheap. It also happened to be Black Monday, the day that the stock market fell dramatically, though I didn't think my arrival was the cause. In the elevator at my hotel, there was a man who was dressed in rags. He jumped up and down and yelled "all right!" When I asked him why he was so excited, he showed me the *New York Times* with the headline about the fall of the stock market.

I arrived a few minutes late at Norman Vincent Peale's office. The directions I was given by a New York City cop were miscalculated. A nice, leisurely three-block walk to his office turned into a nightmare of a three-to-four mile all-out run when I realized how far away I was from his building. It was a sunny day, and my jacket and tie did not help. I walked in late and dripped perspiration on the secretary's desk. I figured the interviews could only get better after that.

Norman Vincent Peale's office complex was huge. The plush wine carpet and tasteful decor made me realize that I was meeting some-one famous.

He came out to greet me. "I shouldn't have made this appointment. I have to catch a plane in twenty minutes! Can you come back?" he asked hurriedly.

"I'm from Madison, Wisconsin," I replied, trying not to show my disappointment.

Norman Vincent Peale stood there looking at me. I don't know what he saw, but he told me to go into his office and wait. I heard him talking to someone I later found out to be his wife. He came back into the room and sat down across from me—still agitated about his flight. He told me to ask my first question, and I could see his intent was to answer my questions quickly and get to the airport.

I don't know if it was the first few questions I asked or just my need to know, but as the moments passed, I could see a change in Norman Vincent Peale. Without his saying so, I knew he had decided this meeting with me was more important than his flight.

His wife came to the door after a few minutes to see if he was ready to go. Without Norman Vincent Peale's acknowledging her or saying anything, she knew that he had decided they were going to miss the plane. When she saw that her husband was engaged in something he loved, she smiled. She walked away and never said a word.

One would think Norman Vincent Peale must have done more than his share of interviews during his lifetime. One would think this one wouldn't have mattered that much to him, but it did, because he could see it mattered to me. He could see that under the pretext of an interview, I was searching.

Through all my travels, I have never met a teacher who turned me away when he or she saw I was sincere. In Nepal, some of the teachers treated me like a king when I showed them my questions. It was as though they had accumulated wisdom their whole lives and had waited for someone to ask them about it. It was as if I were doing them a favor.

The atmosphere settled down, and I was no longer afraid that Norman Vincent Peale was going to leave before I was finished with my questions. He sat across from me and leaned forward to make our talk more intimate. His elbows were propped on his upper legs, and his hands were clasped loosely between his knees. His manner was relaxed, yet he was enthusiastic about the topic. For some unknown reason, I was immediately accepted as a friend. If I hadn't known better, I would have thought we were sitting on the porch of a general store playing a neighborly game of checkers.

For weeks before our meeting, I read all the Norman Vincent Peale books I could find. In one book he talked about seeing the spirits of people who had died; among them were his father and brother. Norman Vincent Peale believes that when we die, our soul goes to a higher and different dimension, and that at rare times, we may break through that barrier.

During the interview, Norman Vincent Peale was sniffling a lot. He had a bad cold. So while we talked and sat across from each other, I looked around the room for a box of tissues. When he saw my head turning this way and that, he reached out and grabbed me. "What?" he said with a spooked look on his face, scanning every nook and cranny in the room. "Did you see something?"

"I was just looking for a Kleenex," I said.

He sat back in his chair. Relieved. Then we finished our interview.

Norman Vincent Peale was an older man, born in 1898. If an old oak tree could talk, it would sound like Norman Vincent Peale. I could tell by the sound of his voice alone that there was wisdom there, a grandfatherly kind of wisdom and presence.

Norman Vincent Peale wrote over twenty books. His most famous, *The Power of Positive Thinking*, has sold more than fifteen million copies and has been translated into fifteen different languages. Two of his projects, *Guideposts* magazine and the Foundation for Christian Living, reach twenty million people a month. In 1984 President Reagan awarded him the Presidential Medal of Freedom, the highest civilian award the President of the United States can confer.

On what beliefs do you base your life?

First of all, there was reason in back of my birth and in back of the birth of every human being. There was a reason I was born. Second, I believe that through my religious faith and through living in what I call the will of God, I can find that purpose. Third, the purpose, in my case, is to help whatever few people I can touch to realize their full potential as human beings.

The highest ideal a person can reach is to reach one's true self, one's *best* self. That is the best I can do with myself. A person approaches this ideal through spiritual methodology. The greatest thinker who ever lived is Jesus Christ. He laid out a way of life that worked, and works. He is the greatest scientist of all time, because he established a formula that can lead to the best possible result. For me, that is the way to achieve this goal.

The chief formula of Jesus was love. I agree with the writer who said Christianity should have been called Love-ianity, because Jesus was the first thinker in history to interject the philosophy of love into human affairs. Before his time, it had been force, hate, and violence. It still is, to some extent. But Jesus taught love of God, love of one's fellow man. He taught that we can attain our goals by love methodology much more than by force methodology.

The greatest obstacle to reaching the ideal of our true self is a certain dualism in human nature. I don't believe that there are *any* bad people, just some good people *acting* badly. That is inherent in the nature of man.

The average person wants to be a fine person but has to contend with other elements. In order to be a good person, we have to battle our animal nature or even satanic influences.

Evil is a challenge for development. When God created man, He gave him a great compliment: He gave him the right of choice. Man could decide to be evil and go to hell, or he could decide to be good and go to heaven. Man looks at evil and, acting as a sovereign judge, decides *against* it. That makes him strong. Every time he has a temptation to do evil, if he weighs it objectively and dispassionately and makes a decision to do good rather than bad, he is stronger. The Indians said every time a warrior scalped a brave, the brave's strength passed into him; the more scalps around his belt, the stronger the warrior. So, if you "scalp" evil and hang this scalp around yourself, you're a stronger person. The same applies to suffering—it makes us stronger.

I believe in the Christian doctrine of heaven. I used to think heaven was in the sky. Some years ago a man named Stewart Edward White wrote a book called *The Unobstructed Universe* and developed a theory that those who have lived and passed from this life didn't go to the sky. They are still in the same space that we occupy but live on a different *frequency* than we do. He used a fan to illustrate. When an electric fan is stationary, we can't see through the blades; but if we plug it in and step it up to a higher frequency, we can see *through* the fan. That parallel provides a reasonable and sensible deduction: Sometimes people have the experience of communication with the dead. For some sensitive reason, they break through temporarily and have communication with the other side, which I feel has been validly proven and tested.

Some people create a hell here on earth. I don't believe in a vengeful God, but if one lives a hell of a life on earth, one isn't used to anything else. I suppose it might follow a person.

Do all religions lead to the same place?

If one follows the teachings of Buddha, one will get to the same place Jesus teaches about because Buddha taught many principles Jesus did. There isn't a particular heaven the Buddhists go to and the Taoists go to and the Christians go to and the Jews go to. They're all God's children.

A person who has *no* religion is making the greatest mistake he can possibly make: He has no fellowship with his Creator, with the good God, with the Lord. When a person of *no* religion dies, I think the Lord God, whose quality *is* mercy, will be kind to him; but a person who is faithful to his religion throughout his lifetime will come to a *higher* level in the hereafter. At least he has had more satisfaction while he has lived on this earth.

What about death...?

I am still learning how to die peacefully and not to be afraid of it.

If you were on your deathbed, what advice would you give your son or daughter?

I would tell my children, "Get acquainted with Jesus Christ, trust him, follow him, live with him in close fellowship all the days of your lives—and on *your* deathbed you will be at peace."

The body deteriorates. We know that. I didn't know Thomas A. Edison, the inventor, but I knew his son and wife, and they told me he had a notion to perform an experiment where he would weigh a body before death and afterward to get the "weight of the soul." He once said the only reason we have the body is to carry the brain around. The soul operates through the brain: With the brain we think, we reason, we remember, we feel the highest emotions. I'm sure every human being has a soul. It is part of the mental and the emotional processes. The body is merely the heart. We used to talk about the heart—the heart is nothing but a vessel that pumps blood. But the *mind* is where you think and decide. If the soul resides in *any* element, it resides there. It is the whole person, the soul is.

The best way I can see you is to look into your eyes and hear what you say. You never "saw" *yourself* and I never "saw" *myself*.

We see only the *mechanism* that carries us around for the total length of our lives.

Some people think personal relationships, like marriage, get in the way of spiritual growth. How do you think marriage can help you...

Oh, my goodness' sakes alive! I've been married to the same lady for fifty-seven years, and she has been a blessing to me ever since I met her. She is the greatest natural-born positive thinker I have ever met. I wasn't. I was a negative thinker. I had to learn positive thinking the hard way. I would have an awfully hard time getting along without her. She has made my personality stronger and better, and I hope that I have added to hers a little. Marriage should be the nurture of two personalities. It should make partners stronger and better people.

Do you feel there is a basic difference between maleness and femaleness, besides the body?

There is a difference between men and women. Women these days are trying to become more masculine; in doing that, they are making a *great* mistake. The good God who made them endowed them with a quality known as femininity. He didn't give that to men, but He gave that to women. Femininity is the most *persuasive* thing, but they are abandoning it. Women are made differently—not only physically but mentally and emotionally—and this difference is *good*. That doesn't mean they aren't equal, because they are, but they should be equal *as* masculine and feminine. They've got the advantage—if they only *knew* it!

What is the most important thing you have learned in life?

I would say that the most important lesson I ever learned was to forget myself, to master myself, and not to be hampered by myself.

I get sad when I don't measure up to myself, which is often. I used to get angry. I don't get angry so much anymore. Anger is a futility; it's a lack of emotional control. The only thing I get angry at is myself—*my* stupidity, *my* ineptness—but not at anybody else, so much.

Why are you doing what you are doing?

I asked the Lord to tell me what my life could do, and He seemed to call me to preach and to write about the Gospel, to tell people that Jesus Christ is truly the way, the truth, and the life. That's what keeps me going. People are the most important thing in the world. It is important to me to help motivate and inspire people and get them excited about what they can be and do.

5

B. F. SKINNER

I wrote B. F. Skinner in 1987 for an interview. I told him I was writing a book on the meaning of life. He answered by saying he wasn't interested in "spiritual" pursuits. I replied that the book was about "truth" pursuits and not "spiritual" pursuits. He then agreed to an interview.

I interviewed B. F. Skinner at Harvard University. After reading about his behavior theories and experiments in a multitude of psychology classes, I was prepared to meet a scientifically dry, cold, and calculating person. The fact that the interview was at Harvard University, synonymous with academic and intellectual achievement, didn't do anything to alter expectations. But B. F. Skinner was warm and immediately put me at ease. He did not make me feel he was a superior intellect, but there were interesting exchanges between us as he corrected me on the psychological terms I used and as he struggled with the way I formed my questions.

I have intentionally left this interview in its original conversational tone. The dynamics of our conversation gives a rare glimpse into the way B. F. Skinner's mind works.

Despite our struggle, I will always remember what he said to me at the conclusion of the interview, especially since his was the first interview I conducted for my book and I was still quite rough around the edges. "The questions were very good, and I enjoyed them. The only problem is that the science of behaviorism uses some very exact concepts. But *we* did a good job," he added with a warm smile, purposely emphasizing the "we."

"We did," I agreed, silently moved by his reply, "didn't we."

The interview with B. F. Skinner precipitated my final disillusionment with the psychology program at the university I attended. At the time, I was working full time along with a part-time job. I also attended classes full time and traveled around the United States finishing up my interviews for the book.

In one of my psychology classes, a requirement for a few extra-credit points was to participate in a graduate student's experiment. Since I didn't have the time to participate, I approached my professor and told him I was interviewing B. F. Skinner in two weeks. I offered to type up the interview and submit it along with a cassette copy of the interview in return for the extra-credit points.

"You're interviewing B. F. Skinner!" the professor said excitedly. "He's one of my heroes." The professor's enthusiasm brought him alive; for the first time I realized he was actually quite young. "Well," he said, "it certainly would be interesting to hear what Skinner says. I'll ask the other faculty at our next meeting if that's acceptable."

Leaving his office, I had little doubt that the psychology department would consider a personal interview with B. F. Skinner a better learning opportunity for me than participating in one of their countless graduate student experiments. It would also benefit the university to have an hour interview with B. F. Skinner on "the meaning of his life" in its psychology library. This interview would certainly be an amazing and valuable insight for any student who studied Skinner.

A week later, I returned to the professor's office. "I'm sorry," the professor said, "our department can't accept your interview for extra credit. We have strict guidelines. If we let you do something different, then every student will want to do something different."

As I left his office and walked down those halls of endless classrooms, my disbelief turned into frustration, and my frustration turned into disillusionment. I realized that what I wanted and needed to learn wasn't what they wanted to teach me.

B. F. Skinner may be the most influential psychologist alive. He is a professor at Harvard University and the leading proponent of behaviorism. He has authored fourteen books, among them *Walden Two* and *Beyond Freedom and Dignity*.

On what beliefs do you base your life?

I don't base my life on any belief except that I assume—it's an assumption, not a belief—that everything in the world is orderly and lawful and can be studied that way. My beliefs are entirely scientific, and I leave science up to astronomers and cosmologists, who have more knowledge about the universe than I do. I haven't any idea where the Big Bang came from, but they are certainly doing a good job of showing how the elements could have been formed and how they could have gotten into space in terms of distribution.

I've learned a great deal about human behavior from what other people have discovered and written and from my research. I believe strongly in science, which is a progressive thing, moving ahead, getting a better and better picture, but never getting the True Picture. Nothing can be known about that—the True Picture—in terms of prediction and controls.

There is no purpose to life. Purpose has been replaced by the notion of selection. Biologists have a pretty good idea of how life and living things could have come into existence under the conditions that must have prevailed at one time on the earth. Beginning that way, variations that affected reproduction were selected or rejected in terms of the consequences, which led to the origin of species. Similar processes have produced human behavior.

We don't do anything because of what is going to happen; we do things because of what has happened. With that, the concept of design or plan goes out. If we are able, we can explicitly plan, but that happened only very late in the history of the species with the development of verbal behavior.

What is the highest ideal a person can reach? What are the greatest obstacles to attaining this ideal?

Ideals are another problem. Individuals work toward the things that make them most effective and happiest. That is what positive reinforcement means to me. There is something beyond that, however, which I've developed in my book *Beyond Freedom and Dignity*. What is beyond a feeling of freedom, a feeling of worth, is the survival of the world, which is what ecologists and others are concerned about now. It often conflicts with personal happiness and, indeed, personal achievement.

I don't like to talk about ideals. In general, we have struggled to escape from punitive control and struggled to find reinforcers. In the long run, we begin to see that in doing all this, our very world and future is threatened. How can we make the future important enough to people? That is the issue, because it is "the future" and can't have any effect on us. All that *can* affect us is what we can conclude about the future—the scientific facts and so on.

I don't know if one can name obstacles to our happiness. When we do things to escape from harmful things, such as punishments given by peers, parents, religions, governments, or industries— when we act to avoid or to escape, we seldom report that we are happy. When we do the things that have been reinforced and that we therefore are inclined to do, we report that we are happy. I would say that the greatest obstacle isn't an obstacle, but the preponderance of conditions under which we have to do things.

What do you think about death?

When you die, that's it. There are no things about death that worry me to death. I have lived eighty-three very productive and happy years. It would be rather ungrateful of me to complain when I die. I won't be here to complain, fortunately.

When I die, I'll do what Oliver Wendell Holmes, Jr., the Supreme Court Justice, did. A friend came to him when he was dying, when Holmes could hardly speak, so he put up his hands and went . . . [At this point B. F. Skinner put his thumb to his nose and wiggled his fingers!]

What do you feel are the three greatest problems in life?

You are asking me to pick particular things. I just don't think that way. There are problems I can't put names on. I've written a paper called "Why we are not acting to save the world." In it, I indicate some of the current consequences that keep us all from allowing ourselves to be influenced by predictions of future consequences. Governments, for instance, can't really take steps to restrict birth except in totalitarian governments like China, where it can be done.

Do you feel that there is still something life has to teach you?

There again, I don't pinpoint things like that. Life is always pushing me toward new ways of behaving, and my work is still developing. I get to my desk in the morning, as I did this morning, and something new turns up. This morning, I saw a new aspect of what I'm doing. I wouldn't want to put an abstract label on it.

Do you still believe that behavior is conditioned?

Conditioned . . . that's a misleading word. I'm not talking about Pavlovian conditioning at all. I'm talking about the effects of consequences on behavior. All we do is based on the effect of three kinds of consequences: those that are responsible for our bodies and natural selection; those that are responsible for our personal repertoires; and those that are due to the elaborate contingencies of reinforcement that came about with the elaborate development of different kinds of cultures.

We started as members of a particular species, and that includes some behavior, such as suckling at our mother's breast. That was built in, as is most of what we do. We have been conditioned to do what we do, and that has been reinforced by what has happened to us.

What we have is an organism that produces an organism that acquires a repertoire of behavior. A person will probably require a great many different repertoires for different selves, which can be confusing. A person who is one self in the bosom of his family and a different self with his friends and colleagues, when he invites a friend home . . . which self should he be at that moment? That kind of thing is puzzling.

Simply put, people have equal opportunities to make the most of themselves genetically. I don't think people are all equal genetically. They certainly are born into very different worlds. Those worlds largely determine the people they become, so they are not free from anything that is being done to them.

Do you believe it is possible to become unconditioned?

Don't use that word *conditioned* again! Human beings begin unconditioned. Conditioning is something that happens on the way. It's a good idea to return to the state before conditioning with regard to the things we do because of consequences from others, the things we do when we take someone's advice or obey a rule or law. I like to have my life full of the things I do because of the immediate consequences, rather than because something is what I'm told to do by another person, the government, a religion, or the economic system.

Why is there suffering? Why evil?

I would have to look at the conditions that cause suffering, that is, the activities of other people. The animal world is full of suffering. Sometimes animals either freeze or fry, and then they consume each other as food, which certainly causes suffering. People suffer from the loss of people they love and feel they are being punished. That is the reason we have suffering, not because there is a being above or a source of evil. What causes evil depends on what you mean by evil: Do you mean things that are harmful and punitive or people who cause other people harm? In Africa lions attack and eat gazelles. From the standpoint of the gazelles, lions are evil.

Some animals kill more than what is natural; they kill for the fun of it. Surgeons hurt people knowing that they are hurting them. It all depends on what the consequences are. A child who pulls the wings off a fly is not consciously doing evil. The fly is just an interesting little toy that does funny things. In an adult, that would be considered abnormal behavior.

What do you think about religions?

Religions view this world essentially as dispensable because in their estimation one can dispense with this world if one thinks of the future world as the main thing. Some religions, like Confucianism, are nothing more than ethical advice. Others are highly hierarchical governing systems that claim power and dictates given to them by God. Those religions have had positive consequences for certain individuals, like a good Catholic who is not worried about broader issues, not worried about getting into heaven. But a good Catholic who realizes how much damage is done by opposing birth control is not getting much out of his religion. These are the issues: What is happening? What is the result? Where do religions come from? Of course those questions have all been studied very carefully in comparative religion.

I'm very much interested in how the Old and the New Testaments came to be written, when they were written, by whom they were written, what the historical setting was that caused them to be written, and so on. This emphasis is, of course, not at all acceptable to those who believe the Bible is the word of God and was put down just as God said.

We now know under what conditions various books of the Old Testament were written, particularly political situations in the Middle East, and we're learning a lot from the new Gospels that are just being discovered. St. John's writings, for instance, were particularly selected and elements destroyed—or they thought they were all destroyed until they turned up in scrolls. That selected part of the Bible is a product of Paul and others who said, This is what the Christian religion says.

I've been told that there is a denial of self in Buddhism. That's very close to my scientific position. The denial of the self is the only thing that starts anything. Nothing is initiated within one; everything is determined by certain external and internal factors.

I grew up Presbyterian. They had me believe in determination and predestination. I was interested in Calvinism—the whole question of whether grace is attained through works. If it is, then grace is not grace. One doesn't get into heaven as a reward. If one works for grace, one hasn't been given it. If one is given it, it is not something one has worked for. Let's say you find a wallet with a thousand dollars in it and take it to the police and they say, "It is yours." You didn't work for that thousand. It is grace; it is given to you. If you went out and worked very hard for a thousand dollars, that would be entirely different, and it would have a different effect on you. When Paul spread the word and was dealing with the Romans, who weren't Jews, could they be good Christians?

I know a little of the history of Muhammad and the fire and sword. The Arabs are doing exactly what Muhammad would be delighted to have them do, I suppose—blowing up as many people who are nonbelievers as possible. It is one of the more dangerous religions today because of the devotion of its believers. They are self-sacrificing to a dangerous point.

Religions obviously have evolved. I don't know whether anyone has yet found a group of people who don't have something that is a belief system about what's beyond the here and now. Religion seems to have been inevitable, human nature being what it is.

Who knows what people would be like without religion. It is hard to say what people would be like if they hadn't eyes. There are blind animals; they make their way around somehow.

If you could meet anyone throughout history, who would it be?

I had a very early introduction to Francis Bacon, and my philosophy of science is similar to his, so I would like to talk with him, but I wouldn't have wanted to be Bacon. I don't like his lifestyle. I would ask him to explain more clearly what he said. He has a very important principle: Nature, to be commanded, must be obeyed. We must respond to nature in order to do anything with it—a very important point.

Another one of his ideas is that books must follow science, not science follow books. Find out how things really are; don't just take somebody's word for it. A very important principle.

If you could change anything in life, what do you think you would want to change?

You want me just to pick out one thing! I would like to change education, which is being badly handled right now, and I would like to look forward to a world in which the only way people govern each other is through such things as education, counseling, advice, therapy.

There are five main institutions today that determine the world we live in: government, religion, economics, education, and therapy (in terms of counseling, advising people what they must do). The first three of these use very explicit techniques. Governments usually punish for misbehavior, illegal behavior. Religions promise rewards and punishments. Industry uses goods as reinforcers and almost always uses them as punishments, too, because one doesn't just work Monday morning to get the check on Friday afternoon. A person works under a supervisor who will fire him if he doesn't work, so one might as well be a slave and have a master with a whip.

Both teachers and therapists must get out of the picture before they can claim to be successful. The student who keeps coming back to his books or his teacher has not been taught; the patient who goes back to the psychiatrist hasn't been cured. So I have in mind a world in which the controlling practices have to disappear to be successful.

Do you believe there is a basic difference between men and women?

I suspect there are differences between men and women that are not due to the environment. There certainly is one major difference: women can have babies. I don't think the sexes were ever completely discriminated between. For example, men have breasts, not because they are useful, but in order for the whole genetic business to form two sexes using the same materials.

What is the most important thing to you? Would you say your research or your family?

That raises a very important question about which I am misunderstood. It was, I think, Montaigne who was asked, "Would you rather bury your books or your children?" He answered, "My children." I've said the same thing—and told my children that. I have done more for the world with ideas than I have with genes. Although I love my children very dearly and am not going to bury them, I hope I don't ever have to make that choice. But I'd make the same choice about myself.

If some Mephistopheles appeared now and said, "I will give you a new life starting as a baby, unconditioned, and all evidence you have lived will be wiped out," I wouldn't take that deal. I've been lucky, and that is much more important for me and for the world than living my life again.

6

R A M   D A S S

Years ago, I lived in the basement of a house I shared with five other people. A woman whom I was seeing gave me a tape on relationships by some guy who called himself Ram Dass. "If you want to have a relationship with me," she said, "listen to this!" I managed to catch the cassette just as the door slammed shut behind her.

I wanted a relationship, so I listened ... to that tape and thirty others she had. Years later, when Ram Dass called me to set up an interview, I had to remind myself the voice was real and not a tape.

I respect Ram Dass a great deal. He was my first spiritual hero, and he continues to be a source of learning. His unorthodox view of life helped me begin the process of freeing myself from an overly burdensome view of myself and the world.

When I met Ram Dass at his home on the East Coast, I arrived early so that I could walk along the ocean and be "relaxed" and "centered" when we talked. I walked about fifty yards when a pack of dogs, mistaking me for dinner, chased me back to my car. A little shaken, my heart still pounding, I went to his house.

"Find it okay?" he asked.

"Yes," I answered, "but those dogs chased me down the beach!"

"Oh ... those dogs," he recalled fondly, "we walk together every morning."

Once inside his home, he made me tea. I was excited to meet him, and it wasn't until he told me I could sit down that I realized I had followed him around the house and into the kitchen like a puppy. Later, I asked him if he had any advice for me. He suggested that massage or bodywork would be helpful and then proceeded to give me a massage. At one point during the interview, while we stood in the middle of the room talking, Ram Dass began to dance. It was out of the blue and totally unexpected. Here I was, hundreds of miles from home, standing in the basement of a man I had never met before and watching him dance. At the time, I was quite uncomfortable. I wasn't sure what to do. So I just watched. We then sat down and meditated with each other.

"Is it all right if I push you a bit?" Ram Dass asked, referring to a probing spiritual analysis of the state of my soul. I agreed, and while we looked into each other's eyes, he asked about the status of certain chakras. My answers were spiritual and mystical in nature until he asked me about my sexual chakra.

"Oh, I do all right," I instinctively replied, assuring him of my healthy male libido.

Ram Dass's honesty is refreshing. He reveals his human failings along with his insights. Often when I've seen religious or spiritual persons at a speaking engagement, for those two hours, they're happy and seem to have all the answers. This leaves the audience assuming they are like that all the time. So when I met Ram Dass, I confessed that sometimes I didn't like being here.

"What do you mean by 'here'?"

"You know—here on earth."

"Welcome to the club," Ram Dass said, smiling in agreement.

After the interview, Ram Dass walked me to the door. "How did you get here?" he asked.

"I drove my Honda. It's got 98,000 miles on it."

Turning to his, car Ram Dass said, "Mine has 110,000."

Ram Dass, a.k.a. Richard Alpert, received his Ph.D. in psychology from Stanford University and taught at Harvard. In the 1960s he was active in research on consciousness, with Timothy Leary, Aldous Huxley, Alan Watts, and others. In 1967 he continued his study of consciousness in India and was named Ram Dass (servant of God) by his guru, Neem Karoli Baba. Through books like *Grist for the Mill* and *How Can I Help?* he has contributed to the integration of Eastern spiritual philosophy into Western thought. In 1973 he founded the Hanuman Foundation, the Prison-Ashram Project, the Dying Center, and meditation programs and retreats. In 1985 he helped found the

Seva Foundation. His primary yoga, or vehicle for realizing liberation, is through service.

On what beliefs do you base your life?

I believe there is a spiritual dimension to life. I believe who we are is not what we think we are and what is seeable. Who we are is more than the body or the personality.

It is possible to liberate awareness from identification with thought, and thus be impeccable in life. Spirit resides in every human heart, and there is life, or awareness, or continuity of awareness, beyond death and before birth.

We come to Earth as a curriculum to ground ourselves, as Emmanuel (who is channeled spirit) would say, and to work on ourselves in order to extricate ourselves from the karma of attachments to our thoughts and emotions. Then we can be as Christ said, "in the world but not of the world." That's what the journey of life is about.

There is law in form; spirit has no form. It infuses form. I don't think there is a "being" that is God. There is spiritual awareness that lies behind form. That awareness manifests in form lawfully, and as we get wiser, we understand the laws and the ways the game works. The simple wisdom of those laws rests in the unitive awareness available to all beings. In that sense, everybody is potentially God.

The Hebrew, Christian, and Islamic traditions are all monotheistic because there is only one awareness. If you don't interpret God as a man with a long beard, you have it. There is "one" behind the many—one awareness and one completeness, which includes the many and also manifests through the many.

All religions are rooted in the same thing. Some religions are very entrapping. If a religion works, it must self-destruct at the end. You have to go beyond religion into the spirit, and a lot of religions almost prevent you from doing that, at least the exoteric part of religions, maybe not the esoteric part. Since all religions are rooted in the same touching of spirit, its truth, beauty, wisdom, emptiness, love, they aspire to the same thing. But I don't know if they'll ever get there.

The purpose of life is to awaken out of multiplicity into oneness. To be one with God.

Except for beings who come to Earth already enlightened, the highest ideal is enlightenment. The Buddha is a good example of that, of somebody who made it, who is free to be a being of compassion and love. That is the highest thing that one can aspire to. Compassion, love, wisdom, truth are the root nature of a person's being. I believe all beings will eventually become enlightened. Maybe not all at once.

A person attains this ideal through three basic practices: quieting the mind, opening the heart, and fulfilling one's karma . . . to become fully alive through honoring the uniqueness of one's incarnation.

Vipassana meditation is the main way I quiet the mind: following the breath. I also do other things. I do mantra, and I spend a lot of time in quiet contemplation with my guru, which is my basic method. It is known as *guru kripa*, or "the grace of the guru." By sitting quietly with him (since 1973 he's not been in his body anymore), my mind lets go of all worldly concerns. His being becomes an object of one-pointedness for me. He's very quiet inside and very irascible and very wild, rascally outside. So when I connect with the quietness of his being, I experience my mind becoming very quiet.

I experience my guru as my deepest self. The dialogue between one's deepest self and one's ego is a continuing dialogue, as well as the dialogue with one's incarnation. One constantly is listening to get the ego and the deeper self integrated into some kind of harmony so that the ego speaks from the deeper self or represents the deeper self. That comes from extricating the self and the ego from identification with desires. But since, just like you, I have a body in this incarnation, so do we have an ego. We are constantly tuning into whether or not our acts are bringing us into harmony at every level of our being.

Sometimes an act satisfies one level but doesn't satisfy all the levels. It's a constant tuning and feedback, and tuning and going inside. It's a willingness to admit errors—being willing to fall on your face and realizing you got caught in your ego again.

The main way I open my heart is by singing the *Hanuman Chalesa*, which is forty verses to Hanuman the monkey. I sing it many times each day, and it takes about six minutes each time. It reminds me of my guru. Also, focusing on his love instead of his emptiness opens my heart.

The pure yearning of another human being for awakening and for the ceasing of suffering also opens my heart. I've worked a lot with dying people. The purity of those moments when ego is transcended causes my heart to become liquid almost immediately. Often, when I am giving lectures, the fact that these people have come together reaching for something, and the purity of that reaching and then coming together—that opens my heart. I realize how much I love beings. I love that yearning quality.

I fulfill my karma by listening to the uniqueness of my incarnation. For example, I am taking care of my father, upstairs, because I am my father's son. A few days ago I was in Washington on the steps of Congress in a demonstration against the Contra aid vote, because I am an American citizen and I am somebody with a compassionate heart.

I work with the dying because I am a member of a species that is generally afraid of death. I work with people who have AIDS, in the hospice for AIDS patients in Boston, because I am bisexual and because I have worked with death for many years. It is appropriate that I play that part to help those who are going to die. We have to honor family, community, relationship, and the family of humanity.

For a long time, I thought one got liberated by pushing the world away. Then I realized one got liberated by being in the world, but not of the world. When I'm driving, I drive. When I am making love, I make love. When I am eating, I eat. That's part of it.

The biggest obstacle to enlightenment is clinging to one's own mind. The second noble truth of the Buddha: it's not the pain or the things the world does to you; it's how you react to the things the world does to you. Including crucifixion, as Christ pointed out.

There are no obstacles out there: All the obstacles are within oneself. A person can get enlightenment in almost any condition. I work with some people who've been prisoners many years, and they are doing beautifully, spiritually. They are surely not in a supportive environment.

Very deep LSD experiences have also taken me beyond my mind into spaces where I feel there has been a break in the continuity of consciousness into pure awareness. It doesn't happen frequently but has happened through LSD.

Do you think if a person was enlightened, people would necessarily know it?

It depends on the function that enlightened being has in the world. There are enlightened beings nobody knows, and there are enlightened beings everyone knows. They have different functions. Some of them work on the physical plane; some of them work on other planes.

There are also people who are very enlightened in one aspect of their lives, but their enlightenment doesn't generalize . . . like spiritual idiot savants! That often happens. People find that certain aspects of their lives take them beyond themselves, beyond their ego. Often when I am lecturing, it is a transforming experience and I am outside my ego. Shortly thereafter (I can always tell because I usually hug about a hundred people after a lecture) when my pelvis gets engaged, I know that I have just come back into my ego.

I am a good example of someone who goes in and out. I even have names for them: Richard Alpert and Ram Dass. But I would say they're coming together, slowly coming together. I am getting to like Richard because I have always liked Ram Dass, but Richard was an upwardly mobile achiever with a lot of sexual perversity and fear. I had a long way to go to let him in. I was busy being Ram Dass for years and pushing Richard away. It is very hard on my friends because they have to deal with that schizophrenia. They cannot expect me to be holy because I might be very caught in illusion and attachment, and they can't expect me to be caught because I may be free. The fun is having friends who help each other get free. That is a very important method for me, the *satsang*, the community of other people.

The deeper my *faith in the spirit*, the deeper my willingness to risk *involvement in life*, passions, all of it. My relationships are deeper than they have ever been because of the emptiness of my form. The emptiness is deeper, too.

I want neither to be "here" nor not to be here. I am very happy here. I am sure I would be very happy not being here. I don't think I would be happier being here than not being here. In that sense, I am happy here. Ultimately, it is all planes at once. It's just that you're seeing me in the body and personality so you're asking about that one, but that's only part of who I am. There's a big part of me that isn't "in" time: it isn't in space or going anywhere and is never born and never dies.

I just am, more and more, and that's who I am. That makes it fun to play on this plane. You've got to be careful not to get too caught up in fascination with it all—because it gets to be such fun. Part of the practice is to go beyond rapture and bliss, or the *janas,* as they call them in Vipassana or Theravada Buddhism.

What about death...?

It's another mind moment. It's transformative. It's an integral part of life. It's a *maha* acid trip. It's a great opportunity to move into an incredible adventure of leaving behind the limits of the forms that one has been encased in since one took birth. The moment after death is an incredible release, except for those who get released before death.

When I talk to people about death, I usually quote Emmanuel and say, "It's perfectly safe, like taking off a tight shoe." They can hear that. They can hear the humor in it and the wisdom in it, and I say it from a place from which I feel its intuitive validity. It's not what you say; it's where you say it from.

There are many people who come to the bedside of a dying person and say, "Don't be afraid of death." But they themselves are afraid of death. Somebody caught in quicksand cannot free another.

The work is to extricate ourselves from the causes of suffering in order to free others from suffering, because others *are* our self. We have leverage on that little part of ourselves, which we free in order to free the greater self. When we are free of fear about death, we are able to free another from the fear of death. That is fierce work on oneself, because it is such a deep fear.

People have fear because of ignorance. They don't know who they are. They think they are vulnerable, but awareness isn't vulnerable. That's what Christ said: "Look, I'll show you: crucify me, and I'll drop back in three days and show you that isn't who I was." Who we are isn't vulnerable. We're frightened only if we feel vulnerable, vulnerable to severe things.

I'm part of Amnesty International, which deals with tortures to human beings—the crushing of testicles and watching one's mother getting raped and murdered. I have just been in Guatemala where the torture is incredible and people are afraid of the pain. When we use the pain instead of getting caught in it, there are levels or ranges of experience that we can transform, although when the fire gets too hot, we cannot transform it anymore. What we keep working with are hotter and hotter fires.

I don't think I am wise enough to know what should be changed. I work very hard to change the life conditions of Guatemalans, Nepalese, Indians, and American Indians. I try to help people who are suffering who come to me and AIDS patients who are dying. But I don't know if these situations should be changed. My heart demands that I do those things. I do what I do because it feels harmonious. I listen, and in the moment I hear the appropriate response to that moment. I don't know how it all comes out or what I am going to do today or who I am supposed to be. That will all become clear, I guess, so what's the point of asking?

What are the causes of evil and suffering?

Evil comes out of fear and greed. There are many planes of reality. The unitive plane includes good and evil; one plane lower is dualism, that is, dark and light, positive and negative energies, good and evil. One way to identify evil is define it as that which takes people away from unity; good is that which brings people to unity. That is the most profound definition I have found of good and evil.

Suffering is caused by the clinging to the mind, having expectations. There is suffering because of neurotic patterns of thought, because of the five hindrances (greed, lust, sloth, doubt, agitation), because of people's inhumanity to each other.

Primarily, suffering is all in the mind. The third noble truth is right. It says the way to end suffering is by detaching from the desires and clingings of the mind.

Why are you doing what you are doing?

Why questions, I find, are questions of the mind. They're not questions of the heart. The heart doesn't ask those questions. We do things because that's what we do. Just as a tree grows and blossoms and dies, so I do what I do.

If somebody calls me, I say either yes or no to whatever they ask. I no longer intellectually analyze it; I intuitively respond. I might get an invitation to do a benefit and say yes; another time to the same invitation I say no. I don't know why I do that. The intuitive heart doesn't ask why; the mind asks why. It always wants a rational explanation as to why one does anything.

I am doing whatever I'm doing to get liberated. I know I have a yearning to get liberation. I know I feel the suffering of other people. I know those things guide my actions, so I guess I can say "because of those things," but that's just a link of the mind.

The why lies in the gestalt of the moment. If you weren't here, I wouldn't be talking to an empty chair, and your listening gives me a chance to reflect about things I might not reflect about otherwise.

If you were on your deathbed, what advice would you give to your son or daughter?

To be true to their own hearts. Gandhi's line is very deep in my awareness, my consciousness these days. "My life is my message," I would say to them. "*Your* life is *your* message." We keep molding our actions into our highest self, our highest awareness. Our actions reflect that part of our being that has to do with all the qualities of decency and responsibility and listening to the universe, forgiveness and caring, compassion. These qualities all follow from "To thine own self be true" (Shakespeare had it pegged pretty well), "then canst thou be false to no man."

It's a life's work. We ask, How do I become true to my higher self? Well, asking the question is the beginning of it. Then we look for answers. Somebody says, "If you meditate, you'll get an answer." So we meditate, and we get part of an answer. Somebody says, "If you meet so-and-so or read this book, you'll get an answer." If we keep asking questions, we'll keep getting answers. The whole world will become an answer to our question. Everything in my life is an answer to my question.

How do I hear my guru, or how do I hear my higher self, or how do I live with the spirit all the time? If we ask the question intensely enough . . . if we are ready to ask the question intensely enough, everything will answer. If we're not ready, the answers will lie fallow and we'll forget, until someday we'll remember, in one incarnation or another.

If you could meet anyone throughout history, whom would you meet and what would you ask that person?

I'd meet my guru. He would be the first one. Lao-tzu and Chuang-tzu and the Buddha and Christ and Kabir and Rumi and Rama and Hanuman and Isaiah would be interesting. St. John, Martin Luther King, Gandhi, all my heroes, all the people who have touched spirit and have tried to integrate it with form, are people I would love to hang out with. But in a way, the quieter I get, the more I do hang out with them . . . like my guru, because the more I see as they see, the more I am as they are. The question is, Am I hanging out with them in form or in essence? The only thing worth hanging out with is the essence, not the form.

Although I love the fun of form, what feeds my heart is the essence of beings, and that is independent of life and death. They are here and I am here, and the words they left and stories left about them are all things that feed the heart. That is why I really use the holy books a lot. I just open books like the *Tao Te Ching* or the *I Ching* or the Ramayana or the Bible and get hits from them. I would ask them to tell me anything I need to know.

What was the most significant thing that has ever happened to you, that affected your life the most? What did you learn?

My birth.
My death will be the next one.
The first time that Tim Leary gave me acid in March of 1961 was significant. November 1967, when I met my guru, was a moment significant in my life. Those were two very significant moments in my spiritual awakening.

I've learned that the limits of time and space are a conspiracy of the mind. It is possible to go beyond those things.

I've learned that human desire has a finite nature and that death is transformative and not the end. People have very beautiful hearts, even though their minds may catch them in ugliness or ego. One must look at another human being at many levels, many realities, not just one.

I've learned that the body decays and that's okay. Relative importances: when in New York or L.A., I know how to get around the city.

What makes you happy? sad? angry?

I've developed a lot of appreciation in life. Most things make me happy. Relationships make me happy. Frustrations make me happy. Helping people become relieved of suffering makes me very happy. Singing to God makes me happy. Making love makes me happy. I like doing charcoal sketches of animals, nature, babies, old people. I am a very happy person. I rarely lose my happiness, only when I am very fatigued or quite sick, and those are the two I am working on now.

Things that make me sad . . . the suffering of other people. The way that the earth is being misused. The fear that's generated by people and the pain that comes from lack of faith in the spirit.

My own clingings of mind make me angry. I get angry at other people for not seeing how wise I am [he laughs], for being confrontational or rigid in their thoughts. I get angry when my car breaks down or when my plans are frustrated. Those are things all in my own mind, so the basic anger is always in myself, not with anyone else. Everyone else is just being who they are, so I don't know what I'm getting angry for.

Sometimes the Richard Alpert side of me gets angry. But my practices of *mantra* and *japa* are deep in me, and I have these beads in my hand much of my waking time. I do "Rama, Rama, Rama," and that usually brings me back to Ram Dass. Sometimes anger makes me lose it; I'll just be doing the beads and not thinking. Once I feel the beads, though, or come back to the term *Rama,* I'm right back in there again. I would like to be like Gandhi at the moment that, as he got shot and was dying, he said, "Rama."

Maybe he said, "Mom"?

No, he said, "Ram." He was beyond "mom."

Some people think personal relationships interfere with spiritual growth . . .

Relationship is one of the most profound yogas one can perform. For two people to come together to reach for that which is unitive behind separation means they can be one dance and not two.

71

I've performed many marriages, and I see marriage as an incredible opportunity for awakening. It is clear that by its nature, it is one of the highest-risk yogas, because of the potential for entrapment through frustration and fear and personal expectations. At the same time, it is one of the highest opportunities on earth.

There are individual differences in the paths of people. For some people sex is an impediment because they can feel the power of those drives inside them. They get entangled in them and can't extricate themselves into awareness during those times.

I myself go in and out of awareness during sex. At times, I lose it completely. At other times I get it back, but I play the game, just as I play with death. Death is the first chakra, sex is the second chakra, and the ego is the third chakra. When we get those three under control, we are flying free. I don't run away from any of it.

If one thinks there is an energy loss during sex, there is an energy loss. But we "are" the energy of the universe, which is infinite, so there is no using up of it unless we think we are finite. What we think is what we get.

Celibacy is true celibacy only when our mind is turned toward the unitive nature of all things; then the desires do not arise. If desires arise and we do not give expression to them, we are merely in what I call the "horny celibate syndrome," and I don't think that gets you to God.

Do you feel there is a basic difference between men and women besides the body?

Not in spirit. In spirit, souls are androgynous. On the level of men and women, there is a hormonal, anatomical, and psychological difference.

The greatest freedom comes when we honor our uniqueness. When a woman is truly a woman, she seems freer to me than when she's trying to be a man. When a man is a man, he seems freer than when he's trying to be a woman. This is said by a bisexual who deals with all these issues inside himself and accepts the uniqueness of his predicament and his feelings. I would rather deal with the truth than deal with what I am not.

The old saw has it that men are more rational and women are more intuitive, but that is cultural training. I find that as we get more spiritual, we get more androgynous, interestingly enough. We get so we are not busy being a man or a woman. As we extricate ourselves from the psychological aspects of the role, then we find, if we're men, deep intuition as well as emotions; if we're women, great clarity of mind.

There are differences. Women have a strong nesting instinct and drive to protect their young, which is a species aspect that is so powerful it grounds them a lot. When a man extricates himself from his ground, there is less to pull him back to earth than there is for a woman.

Hindus see it as the husband's job to keep working spiritually to get out, but he needs the *shakti,* or the energy, of the wife, because the energy created by that relationship gives him energy. And she who might get caught in the earth needs him to help her get free. Together they are unbeatable. That's a very ancient understanding of the difference between men and women and the complement of how they work together.

Ultimately, however, the journey is for each individual to make alone. One can go so far "in" a relationship that one goes "beyond" relationship, where there is just one. It is the great aloneness. This doesn't mean separateness from the other person; it can include the other person. It just means that the term *relationship* has ceased to be terribly relevant anymore. We become free by honoring our uniqueness, and that includes our sexuality, whatever it is.

How can psychotherapy help a person's spiritual practice?

It can allow one to see the laws of the universe in action, because the laws of the universe are holographic in the sense that they are in the small things as in the big things. This law is readily apparent in our own personalities and our own bodies. As we study our personality in a supportive setting with somebody who creates an environment that allows us to feel safe to examine it, we begin to see how the mechanisms of personality, mind, and emotion work. Such a setting allows us to develop and cultivate a witness. Therapy at its best allows us to cultivate a vantage point from which to see the dynamics of personality while free of the entrapment of personality. We can thereby get to enjoy the personality.

With all the therapy I have had and all the drugs and all the gurus, I have never gotten free of one neurosis. What has changed is that, instead of being big monsters I am frightened of, the neuroses become like little schmoes that I invite in for tea. When I see a perversity, I say, "Hi. Come on in." Instead of seeing my personality as my enemy and being caught in the struggle between the id and the superego, I have cultivated awareness. This is why Jung had it over Freud, because he recognized there was something behind the id.

Jung (as did Maslow and Carl Rogers and people like that) saw that there was a higher component of the being than the instinctual impulses and animal motives and desires. Jung recognized something beyond the archetypes, which is the astral plane, the unitive quality in things.

Many people ask me for advice about becoming a therapist or counselor. I say to them, "You will be the best therapist if you see the relative reality of personality, rather than be caught in it as an absolute. Your job is to work on yourself in order to be free of your personality, in order to be able to free another from his personality, because the minute the clients get into their awareness, they can heal themselves. You are to become an environment in which people can heal themselves."

I then say, "You have your choice. You can take the traditional training in counseling that will teach you most of the academic disciplines of counseling, or you can take the more transpersonal strategies that will put you more on the edge of society but will probably help you integrate the spirit and psychology better than the traditional training. Traditional trainings are rooted in what they call science, which has a materialistic ground to it. What you see is what you get."

It's a person's ability to tolerate not having a credential. If one needs a credential to have an identity one is comfortable with, then one should take conventional routes. It's better to be a Ph.D. in psychology than a social worker, for example. But I feel the quality of counseling has nothing to do with that. Degrees are all for legitimizing oneself and climbing the ladder of social institutions, getting better salaries and better positions and getting more respect from people.

The fact that I have a Ph.D. makes people listen to me more than if I didn't have a Ph.D. That's about what it is worth. I get a fairer hearing, if you will. The prejudices people have make a difference, and they are put to rest when I say that I have a Ph.D.

Counseling has to do with intuition, with work on oneself, with the quietness of one's mind and the openness of one's heart. The scene is wide open. Pretty soon, I would imagine, the world will divide into the counselors and counselees, and everybody will be everything to everyone else. Everything will be fine, because it is merely a mirroring-supportive-reflective environment to allow a person to work on himself in my environment.

The mistake of therapists is in thinking they do something *to* other people. I don't have that sense of doing anything *to* anyone else. I have a sense that I am an environment, and people do it to themselves.

When I therapize people, I am not attached to how they come out. Whether they go and kill themselves or go and be happy is not my problem. That is their problem. *My* problem when I am with them is to keep quiet with my heart open, and I must listen and acknowledge the license they *are* giving me and the lack of license to the place they are *not* giving me.

I'll go just as deep and as far as a human being will allow me to go, because to me, everybody is a lover. I mean, I've got no boundaries. Most people say, "I want you in *that* role, at *that* distance." That's fine. I'll play it, or not, as I choose. I do not present myself as a psychology counselor or therapist, because it is too limiting a role for me.

I have an opportunity in this society to play a role. To put people in relation to the spirit is just grace, having that role.

I deal with a lot of people in mental hospitals where the work they have to do is primarily psychological and not spiritual. They have to do that as a prelude to doing spiritual work. I am not the person to do that with. There are people extremely good at dealing with that relative psychological reality, much better than I am because I just don't take it terribly seriously, and there are stages where a patient really wants one to take it seriously.

7

JEAN HOUSTON

Jean Houston's home is amazing. Entering, one is surrounded by reminders of past eras and remote cultures. It is a time capsule, filled with large Oriental rugs and antique high-backed chairs fit for a king, chandeliers and paintings, suits of armor, and a mummy's sarcophagus. The room also describes Jean Houston: Her mind is a sophisticated smorgasbord of ancient and contemporary wisdom. She describes the mind in which she lives with the flair and heart of a Shakespearean actress.

She is close to six feet tall and appears very capable of carrying her share of the load, whether it's living in the bush with the aborigines or climbing mountains in Java.

Her mixture of ancient and contemporary wisdom prompted memories of my visits with Jagir Singh while I was in Nepal. Often, as I walked the streets of Katmandu, people recognized me as Jagir Singh's friend. They volunteered wonderful and mysterious stories about the things Jagir Singh could do, how he could see the future and heal people. "Mr. Bill," they said, "thousands of people are able to have children because they went to Jagir Singh."

One day when I had a bad cold, I visited Jagir Singh. I was sniffling and my nose kept running.

"Mr. Bill," Jagir Singh said, "do you want something for your cold?"

"Sure," I said.

Then he went into the back room, the same room into which I had seen him disappear hundreds of times before. There he would pray over his magical concoctions and instill them with a great healing power. He would then wrap the cure in a small sheet of paper and tell people, "Carry this with you, always," or, "Put this under your pillow." The ritual would conclude with Jagir Singh's hands placed on the person's head and a blessing given. "When I look at a plant," he once told me, "it reveals to me its healing properties."

So I anticipated the whole treatment when he went into the back room: the magic herbs, the prayers, the whole thing. He emerged from the back room with a large box. I had never seen this routine before. He searched the box for awhile, and then his eyes brightened. He reached in and pulled out a bottle of Dristan cold capsules. "Ah, here we go, Mr. Bill—this works very well!"

Jean Houston does not hold to the past or the present. She will use any means, ancient or contemporary, to teach. She combines her scientific background in psychology and anthropology (for years, she worked closely with Margaret Mead) with her great knowledge of myth, religious tradition, and spiritual techniques. She is a modern alchemist extracting a new truth from various traditions and sciences.

Jean Houston has an immediacy about her. She feels strongly that people need to be empowered, and she did that for me. After the interview she told me that the book was a good idea. "But don't put it off," she warned. She expressed a genuine concern at the lack of opportunity most people are given. As a leader in the human potential movement, Jean Houston must be painfully aware of the potentials that are never reached.

Dr. Jean Houston, internationally renowned scientist and philosopher and past president of the Association for Humanistic Psychology, has conducted seminars and worked as a pioneer in human development in over thirty-five countries. She is Director of the Foundation for Mind Research in New York and is the author of more than ten books, including *The Possible Human* and *Public Like a Frog: Entering the Lives of Three Great Americans.*

On what beliefs do you base your life?

I base my life on the fact that I am a citizen in the universe, which is larger than my aspiration and far more complex than all my dreams. I am a co-creator of this universe, but human beings are not the only ones minding the store. We are organism environments, symbiotic within worlds . . . within worlds . . . within worlds. Spiritual realities are the underpinnings, the very template of existence. As I refine my body, mind, and spirit (and that needs constant homework), I have more and more access to these realities, and it is a co-creational process.

I believe that the human being is part of nature and that nature is part of "Godding." There really is no great separation. It's all an interwoven tapestry we can enter at *any* point—through beauty, through music, through craft, through prayer, through profession. The world becomes luminous, then, when we bring the totality of what we are to that activity.

A pattern I often suggest is a kind of tripartite scheme of reality. We're built something like conglomerate rocks. This little local self I'm calling me is bound in space and time: it has gender, profession, a certain birth, a certain death, various kinds of categories and existences. That that local soul has *leaky margins* means we have a much more amorphous reality. We have the reality of archetypes, what we call gods, small *g*. $E=mc^2$ describes the great patterns of connection. We can have access to those. This *we* that is reality is also diaphanous or transparent to what we call "I am." [She refers to a biblical passage in which God describes himself:] "I am that I am"—beingness itself.

Human beings often have needed access to archetypical "realities," gods, and architectural structures, which allow for them to take on larger strength, power, beingness, and capacities—larger coding that allows them to know beingness, themselves. That doesn't mean they can't know "being" as Zen Buddhists do, but the way of Zen is the via negativa—the way of absolute centralized concentration and meditation, which is "me" going to who "I am." But for purposes of muscular concrete reality, we need to go through the extension of being—the via positiva, which is the extension through these archetypical realities.

I believe we are at the most critical place and time in human history. Indeed, these are the times and we are the people who must act. If not now, then when? If not you, who? What we do makes a profound difference. The Christians would say, we're moving from lesser guilt to higher guilt, a higher responsibility.

We have enough complexity, crisis, consciousness, uniqueness of planetary affairs. We are about to become *planetary people:* The global villager, the cosmopolitan, and women are now rising to full partnership, not just with men, but with the planet and the whole domain of human affairs.

The new technology gives us access to a whole global system: The revolution with the understanding of human potential means that we can finally begin to harvest what the genius of the human race is and learn how to use that genius to become who we are.

The spirit of the time is moving so that we are at jump-off time into what is Type One high-level civilization, in which we become responsible along with "God" or "Goddess" or "Godding spiritual powers" for co-creation of the earth and orchestration of its resources. The earth is growing a nervous system, and we are responsible for that. This, then, expands our own psychologies, so that ego (what we thought of as a dominant form of personality) becomes only *one* image among many images of the manifold psyche.

We are becoming much richer than we thought we would. Great literature has always spoken about it, but this *is* it: democratization of our capacities for the first time in history! We are moving toward a world myth. That's why there's fascination with myths in our time and the rise of so many of the ancient myths. Part of my job is not just to go in and speak to different cultures, to help whole cultures, but to begin to get state-of-the-art in human capacities. It's only one small part of what I am doing.

What I really do is find the Great Story in each culture, whether I work in India, West Africa, Australia, or China. I try to find the great story, the coded DNA of that *cultural* psyche trying to emerge, and then to help it emerge so that it's not caught in atomistic forms. The whole spiritual template of the world is moving to greater complexities, to consciousness, and we are about to *become* the gods that we used to write about. Not The God, though we are diaphanous to that, too, but the gods.

We are moving to what I call "we are." What used to be mythical is now becoming existential. What used to be "essence-ial" is now becoming existential. That means, what used to be "essence," the *vertical* level of existence, is rising to levels that it could, perhaps, never be before. The whole planet is being charged and is moving into its next phase. ("The vertical level of existence" refers to one of the symbolic meanings of the cross. The vertical aspect of the cross refers to a relationship with God or a formless higher reality. The horizontal aspect of the cross refers to one's relation to humanity and the reality of worldly form. Thus, the cross represented Jesus' embracing of both realities.)

What is the highest ideal that a person can reach?

In Eastern terms, to see all people as Brahma. To see all people as Buddha. To hear all sounds as mantra. To know all places as Nirvana. In Western terms, the ideal is to see all people crystal clearly as God-in-hiding. It is to hear all sounds as part of the music, the weave of creation. It is to hold this attitude with a loving heart, available mind, and quickened soul.

It begins with where a person is at that moment. As Huang Po said, "Every moment, you are sitting on the Bodhi Mandala, which can, at any moment, erupt into enlightenment." The moment is always there; the totality is always there. Know at every moment that this is it! It isn't a future event; it is the radical now.

Have that excitement, then join with other groups of people. One thing I find is that we need the affirmation of others to keep us going. I really believe in bands of angels, bands of secular angels, who go out to teach and establish learning communities where people gather together and do physical, mental, psychological, and spiritual exercises. That is what my books actually provide . . . or people can make up their own methods. They do what they do and they can keep on empowering each other. Is the purpose to say, "Hey, you're a great guy . . ."? Not at all! It should be, "I see this attribute in you. Let's bring it out so we can, together, become fascinated by each other's glory."

Also, the purpose is to share each other's pain, though not have it degenerate into kvetch sessions. We need each other to spark each other, prime each other, hone each other. That is why every great spiritual form that enters into the world always gathers around it an ashram, or a community, or a sangha. It needn't be a formal kind of community; it can be just a community of a few friends who gather together regularly at a sacred time and place and work for the quickening process in each other. They must know that the quickening is not for narcissistic reasons. Its purpose isn't for one's own atman to groove on one's own brahma. The purpose is enabling people to be deep partners of the earth. We are being called to an immense relationship to planet Earth that we've never been called to before.

There *are* obstacles—selfishness, unkindness to others, laziness, any kind of closing down—they're often the same kinds of things. Growth is always within our capacities. It will spark through us. Sometimes it will drive us mad, if we close down on it too much. A lot of people are going mad now in ways they never have in history. We cannot stay closed down: This evolutionary process, this spirit, is going to get to us any which way it can. Any which way, it does! AIDS, for instance, is the shadow-side of what is happening in the universe. It's the end of the immune response; all barriers are breaking down. The barriers are breaking down between nations, between peoples, between our selves. The biggest barrier is a sense that things don't matter. It's getting caught up in the immediacy of everyday living and not realizing how important we each are at this time in history.

I have done a fair amount of work with people who work with AIDS victims. One of the ways I train them is by saying, Not only have the barriers in the bloodstream broken down, the breakdown is also between the self and the self. AIDS victims are often profoundly open to their own spiritual depths. Although they may not have much time, they have an extraordinary quality of time and access to their own spiritual lives.

My job is to sneak up on them, like a Trojan horse. It's very easy. They think they're going to a seminar on human potential, but suddenly they discover that "They-I" transformational life journey. One doesn't have to persuade or convince; it is just there. It's reaching out and touching a person and saying, "You matter." I do it in a very complex way, through old myths, stories of Oedipus and the search for the Grail, stories of Odysseus or Jesus Christ. People find that their "personal particular" is joined to a "personal universal," to a much larger story that is really reflecting *upon* the story itself.

Subtly, they're no longer caught in their own story, because they have joined a universal one, gone from "This Is Me" to "We Are" of the larger story. They can never lose that feeling. Once you have joined a larger story, that entelechy, or seeding, in you that has been yearning at the crossroads of your existence to enter into time is going to get activated; it rarely shuts down again. It is a very difficult, very complex work that involves constant study and refinement, yet in many ways it is very easy, because it is turning to the natural flow of things, like water flowing downhill. It's like trees rising in springtime, plants coming up. Pour a little water, give a little nourishment, and most human beings are going to bloom.

Everybody won't reach it. A lot of people are committed to their own calcification and get a perverse, almost semi-erotic joy out of courting the crash in themselves. But many more people can be reached than cannot. There is no such thing as reaching everybody. We have too many individual variables. It's like the universe saying, "Is everybody going to live, or is everyone going to die?" Eventually, everyone is going to die. Some things will live first and then die. We're very much a part of nature. More and more people are speaking life. At the same time, the shadows of death are rising fast. We've never had simultaneously such bright sunlight with so many shadows.

What is your idea of God? How would you describe God?

I don't think it is masculine. It's beyond gender, and that's very important to me, as it is to many women. Even though we know that intellectually, scripture gives the sense that power and dominion are ultimately male. It's very important that that changes.

Do you believe there's a basic difference between maleness and femaleness?

Women are aware of many more patterns and gestalts than men; men are aware of the practical way to accomplish a goal, which is simply a different style. This is one of the problems in corporations: Women are becoming good secondary men and aren't allowed to develop their own geniuses for seeing larger patterns and processes.

There are profound differences between men and women. There is no question that there are neurological differences and different stages of development. Tests have indicated different language development rates, and so forth. In the realm of ultimate spirituality, men and women are the same. In terms of historical development right now, they are different. For example, if I had been born before the last four hundred years, what would I have been doing? I'd be stirring the soup, taking care of the kid; if a man, I'd be fighting off the woolly mastodon. People of those times would be aware of many processes and developments, especially the developments of children, which account for the main difference between women and men. Women tend to be much more development and process-minded; men, more goal-oriented.

Look at music. It is very different when women produce their own music. Take "Both Sides Now," by Joni Mitchell. She's humming . . . that's a mandala. It's a circle; it returns to itself. In the eye is a mandala. The planet is a mandala. A mandala generally has a center and direction (north, south, east, and west) and certain kinds of balances and harmonics. In Tibetan form, it is literally a progression, a study to enter into The Source. Women's music is reflective of a mandala. Women's religion is revitalizing with its emphasis on the Goddess in God, our relationships to the earth, and nurturing. It is not suffering. That dual-gender god does not create the world and say "Good." God spins the world or is the world or grows the world, constantly in process.

God-Goddess-Godding-Godseeding is that Mind that creates the universe, which engages us as parents, in a sense, of that Godding. Godding has both the physical extension of the universe and the *psychic extension of ourselves*—and, I am sure, of other ascended creatures as well. I am a great animal fan. I am not about to say that we humans are IT. I swim with dolphins, and they are very advanced. There may be all kinds of forms.

This Godding is also an evolutionary principle that allows for the transmutation of the depth structures of patterns of creation, of great creative potencies manifested—in the realms of time and of space. It is a love that moves the sun and all the stars. It is the lure of becoming. Nothing is ever lost in that Godding. Great moments—the smile of a child, the bark of a dog, the leafing of a magnolia tree—all are preserved. Nothing is lost. In the realm of space and in time, it is all there, the "great code." We have the ability to know that and be part of that.

Part of evolution on the planet gets us to the place where we are conscious of our dominion, of our extension of daughtership or sonship, of our beingness in this God-being. That is the universe, free to make mistakes, not absolute, always becoming.

Rather than experiencing God as separate, I see more of a rhythm, with times of deep identity, of knowing. Whenever people have these times, they say, "I am God." And others say, "You lazy, crazy fool. We're going to crucify you!" But there is a falling out of that sense of identity, and we become being that is connected to "other." This creates an immense yearning, despair, but our sense of loss creates the energy to be restored again. We need to be thrust out from that beingness to create the energy for a creative dialectic. At this stage of the evolutionary process, we need that sense of division from time to time (which, for most of us, is most of the time) to create the energy of yearning. I wrote about that in *The Search for the Beloved*. When I have looked at the lives of people who have achieved enormous amounts of what I call co-creativity, almost unbearably, they have had a relationship to this oneness. So powerful has that relationship been, it has provided them with the energy, the momentum, the passion to get on with it.

When we feel too separated, we seem in utter creature relationship to creator. Then we lose the passion for the possible and begin to set up rules and devise all kinds of schemata and taboos, thou shalts and thou shalt nots. These keep us from remembrance, in a state of holy terror, because we dare not know the power that comes from the truth of identity.

Those people I know who have been able to sustain that sense of tremendous relationship to oneness have been able to do so much more. They have extended themselves into the death realms and the realms of "we are." Thus they give of themselves, juiced and green and yeasted by the great patterns of creation. They feel their relationship is deeply personal. It is not, "myself with God"; it is, "myself with Beloved." I have talked to so many people who have been part of this. Mother Teresa is an example. When I got to know her very well, I said, "How is it that you are able to do so much?"

"My dear, it is because I am so deeply in love."

"But, Mother, you are a nun!"

"Precisely. I am married to Jesus."

"Yes, I understand you're married to Jesus. All nuns are."

"No, you don't understand," she countered. "I really am so in love with my Beloved, that I see the face of my Beloved everywhere—in the face of a day-old child left in a cradle, in lepers, and in the Hindu man dying in a street of Calcutta. I can't do *enough* for my Beloved! And my Beloved cannot do enough for me."

Her Beloved is the cultural archetype Jesus, who has become for her the icon, the symbol of that deep belovedness. What she has is the power of the collective archetype. Many of us do not *have* that power. My relationship has to be far more individualized and much more sought for. I'm not suggesting that it is easy, either way. I'm saying that we're living in a time in which the personal relationship to that Goddedness, which I call "in The Beloved," is becoming far more individualized. As we are moving more and more toward a planetary society, we are getting a very deep and personal relationship to these depths that are no longer the God or the Goddess of the tribe, or even the polite God or Goddess of the cosmopolitan. That pursuit of relationship gives us the passion and momentum to do what we have to do. Without that relationship, most of us simply are not going to have sufficient passion to perform the possible.

What about the difference between the Western and Eastern approaches?

The jury is out on that one. This is the great time of experimentation. People can go the shamanic route, which is highly activated, at times too activated for our forms, with the drumming and the ecstasy. When people change their religions, they tend to go East or West. They don't tend to go North or South. That's why Episcopalians become Bahais and Jews become Sufis, but they don't become Africans or engage in shamanic or South American realities because those are so highly energized.

There are many things happening in shamanic practices right now—that is, with individual, not mass conversions. The latter traditions are so high up, they demand that you dance and sing and dramatize your reality, your ecstasy. But many Westerners have found a problem with deep quieting, unless it is going to be a constant practice. It has to be a constant practice. If it is just one or two intensive blasts, then one will notice some problems because the brain waves are going to be at variance with the new things one has to respond to.

Some people say all religions lead to one place, but nobody's really looked at that one. That's a kind of thing that people say automatically, like a truism. I am not sure. They might, ultimately. Most religions never get that far, to beingness itself, where one is the doer, the doing, the done; the knower, the knowledge, the known; the laugher, the laughing.

Many stages are colored by the culture. For example, if one has a revelation of the Bhagavad Gita, of Vishnu, it's going to be Vishnu "brighter than a thousand suns was Vishnu, Krishna, Vishnu." If it's a revelation of Christ, it will be the rising Christ or the Resurrection. If it is Quetzalcoatl, the flaming serpent. Archetypal realities look very different depending on the context. Ultimate realities will ultimately be the same. It is all the same nervous system, the same relationship to totality. Culture tries to dictate too many steps along the path.

More and more I am drawn to the Western approach, which appears more active. Rabbi Zalman Schachter-Shalomi is one example; he's so Zorba-like.

He's a close friend of mine. He is *via positiva* as opposed to *via negativa*. Vipassana is an example of *via negativa*. That means deep awareness and deep quieting, the cutting-out of distraction. The *positiva* is something Zalman does, laughing and singing and telling jokes and going in a side door to find an ultimate reality and a caring mind. His way tends to be the way of the West. One is not better than the other. When you put both *positiva* and *negativa* together, however, you have some problems.

There are very great shamanic traditions in this country because of the Native American. Very powerful. My seminars have a lot of music and dancing and telling of the great myths and living them out as transformation. They are *via positiva*. A hundred and fifty people come once a month from all over, people who have been pursuing Tibetan meditations and altering their lives. Ironically, Native American practices came so naturally to them! Jewish people, Catholic people—all sorts of backgrounds, but all Americans. They've responded the most because Native American concepts are still reflective of the sensibility and spirit of this place.

There is something about the precious symbols that have arisen over hundreds and thousands of years springing from time and place. Such symbols speak to a person. Jung warned in the 1920s and 1930s that we can utilize Eastern thought, but unless we are truly Easterners, we will not understand what sleeps in the art forms. We are "grown out" of the land and in some sense are grown out of the symbols. So, in the sense of time and place influences, we are all Native Americans, whether we like it or not.

Only after studying the symbols of the East did I begin to understand the Western symbols.

Often, we have to come into our own symbol system by going outside, because we contain so much negative baggage about our own culture, especially in the Judeo-Christian tradition.

What is the purpose of life?

Life has many purposes. The deep purpose for me is to be a minstrel. At this point in time, this day and age, my purpose is so overpowering that I wake up with it every morning, and it is very obvious. The earth is at the greatest period of crisis in history. We are being called to be co-creators. I don't think we can finally destroy our earth, but we can cause an awful lot of damage to her in the next ten or twenty thousand years. Earth may eventually shrug her shoulders and go back to normal. My purpose is to warn that we are neither prepared nor educated to be co-creators, co-transmitters of this planet. We're not living in the year 1845! Suddenly, we have been thrust into an immense responsibility, which I call Type-One Civilization. My purpose is to learn as much as I can about what it means to be a world co-creator.

We have to extend our minds, our imaginations, our capacities, our problem-solving, our thinking, our relationships, our relationships to our bodies. We have to understand our own bodies deeply and to train people in that. We then must work all over the world simultaneously to look at the deeper story that is trying to emerge—because, as far as most people are concerned, when one discusses the abstraction of "earth," even with the picture of outer space being so powerful, people don't respond. They have to feel that they are themselves part of the story. That's what I'm looking for, the "we" world myth for today's age.

The schools aren't going to do it! So I go into whole cultures and train people, not just in human development, but also in their myths. I say, "Let us look at the deeper story emerging that you are part of, so that you will feel a passion to be part of that development! Then, we can determine what you can do in your little or large ways, as the case may be. (Of course, there is no such thing as 'little' or 'large.' Everything is immense right now!) What you do makes a profound difference. You develop the possible human, then help create the possible society that co-creates the possible earth. We are requested—required—by our planet to join with her and educate ourselves to become."

If I had been an abbess in a convent five hundred years ago, my purpose would have been to create a harmonic realm to extol God and Nature and to find out as much as I could about God and Nature. I would have been a Hildegarde of Bingen type. That would have been a natural form for me. Now, my purpose is to extend the life of God/Goddess in the world; to be a Godseed in the world; to emphasize as much as we can the traits of serving, compassion, love, pleasure, while not avoiding pain or tragedy, because they are necessary complements to the former; to find meaning in, as well as patterns of connection between, all of us, even at times when society seems utterly leveled. Those levelings are part of a much larger story.

I was once told that I shouldn't try to change people, that if I touched them, they'd change themselves.

That's true. Each of us bears what I call an entelechy. *Entelechy* is Greek, meaning "seeding, coding, dynamic propulsion." It's the entelechy of the acorn to become an oak tree, the entelechy of a baby to be a grownup in the world. The entelechy of you or me is to be—God only knows what! Sometimes, we get glimpses of entelechy. Part of our purpose is to track into the entelechy of maturation. Once it starts in us, twenty years later we will look back on our old selves as Neanderthals, we'll be so different.

When you touch people, you can be deeply present, witnessing, evoking, midwifing their entelechy. Then, you have to recognize when to stand back and not say, "Let me help you," and not get in the way while this natural process unfolds. That is my purpose—to help spur realization of the entelechy of people and also of whole cultures. That's why I'm looking at myths. Myths often contain the coding of the entelechy, but to help the entelechy of people and the culture to emerge, there is only so much one can do. One cannot do it all, but one can be deeply present and touch.

Do you believe in a spiritual practice? For example, one person I interviewed said that one can work up to enlightenment gradually. Another said one can't work toward it. What do you think?

Both things are true for both those people. There are so many different ways of entering. I remember once, in a deep meditation, I found myself inside a gold honeycomb that went on and on. There were different cones inside, and they were filled with golden light. Each one was a different world. Over a period of eight hours during that meditation, I went through nine or ten utterly different worlds, and I touched only a part of each—they seemed to go on a long time.

I knew that the message of the meditation was that we are part of that extraordinary reality and that there are so many different paths. I don't think there is such a thing as One Way.

The greatest experience of alternate reality I've ever had was when I was six years old. It came about through humor and laughter because of my father, who was a professional comedy writer. He wrote for the Bob Hope show. In my book *The Possible Human*, I wrote about my experience. I had just been threatened with three hundred years of purgatory by a nun, because I'd asked if Jesus ever had to go to the bathroom and whether Jesus, when he rose, was filled with helium. My father found it hilariously funny and made it out to be an enormously funny thing. He took me to see *The Song of Bernadette*, and we started to get hysterical because the Virgin Mary was played by an old starlet he had been trying to romance! We got hysterical and were thrown out of the theater. I went home and prayed in the closet, hoping the Virgin Mary would show up. She never did. As soon as I gave up, wham!—the universe opened up. I knew that my doggies and me in the closet were taking the place of the Virgin Mary and that the trees and the airplanes and my Mary Jane shoes were all part of an extraordinary universe in which everything was significant and moving together. It was very, very good. My father started laughing; the whole universe began to laugh. Those kinds of experiences stayed deep in me. Regardless of how low I have been in my life (and sometimes I've been pretty low), I have never lost that certain knowledge—that we are all part of this enormous pattern of connection.

I have a spiritual practice. I never stop it; it is always going on. There is an undercurrent of prayer or contemplative prayer that goes on with me literally all the time, even in my sleep, as far as I can see. There are some very specific prayer and meditational archetypal relation practices that I perform every morning and every evening, for a certain period of time, depending on what day it is. For the last twenty years I've performed those practices every day.

When one does things with a certain level of mindfulness, it carries over into one's day with a sense of, "I am body, mind, and spirit acting in time." Then, there are practices for each day. I try to make sure, regardless of what happens, that I am in a position to reach out to others who lack opportunity, whether they are ill or undernourished in body, mind, or spirit, or whether they need an impetus to get on with their next stage of growth. I try to reach out to a certain number of people each day with a phone call or a visit. Being available is also part of the living action, living love in action.

Why are you doing what you are doing?

I feel urgency: This is the time and we are the people, and, by God, we have to do what we can. The more we do the deeper things, the likelier we'll feel the agony of the world. The "deeper" is going to be reflected in our lives. You don't get away with anything. That's one thing I've discovered. It's something women know: You don't get away with anything. What I do, and the way I work on myself, is going to affect profoundly my work in the world. As greater so-called refinement comes, I can get away with less and less. The phone call I did not make that could have been a help to a person is going to haunt me, is going to come back and hit me. One can't be bad and get away with things as one used to.

To answer the depth of your question of why I am doing this: I am so blessed to be part of this time that, by God, I'd better do it! It's not just the responsibility for "I" anymore; it's "we" and "us." We are part of a community of body, mind, and spirit that is trying to make a profound difference, that is helping to make the earth move into Type-One Civilization, which really is culture cultivating Godseeds. Maybe earth is a planet, but maybe this is a school. Maybe it's a school of Godseeds. Maybe that's what we are! We are finally coming to that awareness where there's sufficient complexity, crisis, and consciousness to wake us up to this wake-up time. This is the mythic time, more mythic than anything, than the search for the Grail or the descent into Hell. This is the time! Wake up!

I was the daughter of a very funny man who saw life as a paradox, a comedy endlessly entertaining. My mother was a very deep and wise woman, who really looked at life as service. She always saw the spirit in the world. My father was not religious; my mother was. I am from two very different ethnic groups, half Scot, half Sicilian. My mother's name is Maria Luciatti Serafini, and my father's Jack Houston. My mother was born in Siracusa, Sicily. My father was from an old Southern family, the Houstons of Texas, and Sam Houston was my great-great-grandfather. Robert E. Lee was my great-great-great-grandfather. I come from an old, old American family and from an immigrant family, too, and I embody all these cultures. I went to twenty-nine schools before I turned twelve. Dad was on the road, writing the Bob Hope show. I was always seeing many, many different kinds of people . . . often thrust into all kinds of survival situations which I had no business as a little American girl being thrust into so early.

When we see the humor in it all, we always see things in new ways. Humor helps us see the healing, the whole, the larger situation. I have that sensibility. After I had that mystical experience when I was six, I no longer had any freedom. After that, I was utterly committed to a life of helping and looking and finding, of yearning, exploring, discovering, evoking what is possible. We can become citizens of and open to a universe larger than our aspirations, and more complex. This is where we are in history, and, by God, we had better do it!

What about death . . . ?

I don't think there is such a thing. I am not sure there is birth either. I don't think this is a sunlit journey to a sunlit shore. There are multiple options. The universe is just too complicated to say, You live, you go to a place, you get your lessons, and you go to another place. So you come back again, and live again. Life is continuous, and it takes many dimensions and many different forms of continuity, of which reincarnation may be only one.

In the stories of Buddha, he always smiled, so I've thought, if one were truly spiritual, one would always be happy.

Oh, no! Some of the most spiritually inclined people I know have been utterly despairing. Read the great book of Evelyn Underhill, the book on mysticism, where she talks about the great saints and the immense despair they've gone through—even the greatest of them, like St. Francis of Assisi. At the end of his life, in Alverno, over the craggy mountain, he was looking out to God and saying, "Who am I? Your most useless little worm! I am a nothing. Forget about me." This, after his enormous accomplishment of changing the value system of Europe! And he, in utter despair!

Nothing's going to grow without suffering. Consider bread, tasty bread. What went into the bread? Seed went into the ground, and the ground opened up, suffered. Seed breaks out of its pod, comes up, and fruit grows. The fruit is ripped out, crushed. It's then baked, and then that's bread. That's suffering! The ruby is under tremendous pressure for hundreds of thousands of years. Fine leather is tanned. (Rumi talks about that.) Fine wine goes through extraordinary crushing.

If we have the blush of maturity, we don't go back to being a little green apple! Wounding allows for the opening of ourselves. It evolves into the holes that make us holy. I have never known—never—a being of depth who has not undergone some sizable suffering. Wounding also takes us out of the limited, nursery sort of culture, out of our limiting innocence in which we have absolute faith in someone who is going to give us utter affirmation the whole rest of our being. With that kind of philosophy we would never grow! Often, we feel betrayed and abandoned, thrust out. It's horrendous, but then, of course, it allows us to be able to reach out to others, to make networks, like scar tissue, like stars, which reach out to form multiple patterns of relationships.

At a certain point, one realizes the larger pattern that was there, the one not seen before. One forgives; one is capable of forgiving the betrayal. All the great myths portray suffering, and wounding is at the heart of them. Christ must have his crucifixion. Otherwise, no upsy-daisy! He becomes just an interesting teacher without crucifixion. Dionysus must be childish and attract titanic enemies. Prometheus must steal fire from heaven and have his liver eaten out. Job gets boils. Adam loses his rib. Odin trades his eye for wisdom. Every story has, at its core, extraordinary wounding, suffering. Every one. The Buddha becomes almost a dead corpse and almost destroys himself before he wakes. Jesus is in an agony on the cross. Enlightened suffering.

After the suffering one of two things can happen. One can fall into a sterile choice: paranoia, denial, an attempt never to aspire so high again, utter disappointment, revenge (an eye for an eye, a tooth for a tooth). If we get encapsulated in those forms of denial and sterile choices, we do not grow. Or suddenly, we understand larger patterns, and we give forgiveness. "Forgive them, Lord, they know not what they do." Socrates said wisdom comes through suffering. After suffering the entelechy begins to bloom, but the entelechy, like the seed put into the ground, seems to need to be bruised. We need that, and given what life is, it is unlikely that we will not have suffering. We are perhaps the most vulnerable and psychologically wounded people in human history.

Look back at the lives of your great-great-great-great grandma and grandpa five hundred years ago. They knew who they were! They may not have lived very long or had much to eat, but they knew kinship, fellowship. They didn't have to ask the kinds of questions we're asking today. One wouldn't find books like yours being written. They were, reasonably, much happier than we are. But they did not have this incredible exposure. In pictures of faces in the twelfth and thirteenth centuries we don't see faces haunted by the despair or suffering that we see in twentieth-century faces. It's because we are so wounded. What we do not have is a psychology of understanding sacrificial suffering as transformation.

Our local humanity will always feel inadequate to the Godsoul it is housing. In Eastern religions, there's a level of maintaining a type of equanimity that we do not necessarily find in Western religions, not to the same extent, anyway. I think we have some great surprises in store for us. Jesus was really very cranky, to the end. That's why I don't object to that new movie, *The Last Temptation of Christ*. The Buddha was far more eccentric than we are.

If you were on your deathbed, what advice would you give to your son or daughter?

It would be to love one another. In one minute, one isn't going to say very much. I'd also tell them to enjoy the immense and fascinating comedy of existence. There should be love and a certain delight. I'd say that ultimately, it is all worth it!

If someone asked, "But how do I love somebody?" what would you say?

Most people have loved a dog, a cat, or a tree, or nature. Most people know what love is, though it may not be the high, romantic thing they see in the pictures. They know that feeling of the self's boundaries dissolving and the immense reaching out to something, that reaching into oneness—that great communion, swarming, mating, weaving that says, "We are, thank God." People think that love

93

has to be directed to other people, but it doesn't have to be. It can be directed to almost anything.

If you could meet anyone from history, whom would you meet and what would you ask that person?

There are a whole bunch of obvious religious figures I would like to meet, but also people who are not so obvious. I would want to meet Hildegarde of Bingen, who in the eleventh century was able to do so much and create so much.

I would also like to be there for them, not just to ask them questions like, "How did you do it?" but to empower them to see the future: "Oh, boy, you wouldn't believe the influence you've had! I know you feel beaten down, but I tell you, it'll all be worth it." I would like to be there under the cross when Jesus is saying, "My God, my God, why have you forsaken me?" and say, "Don't worry, this love is going to go out into the world and it is going to seed in the hearts and minds of many people and cause them to turn a corner on their existence." That is what I would want to do, to empower them in moments of their deepest despair.

I'd like to go back and empower Adolph Hitler to be an art student! I'd say, "What a wonderful talent you have! You have a great talent—let's pursue this." I'd give him a grant. Art was what he really wanted to do, anyway.

Most people probably would not give luminous answers. I have known some very great beings and have asked them many questions. What they really need from the future is encouragement. So it might not be just the great ones, but also the real lousy ones who needed to be empowered at an early stage, who needed someone saying, "Don't give up!"

Some people think personal relationships interfere with spiritual growth...

To be a monk with a large family is going to be a problem. It's not going to work very well. Joachim DeFiore was a very great thirteenth-century philosopher whose theory greatly influenced many historians up to the eighteenth and nineteenth centuries. He talked about three stages in history. The first was the Age of the Father, and he thought that spanned from Abraham to

Christ. It was the time of the Commandments, the "Thou shalt do these things" era. Then there was the Age of the Son, from Christ to DeFiore's time, and that was the age of the Church, the "I'd like to, but I need help" era. Then the Age of the Holy Ghost, which he thought was beginning around his time, the age of "I will, and I sure want to, and I can." In this third stage, the law would be written on the heart, no longer mediated by the Church. It would be a time of spiritualized monks *of* the world, who could still be *in* the world, the ones who would have access to wisdom regarding the death of their own existences as well as access to the horizontal forms around them.

We all need times of removal from society. There are some people for whom it is appropriate at certain times but not at others. They need a time of removal but then have to go back out into the world. That is why the wisdom of Hinduism allows for the different stages . . . and not just in Hinduism: we find it in the Australian Aborigines, where the elders go sit on a mountain with their eyes wide open, staring into the sky, waiting for the cosmos, knowing that the cosmos or infinity is going to fall into their hearts. Many of us are apt to live a very long time, much longer than previously— many of us into our nineties. We can't just be playing poker and golf in old-age homes in the South! A lot of these later years are going to be devoted to being a sannyasin, to the vertical life, to a kind of monkhood that is not so much monastic, but which can manifest through social service as well.

What is important to you?

Living each day of my life as if it really mattered. Truly to be of service and of deep use is of the greatest importance to me.

The most important thing I've learned is that everything is part of the story. The story has real meaning; it is part of the journey of transformation. We are in a loaded time, a time I refer to with a new word, *kairotic*. *Kairos* is time and *eros* is passion, so *kairotic* is the passion of the loaded time. Passion is energy and momentum. In its negative form, passion is longing, regret—some strong emotion by which one is deeply blocked. It could be violence or a rage that turns in on oneself and destroys the self.

To me, the most important thing is that we are in a kairotic time and that the universe is a very complex place. We have the capacity to be part of that universe and to know it. We are not empty little robots playing out a meaningless role on the sands of time.

Life never stops teaching me on every level. I have a recurring dream in which I am in grade 4B at my current age. I'm sure Jung would have said it was compensation, that most people dream about the opposite of what they really are. I dream about being in 4B because in most people's eyes, my external life appears successful, but my unconscious is saying, "You're always back in kindergarten, back in the early grades, in a state of learning." It's constantly teaching me about patience and about limits, how we can go beyond limits and create the weaves among our different levels. It teaches me that I am eternally a mystery to myself, that others are truly mysteries, and that we can never truly know each other.

There is always wonder and astonishment. One must never take anyone or anything for granted, or think of others on automatic pilot. They contain worlds within worlds, even though their behavior might seem to be saying the opposite. We must all realize that the behavior is just behavior, unskilled behavior. What used to be called sin is now "unskilled behavior."

What makes you happy? sad? angry? What would you like to change?

I love to cook, to read, to teach, to travel. I love my dogs, my friends, and moments that are present and full. I like watching the shadows cross the lawn! Any moment is, to me, available for happiness and for filling with joy—actually it's beyond contentment. It's a state of wonder and astonishment that comes from being fortunate enough to participate in this gloriously interesting universe.

I get sad at people being unkind to each other. People doing each other in puts me in a royal rage. I travel to so many places and areas of countries (including ours) where there truly is a lack of opportunity. I think of young women at fifteen or sixteen who are on crack in hospitals in New York giving birth to babies who will have very little opportunity. That is the big thing I would change— people given opportunities that so many millions don't have. There are many things that spring from lack of opportunity: the sense of inadequacy; the sense of not being seen, not being empowered appropriately.

Sometimes I see everything as being part of *my* scenario rather than having an independent existence.

That's true. The Shakespearean playwright view of reality, the theatrical view of reality, is true. We are part of a play, and I say my lines . . . Then, suddenly, we are in two different plays, and you appreciate the fullness and see that life is that rhythm, that there is a rhythm to our being in the same play—your being in my mind, my being in your mind. We like theater so much because it gives us the projection of this process happening all the time.

I studied hypnosis, and Milton Erickson said that we are in different trances continually.

Cultural trances. Different cultures activate different trances. As a matter of fact, there is no such thing as an altered state of consciousness. Consciousness is always altering! That is the nature of consciousness. There are just very few places that one can tend to on the spectrum of altering states. That's what Erickson meant. What you said before about people being part of your reality—that's a trance state. Sometimes, we wake up from that state to another state where suddenly we see the "otherness" of the old.

The Buddha called these trances *skandhas*, referring to them as different streams of consciousness that were going on all at the same time. What happens in awakening is that suddenly there is a dominant entelechy that says, "Aha!" and looks at the play of its own mind, laughs, and enjoys itself. It is literally like rolling back consciousness.

People said to the Buddha, "Sir, what are you? Are you a god?"

"No," Buddha said.

"An angel?"

"No."

"Then, what are you?"

"I am just awake."

It is that roll-back, where it's not that he didn't have different trance states going on, but that he was aware of them. There was full awareness. There are many ways of waking up, but one of the best is the "Stop" technique. Stop for a moment a hundred times a day. Even when you reach for a glass, stop for an eighth of a second. Nobody will know. Then you organize your behavior and do it with great consciousness. Then, your dreams change, because suddenly you begin to wake up within your dreams and know you're dreaming and begin to orchestrate your dreams: "Bring on the lions!"

This state of wakefulness: Is it almost like the trance being aware of itself?

It could be the trance becoming aware of itself. Or it could be the self being aware of the self. It's no longer "trance"; it's now "self." It moves to a whole different level of reality.

I see in people, and in myself, the tendency to open up and feel connected to things, then the person wants to possess and merge with those things.

That's often a very Western form. In 1924, Jung went to Arizona and got to be friends with Native Americans. He had them draw white people. They drew white people with great big eyes, greedy ones . . . our faces. They said, "You do not understand; you have such greed to possess and be crazy." That is part of the culture; it is not necessarily a natural form. We're taught it at our mother's breast, practically: to possess, to grab, to own, to claim as mine . . . Western culture, white races. I am not saying it is indigenous to white races; I'm saying that it is something in our culture.

After seeking the place where there can be a symbiotic beauty of relationship, one almost has to relearn it so one doesn't go off again into automatic materialism, the materialism of relationships to possess, to grab. A lot of stupid and erroneous psychologists have come out of this very limited, pathologized Western man's measure of what it means to be successful. It's something that we grow out of. It will give us endless torment unless we say, Stop! This is my culture, a habit pattern. I don't have to do this. Stop! And just reorganize our behavior and say, I'd better relate to these people or things in a way of honored reverence for oneness and what's best for them. A few days afterward, that old stuff will come up again. One just says, Stop! and one reorganizes one's thinking with it. One will find, after about three months, that automatic behavior will go away. I don't think it's innate to the human being, but it is part of the pathology of the West, and it started essentially with the Renaissance, with the entrepreneurial ego.

8

RABBI HAROLD KUSHNER

I met with Rabbi Harold Kushner in New York City amid the hustle and bustle of hurried people and honking horns. After showing my credentials to the security guard, I walked past an iron gate and through a courtyard into the building where Harold Kushner taught. As I walked down the long hallway, I left the distractions and noise of the world behind and eventually found the door to his office, which was one among many. He immediately struck me as an intellectual man, with a personal philosophy as organized and well thought out as any I had encountered. His intellect was tempered by a caring that was born out of pain and the need to help.

Harold Kushner and I have something in common: We both looked for answers after the tragic death of someone we loved. *Why Bad Things Happen to Good People* is the title of his best-selling book and also a question he tried to answer.

Rabbi Harold Kushner is the author of *Who Needs God* and *Why Bad Things Happen to Good People,* which was written after he learned his three-year-old son, Aaron, would die from a rare disease. He wrote it so that it could be "given to the person who has been hurt by life." Harold Kushner is Rabbi of Temple Israel in Natick, Massachusetts.

On what beliefs do you base your life?

The thing that shaped me more than any other was our son's being born with an incurable disease. It forced me to question what God's role in the world was and what the purpose of being good was. Where do I find the resources to cope with tragedy? How do I help somebody else cope with tragedy?

Our son's condition forced me to substitute compassion for a fairly intellectual outlook on life. It structured my life so I could love a child unreservedly, without calculating what I would get in return. I learned that I could love freely and uncalculatingly, even though this child would *never* make me proud of his success in life and never support me emotionally or financially in my old age.

Life is holy and special. The death of a child or a young person is a tragedy precisely because life is sacred. That is why I have to take it very seriously. One of the greatest sins is wasting a life.

There is something unique and special about being human; those qualities that separate us from other living creatures are very important. The essence of being human is our capacity to think abstractly and to make moral judgments, knowing the difference between good and bad. When we don't take those considerations into our lives, when we don't feel an obligation to respond to the moral demands made on us, then we are operating on an animal level. The essence of religion, as far as I am concerned, is to develop the human side of our capacities in counterdistinction to our animal heritage (to eat, sleep, mate, rest, and so on).

There is a God. It's more than an ultimate reality. God is an ultimate reality that makes moral demands of us. To me, the essence of God is the sense of moral obligation. I am disappointed in what I see as the consensus of New Age religion, which depicts God as a source of energy that we can tap into. This *moral* concept—this sense of the Covenant, that God will hold up *his* end of things and keep the world running smoothly *only* if we will hold up *our* end of things and behave like human beings instead of like animals—that whole dimension is missing from it.

So you feel that New Age religion lacks a sense of responsibility?

Yes. Responsibility means, of course, the assumption that there *is* somebody to answer to.

I don't like describing God. Jewish theology has never been about the *nature* of God; it's been about the nature of God's *demands* on us. I am much more comfortable with that. But the image of God that I keep is the image of what human beings at their best could be. The part of God that is manifest to us is what we are when we are most human: good, generous, truthful, altruistic, loyal, and self-controlled. The whole list of things that human beings are, at their best, is our way of trying to grow close to God. The reality of God is probably much greater than the image we see, but the image of God that we see is the image of what a real human being is.

This is one of the ways to see God, through trying to base life on the qualities that we consider divine. We contact God through prayer, both speaking and listening in prayer. We tend to emphasize too much the act of speaking in prayer and telling God things we would not otherwise say. We don't understand that the *best* part of prayer is listening, an opening up to messages we would not get if we weren't praying.

We contact God through our relationships. Martin Buber taught that all life is "meeting" and that God is found through relationship. We contact God through study and the development of our understanding through the intellect. That's one way God becomes manifest: through our appreciation of the beauty and wonder in the world.

Psychology and sociology give understanding of how the human being works. In Judaism, there is the tradition of biblical study as an act of worship, not simply as an intellectual pursuit. A Jew reads the Bible not only to see how it comes out, but also to pay homage to God. If the Bible contains His revelation, then you feel close to Him by studying His word. In Judaism, we have developed this whole tradition of the interpretation of the Bible, a whole aristocracy of learning. One is honored in the Jewish community to the degree that one is really learned in biblical sources.

What is the purpose of life? What is the highest ideal one can attain?

We are born with the *potential* for humanity. The purpose of life is to realize that potential. The purpose of religion is to create a community through which we learn what it means to be human.

The highest ideal is to become a human being. There's a catalog of traits that only human beings possess: charity, learning, sharing, exerting self-control in eating and in sexual behavior. These are things an animal cannot develop. One becomes human to the degree that one's life is based on developing these things.

What is the greatest obstacle to attaining this ideal?

There seems to be a moral law of gravity that pulls us down, that makes it easier to sleep late than get up and go to a service. It makes it easier to keep our money for ourselves than to give it to a beggar on the street; it's easier to tell a lie than to tell the truth when the truth might make us look bad. It's easier for us to do shortcuts than to do things the right way; and it's easier for us to excuse and justify ourselves, rather than see the other person's point of view.

The biggest obstacle to humanity is this law of gravity. For some reason, the wrong way is a lot less strenuous than the right way. It's a law of nature. I would like to put the struggle for good and evil on a level playing field and make it as tempting to be good as it is to be bad, as tempting and as convenient to be strong as it is to be weak.

Will all people eventually reach this ideal?

I am not sure *any* people will reach this goal—very few. A significant fraction will not even try, for several reasons. First of all, it seems to me that worrying about how to make our lives meaningful is a luxury we can afford only when we have food on the table and a roof over our head, only when no one is trying to kill us. If we are in the midst of war or poverty or if we are living in high-crime neighborhoods, worrying about the meaning of life is a luxury we have to leave to others.

In addition to that, there are many who have money for food, clothes, and shelter but never worry about being human. All they want to do is pay their bills and watch television and go to sleep. The whole question of developing their humanity never occurs to them! So a lot of them don't even try, and a lot of them can't.

Of the rest, some have more potential than others. Just as people differ in their musical or athletic abilities or innate intelligence, I guess people differ in their inborn ability to develop their spiritual selves. The question then becomes: Are they trying to do the best with what they have? Some will; many won't.

Why is there suffering?

There is suffering partly because some human beings choose to be cruel to each other. There is suffering partly because we have evolved as human beings, as sensitive people. If we didn't care, there wouldn't *be* suffering. There would be death, illness, broken bones. There'd be murders, car accidents, earthquakes, and plane crashes, but there wouldn't be suffering; there would just be things happening. Since we want the world to be good and we want life to be satisfying and pleasant, we're hurt and outraged when bad things happen. It is human sensitivity and caring that cause these events to be perceived as outrageous.

There is suffering partly because laws of nature apply equally to each of us, and laws of nature decree that we are subject to accidents, to sickness, to disease, to falling rocks, falling trees, earthquakes, and fires. God created a world where natural laws operate regularly with no exceptions. This means, if I lean too far out the window, I'll fall out and get killed, no matter how nice a guy I am. If I understand the laws that cause people to fall out of windows, I can then find ways of protecting against this. If I can figure out what causes cancer or what causes polio, I can find out how to prevent it.

The first part is God's role, and the second part exists in order to give us the capacity to be stronger and braver and more caring and more supportive than we'd otherwise be inclined to be, so that we can survive our suffering and help other people survive theirs.

I'm less comfortable talking about what God's mind-set is and more comfortable talking about what happens in my life, because I don't know what God does. All I *know* is what happens to *me* because of God. I don't know if God is trying to rid the world of suffering.

Human beings are not going to live forever. The old generation will get old and die and children will be born and replace them. To rid the world of suffering, people would have to learn not to care that their parents die. I'd have to be able to shrug off the death of my father the way a bird or a puppy shrugs off the death of its father. That way, I would not suffer when the older generation died.

No, I don't think God wants to rid the world of that kind of suffering. That kind of suffering is the price we pay for being humanly committed and for running the risk of love. When I love somebody, that somebody may develop breast cancer or may betray me and cause me a great deal of pain. The only way I can avoid that kind of suffering is by not running the risk of love, and I don't want to do that. So, it's not that God wants to rid the world of suffering; God wants to give us the capacity to live bravely in a world full of pain.

If somebody said to you, "I don't understand how it's in my best self-interest to be interested in other people and concerned for other people," how would you explain that?

First of all, because that's how human beings were created. We act in harmony with our essential human nature when we are sharing and generous. Second, we'll feel better about it, and we'll create a climate where other people will be more likely to do something nice for us when we need it. If we try to do everything for ourselves, there will be a lot of things we can't do.

One of the functions of prayer is to come into the presence of God and to be *changed* by coming into His presence. One of the functions of prayer is to open ourselves up to God so that we ask God for His help in doing something that would be too hard if we had to do it alone. I don't believe that praying to God is like going to Santa Claus in a department store. The purpose of prayer isn't to tell God what I want and persuade Him that I deserve it.

What is your core practice?

My regimen of prayer (both individually and as the leader of the congregation) brings me a lot of messages. Also, I'm institutionally committed as a rabbi and teacher to teach ideas to people, to counsel people, and to comfort people in difficult situations at hospitals and funerals. This commitment helps me to develop a side of my personality that is at the essence of being human. I grew up in a family that valued education and religious involvement, and that put me on the track of becoming a rabbi.

Do all religions lead to the same place?

I believe they are on a course that converges *toward* a single truth, but I don't predict (and I would not welcome) all religions becoming one. There's plenty of room in the world for multiple religions, for several reasons.

One is that human beings with the same illness need different medicines or different protocols of treatment, because they're individuals. Some people need one kind of religion more than another, whether optimistic or pessimistic, intimate or widespread.

Second, religion is not so much a matter of having the right answers, but of being part of the community through which we grow to be human. We all need our own community; we all need a "subset" of humanity.

People raised in the United States grow up instinctively understanding religion in Christian terms, in terms of what they believe about God, God's wishes, and the building they go to in order to pray to this God. In most of the world, that isn't religion. In most of the world, religion is the spiritual outlook on life of the community one is born into. Christianity is almost unique in that it is an individual theology rather than the religion of the country. This is especially true for Protestant Christianity in America.

In South America, Catholicism is the *spiritual* language the way Spanish is the *linguistic* language; it is just part of the culture. That's just how South Americans grow up. In the Far East, Hinduism or Buddhism or Chuang-tzu is the religious expression of the *culture* of the particular country. That language is the mode addressed rather than an individual's decision about how the world works and about what God wants one to do with one's life. What they have are religions as the community through which we come to be human, rather than religion as a set of accurate or inaccurate answers about the nature of God.

Some people think that being a monk or a nun is the best way if you are serious about your soul, and that a family gets in the way...

When we were in Thailand and Nepal last winter, we saw that a lot of the people pledge a month or a year or two years of their lives to the monastic life. It's very good for the country just to be reminded that there is this alternative, but I would emphatically disagree that marriage and family take one away from God.

There is a Jewish notion that holiness is found with other people rather than holiness being found by turning one's back on a sinful world or by just being alone with God. To understand what life really is, one *has* to share it. In marriage, one has to learn responsibility for another person's happiness.

When I was in my early thirties, I would have made career success less important and family time more important. Ultimately, what endures will be the immortality we will have won through our children and parenthood. The books I write, the books you write, the business successes people have, all these are a "familiar." They affect other people whether they are an immediate family or not. We will have shaped children who will go on to shape children. This is our immortality.

Do you feel there is a basic difference between men and women?

Yes! The best book on the subject is Carol Gilligan's *In a Different Voice.* She says that men tend to be abstract and ask, "Is it right?" and "What's the law?" Women tend to be concerned with relationships. Men are comfortable with the competition of winning and losing, whereas women are more comfortable with intimacy and people's feelings. So, women are more likely to play cooperative games where one doesn't win or lose, while men learn to take losing in stride and not get their feelings hurt. Women are innately committed to relationship, while men are innately committed to separating and finding their own way. Jung teaches that by the time men get to the midpoint in life, they ought to go back and let the repressed feminine side of their personality emerge—and learn how to nurture and form relationships. Women ought to let the masculine side emerge and learn how to become more assertive, take more chances.

What about death . . . ?

I don't know what continues after death, and neither does anyone else. No matter how confidently someone talks, it's just theory. Having said that, I am quite confident that our physical bodies decay and that we return to nature and to earth.

106

I am quite confident that the most important part of a human being is not his physical body but his nonphysical essence, which some people call soul and others, personality: beliefs, values, commitments, memories, humor—all those things that are the *real* person and not physical. You can have an arm amputated, you can gain weight, lose weight, or color your hair, and you're the same person. But if you change your values or lose your memory, then you're not the same person anymore. So that's the real person. The nonphysical part cannot die and cannot decay because it's not physical.

I have to believe that the soul is immortal and survives death. But my three-dimensional mind cannot even comprehend what it means for a nonphysical entity to exist. So I can't even speculate where a soul goes. Where does the light go when I turn the switch off? It doesn't "go"—it just isn't there anymore.

I don't understand what it means for a soul to exist, but I know that it does because it can't die. When I die, when my body decays and stops working and is buried and my soul survives, will my soul have the ability to recognize other souls if they don't have any physical shape? If the other soul doesn't have form and if my soul doesn't have eyes, optic nerves, and glands to stimulate feeling, will it be *happy* to recognize the soul of someone it knew in life?

Those questions are meaningless to me. I don't spend a lot of time and energy thinking about them. The danger I find is when religions talk too much about rewards and punishments after death. They run the risk of devaluing life in this world. They run the risk of saying it really isn't so important that you're suffering, it really isn't so important that your neighbor is suffering. It isn't so important that there is apartheid in South Africa or poverty in Boston. It isn't important that the poor are getting the short end of the stick, because, soon, *this* life will be over and they will be in a much more glorious world. But, you see, those things *are* important to me, as they were important to the Prophets Isaiah, Amos, and Jeremiah. Widows and orphans are being oppressed, and the rich take advantage of the poor. Human beings are being hurt when they don't deserve it. That *is* important to me, and I'm afraid if my religious orientation put too much stress on the world to come, it would make it too easy for me *not* to take the problems and the loose ends of this world as seriously as they need to be taken.

If you were on your deathbed, what advice would you give to your son or daughter?

That's a very important question, though I have given more thought to the issue of how I would like to be remembered than to the issue of what I would want to tell people. But I really should think about that.

I would give them this advice: "Be good, be generous, and be cheerful, and in the long run you'll find out that was worthwhile. Even if it doesn't *look* like the right thing to do at the time, in the long run, you'll be glad you did. When you meet someone who is a spiritual person, you will recognize in him a serenity and a wholeness and a sense of fulfillment that you will wish you had for yourself." That's probably the best reason.

What makes you sad? angry?

The unfairness of life. When I see people crippled or dying young, people not having a chance to make the most of their abilities, it makes me sad. And when I see people who *could* make the most of their abilities and just don't care to, I am saddened.

There is an old saying, "You measure the size of a man's soul by the size of the things that make him angry." As I mature, I'm less likely to get angry about trivialities and more likely to get angry over major things. Human meanness upsets me, the tendency of people when they're upset to hurt somebody else in order to restore their own sense of purpose.

What do you think life still has to teach you? What is the most important thing you've learned in life?

I'm fifty-three years old, and I hope that I still have a lot to learn, but I can't guess what it will be. I look back over the last ten years, the last twenty years, the last thirty years of my life, and I could never have predicted what each of those decades turned out to teach me. Couldn't guess at all! So I have no way of guessing what's next.

The most important thing I've learned is that we serve ourselves best when we're good to other people. But there are problems that inhibit this attitude. For instance, there may not be enough of the basic necessities (food, water, space) in the world to go around, and people may fight and kill each other looking for them. Further, not enough people will realize that ultimate self-interest lies in being good to others. They think that self-interest lies in selfishness at the *expense* of others, individually and nationally. Also, modern science has brought us to the point where we have the capacity to make this planet uninhabitable, and some damn fool might go ahead and do that.

What do you see as the direction of psychology? How is it connected with spirituality?

The one thing I'm aware of is that it's going in the direction of pharmacology: treating mental illness with pills. If that works, it works, but it's drifting away from the spiritual side, from the kind of psychology that almost in itself is a religion. To the degree that psychology is about helping people cope with their problems, that's a very religious mission. Religion does it better, because religion can call on ultimate resources. God's forgiveness is much more potent than a therapist's. For religion to bring in the transcendent dimension of holiness makes it, in some ways, much more effective and much more profound than psychology. But there are some things that only psychology can do.

I would like to talk with Sigmund Freud about how the human mind and soul work. Whether I *like* Freud is not the issue. He was a genius. He accomplished something very few other people have done: He single-handedly changed the way we look at being alive. He was wrong in more than half of what he said, but I forgive him for that, because he came up with the *ideas* of the unconscious, repression, and sublimation, which were like realizing that the earth moved around the sun. Once we understand that, we see everything else differently. So, the fact that he got most of the details wrong doesn't diminish that he single-handedly taught us to understand ourselves.

I would also like to meet the Prophet Jeremiah and to ask where he got his message and how specific it was. If I could understand what the Bible means when it says "the word of the Lord came to Jeremiah," I would know a lot more about how the world works than I do now. I would like to ask him what he meant when he said that.

What Jeremiah and Freud had in common is that their humanity transcended their animal side. Freud was asked if he could summarize psychoanalysis in one sentence, and he said, "Where id was, let *ego* be." One might substitute *instinct,* which is what the Bible is saying: The purpose of life is to be different from animals, who live by instinct, and to run life by moral choice.

9

ROBERT SCHULLER

Robert Schuller was frustrated because he realized he had made an appointment with me and I wasn't with a major magazine or publisher. In his letter to me, I was told I would have thirty minutes to speak with him. But when he emerged from his office, his secretaries and advisors clamored around him and informed him that he had five minutes until he had to leave for an appointment. He looked at me and said, "Five minutes."

After we were seated in his office, I quickly asked my questions. He initially answered them quickly, but then he took his time when he saw the quality of spiritual search revealed in my questions. I was impressed with his explanation of death, and as he sat across from me, his eye contact never wavered.

I was surprised at how much I learned from Robert Schuller. I expected his brand of Christian spirituality to be a little too simplistic for my tastes, but his response to my inquiry about death was a beautiful one and one I had not heard before.

Robert Schuller is a large man. Even the way he preaches is larger than life. With his arms beckoning toward the heavens and words infused with emotion, he entertains and captures his congregation. He is criticized for his showmanship, but that is what his congregation wants. If he wasn't that way, they wouldn't listen. Even when speaking to me one-on-one, his showmanship made itself known, but behind the showman, I saw an intensity.

When I was in Nepal, my friend Jagir Singh had the same problem with people expecting a show. After ten o'clock in the morning, he got ready for work (he repaired cars and owned a garage) by going into the back room and changing into a pair of pants and a dress shirt.

One day, after he changed into his Western clothes and while we had tea, an Indian the spitting image of Mahatma Gandhi walked in. He was wearing a light blanket thrown over his shoulder and a small loincloth around his waist. He was all dusty and skinny and had a staff in his right hand that was taller than he was.

"I have walked all the way from India to see the Great Saint," the man said. Although he was tired, his face was full of hope. His body sighed with relief at having reached his destination.

"Well, I guess he means me," Jagir said, trying his best not to offend me. "You're looking for me," he told the man.

"You?" the man said with great disbelief. "You're the Great Saint? But...but, where are your robes?"

"Oh, those. I wear those before ten o'clock. But we can talk now."

"No, that is all right," the man said. "I will come back tomorrow before ten o'clock—when you are wearing your robes."

Robert Schuller is founder and minister of the Crystal Cathedral in Garden Grove, California. One of his first churches was in a drive-in movie house, and the concession stand was his pulpit.

Dr. Schuller is the author of more than twenty books, including *The Be Happy Attitudes.* His Sunday telecast, "The Hour of Power," is one of the most widely viewed programs in television history and reaches over 1.3 million homes each week.

On what beliefs do you base your life?

I base my life on the teachings of the Holy Bible. That's the Judeo-Christian faith, and historic Christianity. The most significant event in my life was when I made a personal decision to become a believer in Jesus Christ.

I believe in a God. The Holy Bible teaches it. Jesus believed in a God. It would be the height of arrogance, the ultimate lack of humility, if I claimed to be smarter than Jesus. He believed in God, and that's why I believe in God.

The description of God is Jesus Christ. Jesus said, "He that has seen me has seen the Father." So, who is God? I look at Jesus Christ. He claimed to be God, and he was accused of blasphemy, and that called for the death penalty. He was warned about it, but he said, "I cannot tell a lie, then you have to kill me." They did. So he died for his belief system, claiming to be God in human flesh. That's what I believe.

What is the highest ideal a person can reach? How is it attained?

The highest ideal is to strive to be as much as possible the reincarnation of Jesus Christ, here and now. That means, if he was God, as I believe he was, why didn't he stick around and never die? For one simple reason: He had a body of bones, meat, hair, blood, toenails, and eyebrows, and he had to urinate and defecate, so he could be only one place at a time. But he got his body out of the way, and now he sends his Spirit from wherever he is today into my life. Therefore, he can live in White and Black and Yellow and Green people. He can live in people that speak all kinds of languages, all kinds of cultures. Therefore, the highest ideal is to try to be a reincarnation of Jesus. So I say, "My mind—think through it, Jesus. My heart—love people through it, Jesus."

Prayer is how we reach this ideal. Jesus has promised that he would give his Spirit to those who ask for it. He said, "Human beings are imperfect, and yet they give good gifts to their children. Don't you think that God, who is in Heaven, is better than imperfect human beings? Will he not give his Spirit, then, to those who ask him?" So ask for it and get it.

What is the greatest obstacle to obtaining this ideal?

A negative self-image. I don't consider myself worthy. I know my faults. I know my shortcomings. I know my sins. I see the imperfections of my life. Therefore, I think, Golly, I can't be another Jesus. I'm not that good. So this negative self-image keeps me from daring to open myself to the belief system that Jesus Christ can actually reincarnate his *Spirit*, at least in me. Of course he can! Look at Mother Teresa. Human beings usually do not allow themselves to open up to the Spirit of Jesus. That's the number-one cause of most suffering.

Someone might object, Does that deal with some of the horrific things that happen to good people? No, but the real suffering, in the final analysis, isn't the blood flowing out of the skin. The real suffering isn't the screech of pain in the night. Pain can be covered with modern drugs. The real torture is the torture of the spirit, the soul, the loneliness, boredom, anger, fear, resentment, worry, hostility, jealousy. All of that is *not* the fault of God. It is our fault, for not embracing the faith of letting Jesus come into our lives and calm us, comfort us, turn our scars into stars.

What about death . . . ?

I believe what the Holy Bible teaches about death. I believe the Holy Bible teaches that everybody lives three lives. The first life is nine months long. Then, we experience our first death. We die to that world. We die to that womb. We're born *into* this world. Now, in this world, we can see, we can hear, we can breathe, we can think, we can feel—which means there is the possibility of the evolution of the *spiritual* quality about us that, for want of a better name, is called the soul, the spirit. I believe in the immortality of the spirit and the soul. When the body dies, the soul leaves it, just as it left the womb before, and is free. We get a foretaste of that when we dream. Close your eyes and your mind drifts and you're on a faraway island. There are palm trees, and you can smell the flowers. Dreams are very, very real. These are foretastes of the experience we may have of this mind-force traveling without having a body to drag along. The soul is immortal; it enters immortality upon leaving this body.

After death there is a division, some kind of justice. Not everybody is going to be in the same place with water and flowers. The Jewish people of the Old Testament have a doctrine of Hades. Jesus believed in it. He talked about Heaven and Hell. I don't know where Heaven is or what it is. I don't know where Hell is or what it is. But I know there is a division, because if everybody went to the same place, then Heaven would be a hell of a place. It would be horrible to have to land with Hitler as a roommate forever. So there has to be justice.

One thing is obvious: Life is not fair. The Holy Bible doesn't say it's fair. Some good people get some raw deals. But God has charge over eternity. Therefore, in the eternal scheme of things, God brings fairness to play, and those who have gotten by in this life so neatly— selling drugs, corrupting people, living in mansions with castles in the ports of the world, flying their private jets, tossing around in bed with their pretty playgirls—*these* people are ultimately going to have to pay, probably by failing to enjoy what eternity is like in Heaven, which is enjoying the presence of Jesus. That's part of what Hell is like.

If a person's major emotional stimulation comes through, say, an erection and an ejaculation, if that's his biggest kick in life . . . Don't get me wrong. I enjoy sex. I'm happily married to my first and only wife. But I get a far bigger joy trip out of experiencing the presence of Jesus in my heart and in my life. That puts tears in my eyes. I cry. I never cried for joy in sexual experiences. The deepest joy is when you can't keep from crying. The lips tremble and the eyes fill with tears. That's a bigger kick. But if your biggest joys come through sex or drugs or chemical stimulations or power plays or ego trips, and then if you had to spend eternity without any of that, it *would* be Hell.

So, I believe in eternal life. I believe there's a Heaven; I believe there's a Hell. I don't know where they are. I don't know what they are. *I don't care!* Except that when I go, I'm ready for the trip.

Do all religions lead to the same place?

All religions don't lead to the same place. They all don't even want the same thing. They all don't have the same purpose and declared objective, and they don't all have the same value system.

Christianity is unique in its Doctrine of Grace, you know. Grace is the doctrine of forgiveness. Jesus rejected his childhood religious training. Jesus was born and raised in classic, historic Judaic teaching. In his Sermon on the Mount, which was a revolutionary statement, Jesus said, "We have all been taught 'An eye for an eye and a tooth for a tooth.' I don't believe that. I have a new religion. If your enemy hungers, feed him." Now, *that's* revolutionary. Jesus said, "Forgive your enemy. Seventy times seven forgive." The doctrine of forgiveness is historically Christian, taught by Jesus. It's still true today.

We can find major religions that are in confrontation. One guy throws a terrorist grenade. The other religion will send its jets in the air and bomb the suburbs. You bomb me, I'll bomb you back with a bigger bomb. "An eye for an eye, a tooth for a tooth" is still very prominent and paramount in some major religious interpretations of some people in the world. It is *not* Christian. You can find

Christians, too, who will fall into that trap, because it's a natural gut instinct. You kick me, I'll kick you back, buddy—until finally you'll learn you can't kick me around. That is not Christian religion. That's what makes the Christian religion so radical, and it's a basic reason why a lot of people cannot accept Jesus Christ.

10

JAGIR SINGH

In 1990, I received letters from Mother Teresa and the Dalai Lama agreeing to interviews. After my initial excitement, I realized I didn't have the money to pay for the trip to India. But I worried that if I waited too long, my invitations to meet Mother Teresa and the Dalai Lama would be canceled. Anything could happen, and this was a once in a lifetime opportunity. Besides, on my way to India, I could stop in Katmandu and see Jagir Singh. It had been four years since I saw him.

I arrived in Katmandu at night and stayed at the Lhasa Hotel. I went up onto the roof of my hotel. What had once been a beautiful view of Himalayan mountains and terraced fields was now sprinkled with buildings and satellite dishes.

The next morning, I walked to Jagir Singh's house. On a muddy street, I saw a dog with only one leg pushing itself along. A Tibetan man bent down and petted the dog. The man smiled, and the dog wagged its tail.

I walked up the driveway to Jagir Singh's house. The door to his house was open, and Jagir Singh was sitting in a chair talking with people. He turned and looked out the doorway, narrowing his eyes as he focused on me. His whole face lit up in recognition, and he smiled. I was a little surprised he didn't sense I was coming.

There were many people at his house, because Saturday is his busiest day. Even while Jagir Singh spoke with other visitors, I could see him smiling. He was happy to see me. He would occasionally look over at me and with eyes twinkling say, "I am so happy, Mr. Bill—you did not forget about me."

There was a young woman showing him her hands. He said something, and she turned them over and showed him her palms. He nodded, and she smiled. Later, when I asked him what he was doing, he said, "She wanted to have a child, and I saw in her hands that she was already two months pregnant."

Later, after the tea was brought out, he said, "You know, Mr. Bill, I was in the United States last year and phoned you forty times, but I couldn't reach you. My friends wondered why I wanted to see you so badly. I still have your letter with the phone number you gave me."

My visit was a cause to celebrate for Jagir Singh. He kept telling his daughter to make more tea. "Very strong tea." He pumped me full of tea that morning; then we ate together. His son came in, and Jagir said, "You remember this man?"

The young man looked at me. "It's . . . Bill! How are you?" he asked. It felt like family to see them. His wife and daughters, all glad to see me.

Five cups of tea and four hours later, I no longer could pay attention to what he was saying. I promised to come back that afternoon. Jagir Singh smiled serenely and said, "As you like."

That afternoon when I returned to Jagir Singh's, he was talking to three men. "But you are a saint," one of the men insisted. "You are not supposed to get angry."

"Don't put conditions on me," Jagir Singh said in a frustrated manner. Then he looked at me, his eyes pleading for understanding. Our eyes met, and I shrugged my shoulders.

In the days that followed, Jagir Singh and I went to many places. At each place, people knew him and referred to him as a saint. Late one night, Jagir Singh said, "Mr. Bill, the last few weeks I have been depressed." I was touched that he allowed me to see his fragile side, an unseen side of the man people called a saint. "I say things to people," he continued, "and they tell people I said something else. I say something to one man, and he tells everyone else. And then, they tell me how I should act . . ."

He looked sad and alone. He wanted only to be a man of God and to help people. But they wanted him to be a saint, which relegated him to a position far above their own and which, coincidentally, excused them from acting more like him.

That night I walked home in the dark and thought of Jagir Singh. His yearning for God had created a separation between him and the other townspeople. "After all," they told me later, "Jagir Singh is a saint, and the rest of us, Mr. Bill, are just men."

11

HIS HOLINESS THE DALAI LAMA

I arrived in New Delhi late Sunday night and spent the night in the Ashoka Hotel. The next morning when I awoke, I could see vultures in the trees outside my window.

I called the Dalai Lama's office later that morning to confirm our Wednesday meeting. I was surprised to hear the meeting had been changed to Tuesday at nine o'clock in the morning. The airplanes and buses for Dharamsala, where the Dalai Lama lives, had already left for the day. The only thing I could do on such short notice was to rent a taxi for $170 and drive all night.

I rented the cab from a young man named Dinesh. His eternal smile was a touch too enthusiastic, like that of a politician or used car salesman. His smile gave me the impression that he was taking advantage of me and that he knew something I didn't. But I had no choice; he was my only option.

The cab arrived later that afternoon. The driver was a nice, quiet fellow who kept to himself. As I got into the cab, Dinesh appeared with his suitcase and smile. "Mind if I go with you?" he asked. Since it was a long ride and Dinesh spoke English, I invited him along. It seemed like another part of the adventure.

After a few miles, my sense of adventure waned as I realized that Indian drivers have to be the craziest drivers in the world. It's not really their fault, though, because the government seems to have saved money by making the main roads too narrow. Consequently, whenever a bus or truck came toward us, often at speeds of fifty or sixty miles an hour, we had to drive with the car half off the road. The vehicle approaching us would also drive partially off the road to avoid a head-on collision. This repeated itself every few minutes for fourteen hours. It surprised me to see only three accidents on the way to Dharamsala.

The Indian roads are filled with motorcycles. They are an inexpensive way to travel in India, and it is a common sight to see the wife sitting sidesaddle behind the husband. The second-class citizenship of Indian women is apparent because there is only one helmet per cycle, and the husband always wears it.

After we were on the road for a few hours, Dinesh informed me that in order to be on time for the interview, we would have to pass through the Punjab. The Punjab is off-limits to Westerners, and it is often in the news because of its political bombings and mass murders. It wasn't unusual to read in the newspapers about a small radical group of Punjabies or Sikhs who stopped a train or bus and then machine-gunned all the Hindus to death. Usually, the Hindus would retaliate by stopping a bus and killing all the Punjabies. Occasionally, there were even massacres by wild animals. I've read about crazy bison or elephants that came out of the jungle during the night and trampled whole villages.

When we finally reached the Punjab, there were Indian soldiers everywhere. We were stopped at the border by soldiers. Dinesh pointed at me and said, "Dalai Lama." I gave the guard my letter from the Dalai Lama, but the guard looked at us until Dinesh handed him fifty rupees. The guard scribbled something on a sheet of paper, which Dinesh later informed me was a receipt. Bribes are so common and accepted in India that the soldiers gave us a receipt so that we would have to pay only once on our way to Dharamsala.

As darkness came, we stopped to refill our gas tank. We were in the middle of nowhere. The Indian night was the darkest and most beautiful I had ever seen. Dinesh took a precaution against running out of gas by filling two five-gallon cans and placing them in the car. The fumes were present the rest of the journey. The driver kept lighting his cigarettes in the car, unaware of the danger. At first, I figured nothing would happen to us because we were on a sacred journey to see the Dalai Lama, but I overcame my naiveté and berated the driver several times until he stopped smoking in the car.

We drove all night and arrived early Tuesday morning. I had been awake for thirty hours, and after talking to the Dalai Lama's secretary, I realized I had forgotten to shave. The interview wasn't until later, so I went back to my hotel and cleaned up. I didn't have time to wash my clothes, however. The only things I had that were clean were a pair of faded green surgeon pants and a red, short-sleeved shirt with a stain that I could never get out. I hoped the Dalai Lama would understand I wasn't being disrespectful.

I returned to the Dalai Lama's that afternoon and was led into the first of three rooms, where I was frisked by a Tibetan man. While I waited, I showed three Indian women the malas (Indian rosaries) I bought the day before. They roared with laughter when I told them how much I paid. An Indian soldier called me outside. The women were still laughing and pointing at me when I left, even going so far as to tell anyone who walked into the room how much I paid. Once outside, the Indian soldier also frisked me. When I told him I had already been searched by a Tibetan man, he looked up and said, rolling his eyes, "He's [only] Tibetan, but I'm Indian."

Then I was told to go to another waiting room, where I sat next to a Tibetan monk. He was a nice man but cracked his knuckles nervously, which heightened my own pre-interview jitters. I later found out he was the translator.

After a few minutes, I walked over to the meeting room. As I crossed the terrace, I saw the Dalai Lama posing for a picture with an Indian man. They held hands in a friendly manner while the picture was taken. After our interview, I asked if I could have my picture taken with His Holiness. He agreed. As we posed for the photograph, I reached out for his hand, not only because I wanted to touch him, but also because I wanted us to look like close friends in the picture. After the monk took the picture, His Holiness continued to hold my hand and asked the monk to take a second picture, which was fortunate because the first picture didn't turn out.

The meeting room where we talked was decorated in bright Tibetan colors. To the right of us was a statue of Avalokiteshvara, the Buddhist representative of compassion. Some people, especially Tibetans, consider the Dalai Lama to be a manifestation of the deity Avalokiteshvara, though he refers to himself as a "simple Buddhist monk." I asked him to bless a bag of Buddhist prayer beads that I brought with me. He took the bag and reached inside, examining the different rosaries with great interest. He looked at them so intently that I figured there was a particular rosary he was interested in.

"You want one?" I asked.

"No," he said, softly blowing into the bag. It was then I realized that he really wasn't interested in getting a rosary; this was just his way of blessing them.

What I remember most about the Dalai Lama was his laugh. It had a rich and deep tone. He was the only person I interviewed who laughed out loud when I asked him about death.

> Oh Dalai Lama,
> your laugh is all I came to hear.
> It bellows from deep within.
> Give me no words, I ask no questions.
> Only laugh.
> If I were to describe your laugh,
> it would be the fullness of living,
> together with the sufferings of Tibet.
> It is a laugh of folly,
> for we do the best we can,
> but still,
> in the end, we must laugh.
>
> The Bible has erred.
> The beginning was not the Word.
> No.
> In the beginning was the Laugh.

During the interview, I tried to relate to the Dalai Lama in a respectful manner, but also in a way that allowed me to be comfortable with the fact that we were both human beings. In the process of doing this book, I have learned that when I put people on a pedestal, I am also putting myself down. It is really my lack of self-esteem that causes me to put another person on a pedestal, and this only increases our separation from each other.

Once in Bodhgaya, India, the city where Buddha obtained enlightenment, I walked with a group of Westerners from the monastery in which I stayed. The head lama of the monastery walked slowly at the front of the group while the Westerners walked slowly behind. No one would walk beside him or pass him. Since I was late for an appointment, I walked quickly until I found myself just behind the lama's right shoulder. I could move no further. The looks and pressure I felt from the group told me not to do what they suspected I was going to do. Then suddenly a Westerner broke from the group and walked right past me and the lama. Obviously, he had somewhere to go, and he never looked back.

Later that night I saw the Westerner and approached him. "You know," I said, "I really admire the way you walked past Lama Zopa earlier today without letting the group get to you."

"Lama Zopa," he asked, "who is Lama Zopa?"

Gelong Tenzin Gyatso, the fourteenth Dalai Lama of Tibet, is the exiled spiritual and governmental leader of Tibet. He received the Nobel Peace Prize in 1989 and now lives in Dharamsala, India.

On what beliefs do you base your life?

The ultimate aim in Buddhism is salvation or *moksha*, which means a mental state of complete purification or enlightenment. According to Buddhism, all sentient beings have Buddha seed, which means that as long as there is mind or consciousness, there is the potential for enlightenment. In order to achieve this mental state of purification, one must practice compassion and wisdom combined.

Regarding the demarcation of who is a sentient being and who is not a sentient being, we generally consider that plants and flowers have life but no mind. And animals, including insects, have life and feeling or mind. So they feel pain and pleasure. Plants do not feel pain or pleasure . . . But I don't know. What do you think? Do plants feel? Are their movements due to chemical reactions or to some feeling? I don't know. That's complicated. But I believe there's a difference between those beings who have experienced pain or pleasure and those beings with no experience. I think plants have no memory. Insects have some memory, and memory is a quality of mind.

Buddhism is based on *karuna*, which means compassion. The practice of compassion is the most important basic practice. One develops compassion through one's own experience and through realizing that no other beings, not just human beings, want suffering. Through this realization, one can generate love and compassion. But first there has to be the realization of one's own level of suffering. There are pains that everyone agrees is suffering. There are pains nobody wants.

Once you have a conviction that no one wants suffering, you understand the desire to avoid suffering. When one sees that other sentient beings do not desire suffering and yet do indeed suffer, one feels very unhappy. And other sentient beings have that feeling. You can sense that. All sentient beings—particularly human beings but also all animals and insects—appreciate affection, compassion, and love. By identifying with others, one develops love and compassion.

When one thoroughly assesses the value of anger versus the value of compassion, one sees the value of compassion. Through daily experience, one sees that compassion not only helps other sentient beings, but helps oneself, because through compassion and a warmhearted mental attitude—one gets more reliable friends, more smiles, even fame. If one shows other people a warm heart and genuine attitude, then they generally respond in turn.

We can see the negativity in anger or ill feeling because it is harmful to others. Anger also hurts one's own future because when anger comes, it immediately destroys mental peace, calmness, and mental comfort during that moment. That creates a negative atmosphere in one's own house and thus destroys other people's mental peace and happiness—as well as that of one's dogs or cats.

So you see, just one very short-tempered person within a family—someone who possesses ill feeling, for example—may destroy an otherwise calm and happy atmosphere for anyone who is in that family or comes in contact with that family. This we can see.

We must practice subduing negative feeling and increasing positive feeling, positive thoughts and qualities.

The biggest obstacles to our ideals are ignorance, hatred, anger, desire, and attachment.

What is the purpose of life?

Happiness.

What decides happiness?

Good and bad. Positive and negative, though from the Buddhist viewpoint, there is no absolute positive or negative.

Any activity or action or practice or condition that results in happiness is positive. Any conditional thing that brings negative experiences or unhappy experiences can be termed as negative. For example, poison is negative because it brings us pain, it kills, and it causes illness. And since people generally cherish life, killing is very bad because it ends life. Medicine is good because it removes pain, whereas anger is uncomfortable and it brings suffering, so it is bad. Compassion and a good heart bring us happiness, so they are good. A god or Buddha or bodhisattva helps us to become good through the practice of compassion and love. Therefore, these beings are good. The basic demarcation between positive and negative is by seeing if it results in happiness or suffering.

I believe happiness and joy are the purpose of life. If we know that the future will be very dark or painful, then we lose our determination to live. Therefore, life is something based on hope. Hope certainly does not mean pain. No one hopes for pain or suffering. Hope means something good. Life depends on hope or expectation, and that means something good, happy, or joyful, so therefore the purpose of life is happiness.

An innate quality among sentient beings, particularly among human beings, is the urge or strong feeling to encounter or experience happiness and discard suffering or pain. Therefore, the whole basis of human life is the experience of different levels of happiness. Achieving or experiencing happiness is the purpose of life.

Do you believe in a God or Ultimate Reality? What is it like?

That depends on the interpretation of God. If God is Truth or Ultimate Reality, then there is God according to Buddhism; there is a Final, Ultimate Truth.

If God is the Creator and, at the same time, if God is all-knowing or all-merciful, then the Buddhists do not believe in God. From the Buddhist viewpoint, one's self is the ultimate creator. We believe in self-creation. If one interprets God as compassion and love, then of course there is God.

Do all religions lead to the same place?

No. That is something different. Christianity believes that after death there is a final judgment and that salvation means one reaches the presence of God and heaven. According to Buddhism, enlightenment means complete purification, a completely purified mental state. More precisely, ultimate enlightenment means emptiness of mind. [Which means the interconnectedness of all things.]

Perhaps Christianity and Buddhism just describe the same place differently?

I don't think so. According to Buddhism, the ultimate goal of realization is Nirvana or *moksha*. Nirvana is the nature of "suchness" or emptiness, and this is achieved through meditation on the nature of emptiness itself. The nature of emptiness means the nature of the law of cause and effect or the interdependent relationship of all phenomena. By understanding the interrelatedness of all phenomena, one can realize this ultimate state.

After a human life, some say a final judgment will happen. Some say rebirth. There is a different system. If we are not sure about God or rebirth, it doesn't matter—leave it—because we can agree on things that we can experience, see, and feel, such as being a good human being. Being a good human being means having a good heart. There's no controversy or debate on that.

In Buddhism, however, there is hardly any place to accept or believe in a soul and creator. Once one accepts the idea of a creator, that is absolute. A creator does not depend on another factor. It is absolute. So therefore it is difficult for Buddhism and Christianity to come together.

Also, the Christian practitioner believes that if you do not accept the Creator, then the whole faith will crumble down because the main faith is in God. On that basis, love for God is the love for fellow human beings. That is the basic teaching. Someone who does not accept God as creator finds it difficult to practice Christianity.

But generally speaking, both teachings aim for a better human being, a warmhearted human being. Here, they are in complete agreement.

All religions and teachings teach us to be a good human being, to be a warmhearted person, to be honest and compassionate. The most important thing is to have a good heart, to be a good human being.

A good heart is the source of happiness and also the source of strength. It is the source of success, patience, tolerance. It is also the source of good health, good sleep, and good appetite.

If your heart is filled by anger—then no sleep, no appetite, no smile. Then you ruin your own health, ruin your friendships. Even your furniture will be damaged, because you'll get so angry you'll go like this . . . [He laughs as he pretends to pound on the table.] Anger and negative hatred are the source of all bad things. Of course, sometimes I get angry. Big events do not create anger, but small, small things create anger. The invasion by the Chinese is a tragedy; it's negative, ruthless behavior. But I don't feel angry. I feel very sad. And I feel compassion. But when staff members here do a small thing, such as incomplete work or insufficient work, then I feel very irritated. Then I use harsh words! [laughter] But, one good thing is that it never stays long. It comes and it goes. Strong ill feelings that remain a long time are almost nonexistent.

If you could meet anyone throughout history, whom would you meet and what would you ask that person?

As a Buddhist practitioner, I have a keen desire out of devotion to meet the Buddha.

I have some regrets that I never met Mahatma Gandhi, because I was ten or twelve years old when he was alive. So, there was a possibility, but it never happened. I wouldn't ask him anything. I would just like to meet him out of respect. And sometimes out of curiosity, I wonder what kind of person Hitler was.

According to Buddhism, there exist limitless galaxies. It is very exciting to visit another country, so it would be that much more exciting to visit another planet. I wonder, How many planets in our galaxy have a situation similar to our own? Are there other human beings or other beings in our solar system? Do they have the same experience of pains and pleasures?

Some people think personal relationships interfere with spiritual growth. For example, I heard of a Zen teacher who said if you are serious about spirituality, you become a monk or a nun. What do you think?

Yes, that is true from the Buddhist viewpoint. As we already discussed, the obstacle to enlightenment is negative emotion, such as sexual desire and attachment.

It is difficult to remove all negative emotion from our minds. For that, there are two stages. First we must take a defensive measure, and then we take the offensive. The defensive measure means that, although one cannot remove all negative emotion, at least one can remove acting on negative emotion, such as killing, stealing, and sexual misconduct. As a monk, you see, one must control these things, which means something like taking a defensive measure. Then, on that basis, eventually we can go on the offensive against the negative emotion. Therefore, in the Buddhist tradition the monk and the nun are considered the main followers of Buddha, who himself became a monk. Of course, this does not mean that if you want to practice Buddha *dharma,* you must become a nun or monk.

What about death...?

It is very good! [laughter] It gives me inspiration and hope. You see, negative things are very destructive and disturbing, but they can be eliminated. And the positive qualities can be promoted to infiniteness. From that viewpoint, the negative is something temporary; the positive is something permanent. So there is more hope, isn't there?

Whether someone believes in God or not or rebirth or not doesn't matter, as long as one is a human being—a good human being.

If you could change anything in life, what would you change?

As a Buddhist monk, as a Dalai Lama, as a Tibetan, I have lost my own country and witnessed so much suffering in my country. I wish I could make a happier world—harmonious, friendly, and peaceful. I have witnessed much trouble and suffering on this planet, which gives me more conviction in my beliefs about altruism and compassion. Through the Buddhist teachings and daily experience, I have come to the conclusion that a good heart is very important. I feel the human brain can produce unlimited altruism.

What makes you happy? sad?

When I think about the potential of the human brain to produce such unlimited altruism, I rejoice, but I feel sad when I see that potential uncultivated.

There are many occasions when I explain the value of a good heart and good thoughts. I often cry when I think about these limitless qualities of love and compassion or altruism. When I meditate on these qualities, I experience sadness as well as rejoicing.

Altruism and the understanding of emptiness are my two main practices. Emptiness means absence of independent existence; it means interdependent nature. Things are relative, and that concept is very important and very good and useful in our daily lives.

July 26, 1990

The morning after my interview with His Holiness, I made a copy of the interview and gave it to the Tibetan lady at the front desk of my hotel. I know how much they love him. To them, he is a gift straight from divinity itself. They believe he is the aspect or the quality emitted from divinity called compassion. They listen to his voice and his words with a devotional awe not seen in the West. Perhaps the atom bomb elicited the same awe from Westerners—but surely not the devotion.

When I returned to the front desk, there was a small group of Tibetans gathered around taking turns putting on the headphones in order to hear the Dalai Lama. They were laughing and excited, and I felt good that the interviews were bringing happiness to people.

Afterward, I went to see the Dalai Lama's secretary, who gave me a letter from the Dalai Lama. It was addressed to former President Havel of Czechoslovakia, and the letter said, "His Holiness feels that the book will be of benefit to many people . . . and has found Mr. Elliott to be very sincere and genuine." The Dalai Lama suggested in his letter that President Havel also do an interview.

Later that afternoon, I went to see Yeshe Dondon, a famous Tibetan doctor. At his office, he had signs on the walls that said, "Service before self" and "No admission without permission." I wondered how one got permission without admission. Yeshe Dondon gave me pills for my sister who has arthritis and for a friend who is diabetic. He told me their symptoms would be gone after a year.

Each day when I walked to the Dalai Lama's monastery, I saw the monks, lamas, and other Westerners walk past the beggars. Since I was there only a short time, I gave the beggars fifty paisa or one rupee each. This is equivalent to five or ten cents. It doesn't sound like much, but one or two cups of tea or coffee can be bought for one rupee. A meal can be bought for five or six rupees. Each day, the beggars saw me and said, "Hey, Baba...hello!" Most of them had fingers or limbs missing, which was probably due to leprosy, but I have heard that some amputate their own limbs in order to be more successful beggars.

Most Tibetans I met were lovely people. On my way to the monastery, I would pass them on the street, and they would look directly into my eyes, unlike some Indians who stared at me with intense and piercing eyes. The Tibetans were less threatening, and they were friendly and warm. When I returned their smiles, although I had never met these people before, they would stop and, reaching out, take my hand for a moment. Since I did not speak Tibetan, no words were exchanged. We would smile at each other and touch, with both our hands and eyes.

After spending several days visiting Tibetan monasteries, I thought about my friend Ted. After years of searching and study, both he and the Dalai Lama came to believe that a good heart is most important. Each arrived at this conclusion, but one had to go mad in order to do it.

In the Tibetan monasteries I visited, bright colors and images are creatively displayed. There are numerous Tibetan deities, some meditative, others wrathful, and some even seemingly demonic. Having studied Tibetan symbolism, I see that even the most terrifying deities have a small picture of a Buddha or saint contained in them. I understand that these menacing deities are not meant to separate us from divinity, like Lucifer in Christian mythology. On the contrary, Tibetan deities are meant to help us separate ourselves from ignorance, namely, the ignorance of believing in a false self and false notions about life. If we let go of these false notions, these deities can give us the strength and energy to carry on. If we cling to our ignorance and false beliefs, they will appear menacing and do their best to rip us away from them.

One could imagine what would happen to the mind that created these fiery tantric images if it did not have an outlet or direction to express this bursting energy in a sane way. I have seen the art of a few tortured schizophrenics, and while there is a resemblance in their drawings to some of the fierce Tibetan deities, they always lack the small Buddha contained in the heart of the figure. Perhaps this is the crux of the problem that separates some mental illness from mysticism. The Buddha figure represents compassion and the wisdom to know and to remind us that ultimately these deities are creations of mind, while the tortured mind of insanity has no such reminders.

In Tantric Buddhism, a person is not allowed to engage in deep meditation on any deity without understanding that the deity is ultimately empty of true existence.

I moved from my first hotel so that I could be closer to the monasteries. When I checked out, I was charged ten rupees extra. When I asked why, I was told that my cabdriver never paid for the five teas he ordered.

That night I left my hotel with the idea of spending part of the night meditating in the temple. When I arrived there, a monk seemed to be quite angry and disturbed that I wanted to meditate at night. He looked as if he were ready for bed and didn't want another crazy Westerner keeping him up all night. "Come in the morning, and you can stay all day," he said, irritated.

Several young, well-dressed Indian men were making a disturbance in the temple. They were taking pictures of one another in front of the Tibetan holy figures and altars, all the while laughing and pushing each other, as though they were on a vacation at the Grand Canyon or Lincoln Memorial. They told me they were in college and asked me to pose with them for their pictures. They called to the monk I had just talked to and asked him to adjust the overhead lighting. The monk just ignored them.

On my way home, I stopped at a bar. There were four Tibetans and a bunch of Westerners sitting at a table, drinking beer. In the corner of the restaurant were cases of beer stacked five feet high. Above the beer was a picture of the Dalai Lama.

12

MY GREATEST
TEACHER

It seems like a lifetime since I returned the hat, but it was only seven years ago. I returned it to Dave, who had taken it from a lost and found box at school.

It was a common plaid English cap, but for me, it was a special hat. I hid behind that hat for three years. It hid my pain. During the three years I wore that hat, I never took it off when there was another person in the room. Even now, I remember the agony, the pain, the self-hate—the isolation.

I wore the hat because of a hair transplant I got when I was twenty years old. A hair transplant is a lengthy process. Over the course of a year, I visited a plastic surgeon once a month. At each visit, he transplanted hair from one region of my scalp to another, which is a nice way of saying he drilled holes in my head and replaced the empty pits with hair grafts taken from other parts of my head.

"Before you know it," he said, "the hair will be hanging in your eyes." I clung desperately to that hope, which supported me until it slowly dissolved, leaving me alone with a self I hated.

Even now, it is hard for me to believe how far gone I was. I was "done," as I sometimes say. I was like one of those clowns who has painted himself into a corner—I had nowhere to turn.

Day and night I walked around with that hat on, afraid to let people see me without it. I remember the absolute loneliness I felt while sitting in the plastic surgeon's office after he had drilled holes in my head. I could feel the drill against my head, hear and feel the tendons and skin ripping. I smelled the skin burning from the drill. I even felt the drill against my skull—when it would move no longer.

Once, the doctor left the room after the drilling and cutting. The blood trickled down my cheek. The office door was ajar, and a couple walked by and looked into the office. They *saw* me. I was humiliated, yet I sat there and managed to smile through my wincing and tense face. Afterward, I left his office wishing I were invisible, that I didn't exist. But I did exist, and I hated myself for it. I hated existence.

I lived alone while the plastic surgery was being done. I was fortunate to have saved enough money so I didn't have to work. I spent a lot of time thinking. I figured that after the hair transplant was done, I'd go back to being who I was, as though nothing had happened, probably without telling my friends about what had happened.

I gradually realized that the hair transplant wasn't working the way I thought it would. My poetry spoke of my deepest despair:

> Its walls are woven of darkness and oak,
> the floors of loneliness and mire.
> The roof is a rhyme—lulling to sleep;
> the door is but a liar.

> Born of songs that eternally weep;
> its veins are poisons that claw and seep.

> Come lie within me;
> hide from tomorrow today.
> Feel my darkness within your soul,
> and never wander astray.

I began to have fantasies about dying because I never thought I could be happy again. I didn't want to commit suicide, but each night when I went to bed, I prayed that my life would end. Sometimes I lay in bed wishing I were dead. I even imagined myself as a corpse, leaving the world and its troubles behind. I thought it might be possible to die by letting go of my connection to the body, emotions, and thoughts. Detachment from my body, emotions, and thoughts was made even easier when I saw I had suffered *because of* possessing those three things. Maybe without attachment to them, I would stop breathing and disperse, and there would be nothing left of me.

I had that fantasy many times. Sometimes, the room grew dark, even though my eyes were open. There was always a hope of dying. I started to enjoy the feeling of well-being the fantasy gave me. I felt light and ecstatic. After the fantasy was over, however, I was distraught at finding my problems hadn't gone away.

One day, experiencing the fantasy, I found myself in a deep place. My sense of body or self had faded away. There was darkness all around, and I felt as though I barely existed. Gradually, I realized I wasn't alone: A presence was there in the darkness with me. I recognized that this Presence was connected with God and that it was loving.

I expressed my suffering and lack of understanding to the Presence because I wanted to know why I had to suffer so much. It assured me that *if I was honest and sincerely tried,* it would show me.

After that experience, I started to come out of my depression. Each time I encountered a fear, I just remembered that loving Presence and then had the courage to walk through the fear. After three years, however, I still wore my hat.

Even now, I often wonder how I avoided the insanity I wrote about.

> Death without dying,
> hurting without pain.
> Art thou crazed,
> perhaps insane?

In the summer heat, I wore the hat to hide my head, and since I thought a hat looked weird with a T-shirt, I wore a jacket. I thought my head would be less noticeable with a hat on it and the hat less noticeable with a jacket. I smoked a lot of marijuana in order to forget why I wore the jacket. One deception after another, designed to hide from myself.

I used to lift weights a lot at a local gym. Since I couldn't work out with my hat on, I wore a bandanna. One day a guy said, "I wish I was more like you."

"Why is that?"

"Because you dress any way you want. You don't care what people think about you. I would be afraid to wear a bandanna like the one you wear. People might make fun of me."

I was filled with a kind of horror at the pitiful irony of what he had said. After three years, I knew it was time to stop wearing my hat. I began to go for walks at night without my hat. In the darkness, no one could see me, and I could gradually learn to feel comfortable without it. Feeling the night breeze on my head was a new sensation. I felt elated and scared at the same time. I felt I was alive again.

I had recently moved into a house I shared with five friends. One day, I decided to let them see me without my hat. I gathered my courage at the bottom of the basement stairs and climbed the stairs after remembering the Presence I had experienced years before. I was afraid, but I was tired of being afraid, and it was time for it to end.

"Morning, Bill."

"Hi, Bill."

There were no stares. I don't think they really noticed. After all this time, it was no big deal. Then I began to wonder . . . How many things are like that? Before we do them, they seem impossible. Afterward, it's no big deal. How can anyone really understand the personal hells we must each go through? Perhaps the inner experience of shame and suffering *is* common to all, even though it appears in many guises and forms.

Last year at my nephew's high school graduation party, I remembered my high school graduation party. There was a picture taken of me with my two best friends. Afterward, we told everyone about the law firm we would have someday. It would be called Elliott, Zachary, and Harrington.

Although we were best friends, we were always competitive with each other. Because of that, I felt I could never let my guard down or show them my vulnerable side. I couldn't bear to let them see me after I flunked out of college and started losing my hair. I thought people liked me because of the image I presented. Now, I was depressed and insecure. The image was shattered. Since I didn't have it all together, I thought they would laugh at me.

So I moved away and didn't answer their phone calls. When they came over, I didn't answer the door. When my best friend, Ted, finally came over, I told him I didn't want to see him anymore.

"Bill," he pleaded, "what's wrong? Are you depressed?"

"I just don't want to see you anymore," I replied without looking at him. I never saw him again.

That night at my nephew's graduation party, I felt it *was* time to see Ted. After all this time, I could explain to him what had happened.

I hesitated. What if he were a rich and successful lawyer with a beautiful wife, big house, and Mercedes? Could I handle that? After all, I lived in a mobile home. What if he saw I wasn't the hotshot anymore? Maybe *he* was the hotshot now. Even though the hat was gone, I realized I was still hiding.

I called the only Zachary in the phone book. It was his sister. "Hi," I said, "I'm an old friend of Ted's."

"I don't know where he is," she replied. "You know about the trouble?"

"Trouble?" I asked. "What trouble?"

"He started having problems his second year in college..."

I hung up, and the terror made its way from my stomach to my throat. Although it was after eleven o'clock at night, I jumped in the car and drove to the house where he grew up.

I ran to the door and knocked. A boy, the same age as Ted when I first met him, looked out the window. I said I was a friend of Ted's from high school. The boy's mother could be heard in the background telling him not to open the door. For a second, the boy was Ted. In his eyes, I could see the trust, but though he wanted to open the door, he listened to his mother. I could see his silent pleading through the window: "Please understand, I want to open the door—but I can't."

The next day I went back to the house, and Ted's mother explained about Ted. Ted had been diagnosed as a schizophrenic his sophomore year in college—six months after I had refused to see him anymore. He was in and out of hospitals during the time I had been wearing my hat.

That night when I got home I called Ted at the institution. "Ted, this is Bill Elliott."

"Yes," he said very matter-of-factly. After all those years, I expected more recognition or surprise in his voice.

"Bill Elliott," I continued. "I was your best friend in high school."

"Yes," he said simply.

"Do you remember me? I smashed up your dad's car. Remember?"

"Yes. You were known as 'tenacious,'" he said. "I have to go now." It was the voice of a robot. It was the same voice that Ted joked with in high school, but now he wasn't joking.

Ted had been a good student and athlete. While I had always just tried to get by, Ted had tried to excel.

"What happened at school, Ted?" I asked.

"I didn't finish." Although his tone of voice hadn't changed, I could sense his shame.

"Are you married?" he asked.

"No."

"Are you in trouble?" he asked, concerned.

"No," I said, remembering all I had been through. "Not anymore." I could feel his relief. Here he was, in a mental institution, and he was worried about me.

"Do you have a good heart?" he asked.

"Now I do." The tears began to run down my face.

"Good," he said with finality and approval. For some reason, it really mattered that he approved of me.

"Ted, may I come see you?"

"No, don't come here."

"May I call you again?"

"I would prefer you didn't." I could hear the shame. He was ashamed of his condition. "I got to go now," he added. There was a finality in his voice. If he had hung up then, I don't think I would ever have been able to reach him again.

"Ted, I have to tell you something," I said, as I started to cry. "You were my best friend. You're still my friend. Do you remember the last time you came to see me at my sister's house?"

"Yes, I remember."

"I didn't want to see you because I was ashamed of myself. I was losing my hair and was really depressed. I didn't want anyone to see me that way."

"Well, I have to go."

"Ted, may I call you again?"

"Yes," he said, and he hung up.

Ted had been my competitor in high school, and even though it had been twelve years, I had carried on an unconscious competition with him that for years had existed only in my mind. Now, Ted and I have arrived at the same place, the place where the most important question is, Do you have a good heart?

13

MOTHER TERESA

The bus ride from Dharamsala to New Delhi took almost a day. We traveled a winding road through mountains that were both breathtaking and deadly. It wasn't unusual to see the remains of a poorly driven bus at the bottom of a ravine or cliff.

In New Delhi, I hopped on a train to Calcutta. I've always enjoyed the rustic barrenness of Indian trains, especially third class, where the seats and sleepers are plain wooden boards, hanging by chains. Third class is an austere experience that connects a person to the simplicity and salt-of-the-earth, day-to-day existence of Indian life. Years before I had traveled third class and loved being among the common people. This time I again opted for third class, and although I paid for a sleeper for myself, there were other people sharing the space with me. The train was packed. We sat shoulder to shoulder in a car without air-conditioning, and everyone sweated together. After a day of intense heat, my romanticism melted away. I slipped off the train anonymously, paid extra, and boarded the second-class air-conditioned car.

I was given a sleeper across from a wealthy Indian businessman. I tried to make small talk, but he didn't say much. He had an air of superiority and seemed distant. The only thing we seemed to have in common was our balding heads. "So," I asked, "when did you start losing your hair?"

He looked at me, and his face softened. It was the first time he had smiled. We spoke for the next few hours about baldness cures and politics.

"Would you take a pill if it cured baldness?" I asked.

"Most definitely!" the man replied without hesitation. We laughed together and lay awake in our sleepers till deep into the night, talking like two brothers.

When the train arrived in Calcutta, I asked an Indian man for directions to my hotel. He showed me the line for taxis and waited with me. After thirty minutes, a taxi came. When I asked if he wanted to share the taxi, he said no, that he waited in line only to make sure I continued my journey safely.

Within the first few minutes of arriving in Calcutta, I got sick. I stayed inside my hotel the entire day. The next morning, I felt better and went outside, but within minutes, I was sick again. I was sick for three days.

The night of the first day, I was delirious. I was so sick that before I went to sleep and while waiting for a doctor, I wrote my Last Will and Testament. That night, I dreamt that my mind had broken into clear, small cubes. In each cube, there was an electrical charge that was pulsating on and off. When I awoke, I wasn't sure I could even speak.

The first mass at Mother Teresa's mission started at 5:45. As soon as I stepped out of the taxi, beggars surrounded me. "Are you a Christian?" they asked.

I nodded in affirmation.

"Me, too. Let me show you her door."

The mission's door was halfway down the alley; there, the beggars held out their hands, expecting payment. It was hard to refuse a beggar in Mother Teresa's doorway.

The chapel inside the missionary was very simple. There were few chairs; most people sat on the cement floor. Mother Teresa sat near the back wall deep in prayer and looked as though she had been sitting there for a hundred years. She seemed so normal, so ordinary. How did a person of her simplicity ever become famous? Even at her age, she sat on the same cement floor everyone else at mass sat on, except me—I cheated and brought a blanket.

After awhile, Mother Teresa got up and walked to the altar. She wore a blue and white habit, and her walk was like that of a bride about to be married. There were no unnecessary distractions in her walk. It was simple and deliberate.

Perhaps in Mother Teresa's walk was the secret of her life. Mother Teresa didn't appear to be a visionary with grand ideas and the need to complete them. Instead, her life was a series of steps; with each step, she accomplished what God presented to her. And because her Beloved was *here* in the midst of life and not in the future or some heavenly realm, Mother Teresa was also *here*, in this present moment. For Mother Teresa, each step on her way to the altar was done in God's presence. Each step was a communion.

After the mass, I lost Mother Teresa in the crowd of people who gathered around her. When the people dispersed, I told a nun I was there to see Mother Teresa.

"Oh," she said, motioning to her right, "she is right here." I was surprised to see that Mother Teresa had been standing only a few feet away. If you didn't know she was a "saint," you probably wouldn't look twice at her.

I told her why I had come. "I don't do interviews anymore," she said, waving her hand. "So many interviews."

My excitement suddenly turned to disappointment. Without Mother Teresa's interview, I felt that the book would be incomplete. It wouldn't be the way I planned.

I wanted to ask her again—to use my traveling such a distance and to use my suffering and the suffering of the world in order to persuade her to do the interview. I wanted to beg her, because I didn't want to go home feeling I had failed myself and anyone who might read this book.

I handed her the letter she sent me. Perhaps she didn't realize she had already consented to do an interview. She glanced at the letter and gave it back to me. Then she took my hand and held it lovingly in both her hands and pulled me close to her. Her gray eyes looked into mine.

"I'm not feeling well," she said. "And I'm tired."

When she said that, it was as though God was telling me she was going to die. My concern for myself suddenly shifted to her. And by looking into those eyes, I saw it and took it in as though it were a gift: It was *suffering*. In some strange way, I felt the vast suffering Mother Teresa had witnessed. It was a suffering I had experienced before but rejected, because it had been too much for me. Now, years later, the suffering had returned. It had come full circle; only now I had grown enough to accept it.

"Do *everything* for God..." Mother Teresa continued. "God has given you many gifts—use them for the greater glory of God and the good of the people. Then you will make your life something beautiful for God; for this you have been created. Keep the joy of loving God ever burning in your heart, and share this joy with others. That's all."

I barely heard her; there was something deeper overwhelming me. I had come all this way with my mind set on interviewing Mother Teresa, but now that all changed because she was asking for something from me. Her eyes conveyed this. After having understood so many, I realized that Mother Teresa also needed understanding.

There was a line of people outside waiting to see Mother Teresa. A line that never ends. What will they do when she dies? Who will be our Mother Teresa then?

I tried to forget the thought of Mother Teresa dying, because dying was something our society didn't talk about—especially when talking about Mother Teresa. But I couldn't get away from it. And the moment seemed to take on a timeless element. Everything seemed to be happening quite slowly. Looking down, I could see Mother Teresa's hand in mine. Looking back up at her, I saw her eyes. She was such a small, simple person, perhaps not even five feet tall, and yet there was something else in our interaction that was making itself known. I was being stretched further and further.

It was a feeling I had had before when my mother was dying. It was utter disappointment, a disappointment from which no one could save me. And this disappointment stemmed from the fear that I was being abandoned in this world.

The child in me had once wondered, What will I do without my mother? Now, as an adult, I wondered what I would do without Mother Teresa. What would the human race do without a Mother Teresa. Who would be our Mother after she was gone? All this passed before me in a moment—a moment that ran the length of my life.

Mother Teresa in all her wonderful loving presence now appeared to me in a different way. She was no longer a saint; she was more than that. She was a human being. She was what we, as human beings, were meant to be all along. She was so deeply human and ordinary that she had touched that part of humanity that touched God, a humanity that can suffer, cry, laugh, and even die while staying connected with that essence that infuses us.

There was a bittersweet quality to this moment. A year earlier when I met Brother David, he said, "The difference between you and me is that you are young and expanding and I am old and contracting." He had said this with a genuine smile, but the shadow of sadness had framed the moment.

"Anyway," Mother Teresa continued, and I suddenly became aware again of her presence, "you have the Dalai Lama. He's enough!"

As she said that, she waved her hand in the air as though to say, "Go on. It's going to be all right; you've got everything you need."

She turned and walked slowly back to her room. Her walk was just as it was the first time I saw her—nothing special. In some ways, her presence was also nothing special. It was a presence of utter simplicity. I doubt whether there has ever been a human being as ordinary as Mother Teresa, but it is precisely this quality that has made her so extraordinary.

Out in the hallway, people sat on benches that lined the walls. They waited to get a glimpse of Mother Teresa and smiled at me when they realized I had met the person they came to see. Today, I was proud to be a human being—because Mother Teresa was one.

> Back in the street the beggars besieged me.
> Though I gave them money, they pressed me for more.
> In my frustration I waved them away
> because I was overwhelmed,
> and even Mother Teresa was tired.

The next day, I went to see Mother Teresa again. I wanted her to bless the malas, which are prayer beads similar to Christian rosaries. I figured it would be a nice gift for my friends—prayer beads blessed by the Dalai Lama and Mother Teresa.

I met with the nun who was Mother Teresa's assistant. I asked her to give the malas to Mother Teresa to bless. "Oh, no," she replied, "I can't do that."

When I asked why, the nun said they were Hindu and not Christian rosaries. I tried to tell her that they were Christian to me, but she didn't seem convinced.

"Can you take them to her anyway?" I asked. But she refused again, until I told her that I didn't think Mother Teresa would mind. She relented and begrudgingly took the prayer beads to Mother Teresa.

I sat in the dimly lit waiting room. I found it hard to believe that one of Mother Teresa's nuns would make this distinction. If here, in such a place as this, people still believed in the illusion that religions are so different, what could we expect of the outside world?

Just then, the nun returned, smiling. She said Mother Teresa had blessed the prayer beads without hesitation.

14

LAURA HUXLEY

I found my meeting with Laura Huxley to be a pleasant surprise. She took a genuine interest in me, so much so, that during much of our talk, she interviewed me. When I asked her about the advice she would give to her son or daughter on her deathbed, she mimicked the movements of E.T. and pretended she had a long finger. She pointed to me and said, "Be good and laugh."

I told her that after my parents died, I started thinking about life. I watched television, and the message television gave me was to gratify my ego. Adults seemed to be doing that, and I mistakenly thought that since adults were older and had been here longer, they knew the purpose of life.

But Laura Huxley interrupted me and said that gratifying the ego was one of the many truths in life. When she replied in this way, I realized how I had gotten caught up in the mistaken notion that the ego was evil and that it should be cut off from sharing in the enjoyment of living. I had used my ego as a whipping boy. It was in my way, and so I felt I had to destroy it.

In spirituality, a person learns that the ego has something to do with the separation from life and God—so we often make the mistaken assumption, which is also taught by some spiritual traditions, of casting out the ego. I think it isn't the ego that's the problem, however, but how we relate to it.

Over the last few years, I have slowly gained a healthier perspective and understanding of my ego. We've actually grown quite close. I've come around to the notion that originally people were connected to life and to God. That part of life is constructing an ego in order to live in the world. The problem begins when we forget that we were something else before we identified with an ego. Then our ego becomes the center of the universe, ruling our lives.

Our talk took place while Laura Huxley and I walked through the Hollywood Hills. Every so often, we paused as Laura petted a dog or greeted a neighbor.

After the interview, we sat on her terrace. Night was coming, and the sun was setting. Laura Huxley has such a beautiful way about her. Even at her advanced age, the beauty of her youth is still present.

As we sat facing each other in the twilight, we looked into each other's eyes and I became aware of a strange feeling. It was the feeling I usually got on a date, the kind of romantic feeling one gets just before kissing someone. I told myself I had to be nuts. I mean, I was interviewing Laura Huxley—it wasn't a date, and besides she was much older than I, old enough to be my grandmother, and I shouldn't think like that . . . but still, the thought was there.

At that moment, she looked at me and smiled. "You are a beautiful man," she said. Then she leaned over and kissed me.

Laura Archera Huxley is a therapist, author of *Between Heaven and Earth* and *You Are Not the Target* and wife of the late Aldous Huxley.

What beliefs do you base your life on?

I believe there is a central Thing that might be called God. I believe we are connected with That. But It's very, very deep and not easy to define. There is a wonderful Jester that underlies everything, and Its fantasy is so enormous, we cannot even envision It.

Things have a certain rhythm; they follow laws, which are impossible for us to grasp, but they are there, although we cannot put them down as definite laws simply because we are not smart enough to do it.

There are two ideals. One is to encourage life and not to hurt anything, whether it be human or animal or things or objects. The other ideal is for the person to melt into and participate in this extraordinary life. There are thousands of ways to reach this ideal. Although we can profit by all the people who are enlightened, it still is a personal issue. Sometimes a person gets what is called "gratuitous grace." Aldous spoke about that a great deal. It just happens—but it doesn't seem to stay.

What is the greatest obstacle to obtaining this ideal?

We are usually our own biggest obstacle. Even the fact of trying so hard to get enlightened is an obstacle. If one says, "Now I am going to be enlightened," then one is actually making it harder.

One has to want it, but there's no need to push it. It's play. That's why I say there is this tremendous Jester; I call it "Jester" because I don't know any better term. Everything is a paradox. It's a dance of life and death, death and life. Life and death . . . it is a dance.

What do you feel life still has to teach you?

If I lived a thousand years, there would always be something new to learn. There is so much to life. You're twenty-nine, and people say the time we live in is difficult—but still it is exciting and fascinating. It's like a Renaissance. Things are popping up all over the place, and people have to have the ability to choose, although that is difficult. If I were twenty-nine years old, I would explode all over the place because there is so much to experience.

If you could change anything in life, what would you change?

To begin with, I would change people's approach to making children, the casualness with which people procreate. It should be made clear that there are two functions: to make love and to make love in order to have children. I wrote a book on preparing for conception and the time in the womb. If people's approach to conception could be changed, then I think we would have a different world.

I understand that you knew Krishnamurti, the famous spiritual teacher...

Krishnamurti was an extraordinary person. I feel that he really suffered a great deal because to him the things he was saying were so obvious, as though I were to try to convince you that there is

146

a car over there [pointing to a car]. He spoke for seventy years in order to convince us that there is a car. He was maybe in a mystical state all the time, but I don't think he could transmit it.

Maybe he did reach some individual. Maybe someone became enlightened through contact with him. I don't know; I have never heard of that. Besides he didn't want to enlighten people, at least that's what he told me. Once he took me aside at a party and said, "You know, I think those people that do therapy—they are a *curse*." He didn't want to enlighten other people. He only wanted to say this fact existed. That it was through oneself not through him or anybody else that It could be experienced. He was an extraordinary individual; you could feel it.

He was an extraordinary-looking man, such beauty. When I met him, he was very old but still very beautiful. He had a great deal of power and was totally dedicated.

If I could imagine being in his high state of being and seeing that everybody is making a mistake and acting crazy . . . well, I think he felt he had to do something about it. He couldn't just enjoy himself. That is what a bodhisattva is. Krishnamurti didn't need to go around teaching and talking for seventy years. He didn't like it, and he told me he didn't like it.

You have been very lucky to meet Ram Dass and Jean Houston. They are very special people. Ram Dass went to India and grew a beard—okay. Then he came back and cut the beard. I always tell Ram Dass that he was just as lovely before he ever went to India. He was just the same. Although he doesn't like what I said, he was always very loving, very brilliant, and very humorous. Really extraordinary.

Even people for whom spirituality is a priority get too serious and irritable and angry. Maybe what happens with a spiritual person is that things are just more manageable. Bad moods last less time, but they're still there. (The idea that anyone is *all good* is ridiculous, but churches could not go on if people didn't think like that.)

Giving interviews is a very good therapy for you and the people you interview . . . for me, too, because I didn't know the answers, but at least I know I didn't know the answers. You say that some people you interviewed claimed they never got sad or angry anymore. Well fine. I hope it's true. It seems to me that even people who attain a high state of being still have some questions.

At this point Laura Huxley began to ask me questions about how I started to think about the meaning of life. I was touched and flattered by her interest. I told her about my parents' deaths, my depression, the two years I lived by myself, and the way I came out of depression totally different.

"Those things then gave you a push," she said. "You sort of healed yourself in those two years. You decided to get well, and you let go of one thing after another. It is remarkable how you've changed your life. Life is transformation. You've transformed your difficulties into something very positive. That's what one has to do in life. You stayed alone for a while, and what you did were good ways to transform a tragedy into something positive."

15

STEPHEN LEVINE

Stephen Levine was the only person I interviewed by phone, yet he had a great impact on me.

Since I knew he was a meditation teacher, I wanted to be calm and centered for our interview. I prepared by doing meditation and Hatha Yoga for a couple of hours. But he was unable to call that day.

A few days later, I was running around like a madman, preparing for a trip and applying for a graduate school deadline at the last minute. I had been awake for two days and was wired on coffee. I was disgusted at having made the same mistake for the tenth time on my grad school application and was trying to do ten things at once when the phone rang. Aggravated, I picked it up and said, "Hello."

"Hi, this is Stephen Levine," the voice said calmly. "Can we do the interview now?"

Stephen Levine called from a pay phone at a general store. He told me that his legs were propped up on a sack of grain and his back was against the wall. That atmosphere flavored our talk about the meaning of life.

He helped me to see how I had grabbed onto the spiritual path with a neurotic passion. I had held tightly to the notion that I had to be "good" instead of being "myself." But of course, I couldn't be myself, because I was ignorant and unenlightened, as I had been told over and over again at the monastery I had stayed in years before. Only when I was enlightened could I help people and trust myself. Therefore, I couldn't trust myself. This way of thinking had left me indecisive and full of fear. I was afraid to act because I would make mistakes. And most of all, I couldn't accept this me who was ignorant. I could accept only my good side, my spiritual side, a side that at one time saved me from myself.

Now, however, I was in search of wholeness, and this spiritual side was keeping me from myself. I was in danger of becoming what Stephen Levine called "another constipated yogi." Stephen Levine's great sense of humor is very evident in this meeting. It helped me get some perspective.

Stephen Levine is a husband, father, writer, and teacher of meditation who for several years has counseled the terminally ill. He has worked extensively with Ram Dass and Elisabeth Kübler-Ross, and for seven years he directed the Hanuman Dying Project. While continuing his exploration of healing techniques and therapies, he is presently leading retreats with his wife, Ondrea, and acting as a consultant to a number of hospice, hospital, and meditation groups in the United States and Canada. He is coauthor (with Ram Dass) of *Grist for the Mill* and author of *A Gradual Awakening, Who Dies?,* and *Healing into Life and Death.*

On what beliefs do you base your life?

We live in a world of immeasurable suffering. Understanding isn't enough, because everybody seems to have some level of understanding. We know that our way of being isn't always in sync with what we understand. Mercy and awareness are called for at every turn. It seems when I relate to my own mind, I see the need to go deeper. And when I go deeper, I must have great mercy so as not to stop and get hung up or hold on to the pain of long years (or maybe even incarnations) of latent grasping tendencies. So, there needs to be a lot of softness in the penetration, in delving deeper into the mind.

When the mind is clear, it is all heart. In fact, Ondrea and I sometimes are very close to the Zen tradition. The term "no mind" arises again and again in that tradition, and we laugh and say, "Where there is no mind, it's all heart." As far as belief . . . it is just to try to be a little kinder and to try to pay a little more attention.

Do you believe in a God or Ultimate Reality?

It is all an ultimate, an alternating reality. I'm very comfortable with the use of the word *God,* partly because I don't have the foggiest idea what it means. I have a very intense relationship with Maharaji, Neem Karoli Baba [who died in 1973]. His being in a body or out of a body is superfluous. It is what he represents—the capacity for the human to become the Divine or the Divine made manifest in the human. I'm not sure if there even is a difference between the words *human* and *divine;* it might just be what models we identify with.

I don't think of God as some long-haired fellow or blond-haired woman in the sky. I think of God as the common denominator in all things, the underlying essence, the underlying reality. I like the idea that one hears in the Christian belief system that we are all cells in the body of Christ. That's a very nice way to say that we are all God, that we are collectively and individually God. But God the torturer, God the person you kill for, I don't find anywhere in my heart or in my mind. That's not God. That's the "me" that you kill for; that's the "me" that tortures. That's the separate, not the Universal. I think of God as the Universal.

I used to have an understanding of reincarnation, and I have had certain experiences with people who were dying in which I got a glimpse of things that were happening afterward. (These experiences aren't uncommon; it's nothing special.) I used to wonder: Why would anyone voluntarily reincarnate onto this plane of reality with the enormity of injustice, starvation, abuse, and indifference, the cold indifference, of this plane? For years, I could not think of a reason—I said, "For another hot fudge sundae?" I mean, is that what life is for, one more time to have a body to hang clothes on?

I couldn't believe I would ever voluntarily reincarnate on this plane again. Involuntarily maybe. As they say in the Tibetan tradition: After a person dies, one falls asleep, passes out at the sound of one's great nature, trips, and falls headlong into a womb, except for the people whose lives are ethical, investigative, and kind. The Bhagavad Gita states, "They are born into the wombs of perfect yogis," which sounds great.

Then it occurred to me quite clearly: I can see reincarnating for love and also for joy (not just to see the shadow) because in this plane of mercilessness, at times there is such a need for kindness, a need for deeper awareness, that I could see incarnating just to increase those facilities, to share those with other beings in this lifeboat.

What is the purpose of life?

Where's Woody Allen when you need him? [laughter]

I don't know what the purpose of life is. You know, one of the troubles with purpose is that when you start to add meaning, meaning slows things down. This isn't something I'm telling students who don't ask, because I don't want to take away their ground until they're ready to let it go. But adding meaning to things keeps us in the mind, in the place of confusion and separation.

I see this particularly when we work with people who have lost loved ones. A mother who has lost her child might say it was so meaningful that the child died on *that* day, wearing *that* dress, in *that* car, on *that* street corner, at *that* time. So much meaning is added that it becomes a buffer zone between us and an extremely painful and confusing reality, a bewildering plane we live on.

If one is comfortable with not adding meaning, one can get closer and more quickly to the heart of things. Meaning means opinion. Then, it becomes my opinion against your opinion. Then, we have the German World War I belt buckle that says, "God is with us." Anyone who's ever gone to war has thought God was on his side, that he had the right understanding, the right meaning.

If one can be softer with meaning, the mind might bring it up. If one can relate *to* the mind instead of *from* it, then things are smoother and there is more compassion, although there certainly are such things as meaningful experiences, experiences that open us more deeply, that help us let go on a more profound level. There is certainly nothing we know now that we couldn't know at a deeper level, and it is often meaningful experiences that show us the way. But to *add* meaning, I'm not sure it is a skillful way to live.

You often hear that some paths are faster than other paths. What do you think? Can a person do better than to be "here and present" with awareness?

You know, "here" and "now" are both concepts. Already, as the third Zen Patriarch said, "we have set Heaven and Hell infinitely apart."

Each school of thought, having become a school of thought, may be caught a little off-kilter. Something has solidified behind schools of thought. The concepts aren't as open as they might be.

I have pictures of Maharaji and Ramana and Sarada Devi and Jesus and Mary at different places in the house, and they remind me to be here, now.

When any school starts to pick on any other school, it's evident that there is a lack of faith, and the same old insecurities we all have so profoundly have found their way into spiritual practice. All the practices could use a little more ground and a little more space. It really is a balancing act, not an either-or.

What is your core practice? What is important to you?

Vipassana, which is a meditation practice, is the practice that I do and have done for twenty-five, thirty years, and I find it wonderful. I love to sing to God, and when I sing to God I start shaking in a way I never do when I meditate. I mean, profound *kriyas*. What that is all about, I don't have the foggiest, but it's enjoyable. Vipassana is an absolutely terrific practice, and I would recommend it to just about everyone.

I see as many confused Vipassana teachers with secret lives as I see Tantra teachers with secret lives. In Asia there are Vipassana teachers who won't talk to each other because of a slight difference in their teaching. The lesson for me is to be merciful with myself and to realize how hard it is to go to the source of things, to be kind and try not to judge others. I advise anyone who says the path is easy to let it take a while, study it a little more, and then one will see it's just not easy and there is a lot of stuff we have accumulated. As soon as we start judging somebody else, we're in trouble.

We each must do our work, be kind to ourselves, not think there is one right way, because the "right way" is the wrong way. There is only *one* way: what is happening right now. If we can meet it with mercy, with a little more awareness, there is a chance for a little more freedom. There is no freedom in saying, "My way is the only way." More people have been killed in the spirit of "my way is the only way" than probably for any other single reason, any other meaning. So much cruelty is done in the name of "my way is the only way."

Sometimes I have been told that in spiritual practice I can't trust myself because I (my ego) might be fooling myself.

Fooling yourself? What *is* fooling yourself? The whole thing is to do whatever you do with kindness and mercy. Just go and do whatever you do, because it isn't really *what* we do, but *how* we do it. It isn't whether we can sit for seventeen hours without moving; it is *how* we sit for seventeen hours without moving and *why* we sit for seventeen hours without moving.

Also, don't get into the holy wars. I felt at times I had to pull back a little from the coolness of Vipassana. I felt it didn't have enough warmth, enough *metta,* which is loving-kindness, particularly the way it's been taught in this country, perhaps as a reaction to the fact that in Asia the common practice is not Vipassana, but Metta. The Asian transplant forgot the balance that was already preexisting in the East, but not in the West, of the Metta practice. I knew there was a point at which I just had to say, "It's okay to be wrong." As I began to do service work, I had to go into areas of people's psychology that I had been taught, had experienced, and had heard ad nauseam, but that were empty and beside the point. But now I had to honor them with love.

When we get to love, there is so much we don't know. It is just open, open, open space that never stops, and sometimes it is all right to be wrong. It becomes, Why are you doing it? Is it for the benefit of all beings? Are you doing it for yourself? Of all the teachers I know, none is open all the time. I've never met anybody who is open all the time, whose heart is open all the time, and whose mind is clear all the time. I have many remarkable friends who are very fine teachers, and I've seen every single one of them over the last twenty-five years confused at one time or another. So, here we are; we're just human.

Vipassana can seem to recommend coolness, but the things that attract one to Vipassana teachers are their warmth and kindness. Look at the Tibetans . . . there's a technology of the spirit that one would think would make the people cold because of the enormity of that supertechnology in the Tibetan Vajrayana practice. But the Tibetans are some of the warmest, kindest, most beautiful, most intuitive people I have ever met in my life. I've met Trungpa Rinpoche, who was a Tibetan lama, and certainly his books are some of the clearest water around. We have to go beyond our practice. Who needs another constipated yogi? There are lots of them, and there are those who argue about who teaches best.

I don't see any more enlightened people who are Buddhists or Hindus or Christians. I mean, there is a Thomas Merton here and there; there is a Lama Yeshe here and there; there is a Sarada Devi here and there. I can think of these various sweet, clear beings. But it isn't simply their *practice* that made them that way; it is their *intention* that brought them to that. It is their willingness to experiment, to go to God beyond old conditioning, beyond old anything, beyond old seconds just passed.

It's like what Jack Kornfield told me. He was with Kalu Rinpoche, and Kalu would go out and talk to the group at a retreat about the four different elements. As he would talk about fire, everybody in the room would be sweating. He would talk about air, and everyone would feel the lightness. He would talk about water, and everyone would feel the fluidity. He would talk about earth, and everyone would feel the pull of gravity, the solidity and density, that quality. Jack said that after each one of those talks Kalu would come back behind the stage, kick his legs up on the soft chair, and turn on the television set. That is someone who is just where he needs to be. There aren't many beings like that, and it isn't simply the practice; it is the heart that *does* the practice.

One friend told me that his teacher taught him to be "mercilessly aware." We have to take this whole thing a little lighter. It's too serious. I've even been told by some teachers not to broaden the practice because it isn't good for the tradition.

What is the highest ideal a person can reach?

To reach our own true nature.

I don't like the word *enlightenment. Lightenment* would be a better word. Complete and infinite Lightenment.

I know people who have been practicing an awfully long time, and they are not enlightened. But how would I know? I'm not enlightened. I really like Suzuki Roshi's teachings. He talks about the "moment," the "enlightenment before enlightenment." It's just a moment of clarity and kindness and presence. If there is a goal, that is it.

This goal is attained a moment at a time . . . but even the word *attained* is a trap. These are all trap words. See, I've been at it for a long time, and I'm not enlightened. But I've had moments of understanding beyond my wildest dreams, and it isn't even understanding. I've had moments of pure being, but the underlying conditions that perhaps caused me to take birth have arisen again in a different context, as time goes on.

What makes you angry? happy?

It's not that the mind doesn't experience anger or fear or doubt; it is just that when it comes up, it doesn't stay very long. Those original provocateurs, those latent tendencies, are still there. I see times when my heart is closed, and then the work is, Can I be open to my heart's being closed? Or do I judge it? Or do I close my heart *to* my heart being closed?

When we walk across the floor and stub a toe, our conditioning is to send hatred into the pain, to loathe it and really to try to put it out of our world—just the opposite of what it is calling out for. It is calling out to be held, to be cradled, to be accepted, to be touched with mercy, and to be explored.

Our conditioning is so far off the mark, 180 degrees. We can have a time during the day when we might be way off the mark, when our mind is grasping and we are very self-concerned, maybe even self-pitying or self-doubting. All of a sudden it will clear, and we'll see how it was absolutely nothing but bubbles floating in vast space. But it is not that those bubbles don't arise.

If one can be freer and freer, what difference does it make if we get enlightened or not? If people have anything better to do than to open their hearts and to clear their minds, then let them try it and pay attention to whether or not they cause themselves and others suffering.

Are they happy? That word *happy* . . . Fools rush in where angels fear to tread, but I'd say the only time I'm really happy is when my heart is open and I don't care what I'm given, what desires are satisfied, or even if I'm feeling particularly clear. If that thing, that spaciousness, that wonderment isn't there, I'm not happy. To the mind, the heart and mind are two things, but to the heart, they are one.

Grasping is what gets in the way. Buddha said it was laziness, and I would say that is probably so. I see that in my case. On the other hand, what we do has to be done so gently, so lightly. If we get too fierce with ourselves, the force just closes the heart. It is a balancing act. It is really holding to self as separate, as real, not going deeper. There are *the hindrances* and such, but the problem is not the hindrances. The problem is *identification* with the hindrances. One can say that the root of the problem is our ignorance in thinking the mind is who we are or the body is who we are.

Will all people reach this freedom?

Not in the town I live in [laughter] . . . I don't know, but does it matter? Everyone can have more joy, ability to serve, clarity.

Look at the people you work with. We don't recommend that people teach Vipassana to schizophrenics, for instance. Each person has to use the Braille method: just feel yourself along, one moment at a time, letting go of the last moment and opening up to the next moment in the flow, so you are not so lost in the content and stay more open to the process. The more open you are to the process, the more you get a sense and experience of the space in which that process floats. I would be hard put to find another word for that space other than God or True Nature, but that is nothing to fight a holy war over, because it is unnameable, and it has no edges on it. There is no way to define it.

What about death . . . ?

Death is the space between thoughts. If someone asked me, What is death? I would say, What is life? Tell me what life is, and I'll tell you what death is. You tell me where the light is, and I'll tell you where the darkness is. Not that death is the darkness. Maybe life is the darkness, but death is a moment during life, and it isn't the end of life. It is a point in the process, and who knows?

If I pay attention to what is going on now, I'll be present then. Whatever navigation or necessity or dream of necessity to navigate—whatever is needed, I'll be there for it.

What is death? I don't know. I know beyond a shadow of a doubt that we survive this body. I know it through direct experience, which I've written about in *Who Dies?* and other books.

I don't know what happens after death, but I know there is an after. I know what the process of dying is. I can tell you what the first earthly half-hour is. [laughter] But I don't know what goes on after, because I haven't been there.

Why do you think there is suffering?

Because people ask questions. [laughter] Why is there suffering? No reason. That question was asked of Ramakrishna, and he said, "To thicken the plot." That same question was asked of Suzuki Roshi, "What is the reason for so much suffering?" and he said, "No reason." There just *is* suffering. Certainly where there is grasping there is suffering, but grasping isn't always voluntary; otherwise, everyone who wanted to be would be enlightened.

I asked the same question of someone in Nepal, and he said, "Why is water wet?"

Right, exactly. Or if we ask about evil—these are all *concepts!* Why is there joy? I don't know. One answer could be, because there is confusion.

For about the last three years as part of other work, I've worked with hundreds of women who were sexually abused as children. I worked with the dying for about ten years before getting involved with sexually abused women, and I must say, being with people who were dying was very easy compared to being with people on whom others had imprinted such enormous, unbearable suffering, such evil. Regarding the *question* of evil, I have no idea how or why. Actually, I *know* more how someone could do evil, because we can see inklings of that cold indifference in ourselves when desire arises, but why should that be? All I know is that I have learned more about seeing myself as Hitler than I have about seeing myself as a victim of Hitler.

I remember my boy coming home one day and saying that one of the teachers was unfair, that the world was unfair, and I said, "Yes, but the teaching in that is: If *it* is unfair, let *us* try to be fair." Maybe what we can learn from evil is to let us try not to stimulate or act on those evil qualities in ourselves. Let us be merciful. Let us use evil to remind ourselves not to cause anyone else evil, because evil reinforces self-injury. Let us remember, every time we hear about someone hurting another, how important it is to be kind to others and merciful.

Everyone has the same potential. I hear some teachers speak of a "complete path" and an "incomplete path." It isn't the religion; it is the spirit of the religion. You could probably look in any religion and find faith. I don't include Satanism as a religion. It is an aberration. Belief systems are terribly dangerous.

If you were on your deathbed, what advice would you give to your son or daughter?

Don't fight over the will. [laughter] If I haven't said it before then, I'm in trouble, and they're in trouble.

I would like to pay attention and to be kinder, be more mindful and less fearful.

What do you feel is the most important thing you have learned from living?

Not to do this one again. [laughter] Never go to a retreat. Every time I prepare to go on a retreat, I can't wait, but after I start, I think, How could I have forgotten how difficult it is? I think of how much I have changed. I've probably changed more than most of the people you have met. When I was a teenager, I was a black leather gang fighter. I've learned not to be indifferent. *Sometimes*, I know not to be indifferent.

Certain experiences during meditation have changed the nature of my mind forever. That, and letting my heart break.

What makes you sad? angry?

The thing that makes me saddest is to see cruelty in the world. Frustrated desire makes me angry. In Buddhism there are different types, different tendencies, and I am probably an "anger type." That is why love and loving-kindness are so important to me. It's not, "Don't be angry," because if we try to squash anger every time it comes up, we are just going to be more angry and are going to put our anger below the level of awareness. My advice to work with anger is to be as mindful as possible as soon as possible when we notice the first wave, the first ripple of anger.

Is there a basic difference between maleness and femaleness, besides the body?

There's no difference between men and women; apparent differences are just conditioned. If you believe there is a difference, then you're saying, "We are the body." No, absolutely not. It's fear or ignorance, maybe mine or theirs. [laughter]

There are spiritual teachers who say that if one is serious, one becomes a monk, that relationships get in the way.

In the way of what? Does that mean that desire stays latent, then? What kind of enlightenment is that? If so, we all know of teachers who are high in certain areas but are sexually unethical. Relationship is one of the hardest yogas a person can take on, and it will stimulate every place one holds and all one's latent tendencies—particularly places of control. That's where yogis and meditators have to be especially careful, very, very watchful, because, without watching those qualities, they act out in such subtle ways and enslave the students. Some teachers give people ways to be instead of exploring what *being* is all about.

I find relationship a tremendous teacher. I've got an incredible relationship with Ondrea, who is my third wife. We have three children and have been together nine years, and it is wonderful. I really have a collaborator on the spiritual path. In fact, we tend to want to avoid talking about our relationship to people, because it makes them feel sad. Rainer Rilke said in his letters to young poets, "Don't frighten people with your confidence and joy."

My relationship with my children is one of the most remarkable things that ever happened to me. Whatever heart space I have probably would not have been forced to explore itself so much had I not had children. I didn't expect to have children in this incarnation. I was into Buddhism when I was nineteen years old, and I didn't have my children until I was in my early thirties. Talk about a fierce teaching. It is easier to sit for three years in a cave than to raise a child from the time he is born to three years old.

I can see that a lot of people just don't want the hassle. They start to make excuses for themselves, saying, "Oh, it's not useful." If they don't want a relationship, great. They certainly, absolutely don't *have* to. If they want to put all their energy into painting or gardening or soldiering, it doesn't matter.

There is a wonderful story about a yogi who had been practicing for many, many years. I think Vivekananda told this story. This yogi had been meditating in the forest for many years. One day he was sitting, and a bird was fluttering right in the way of the sun. It was casting shadows on his face and making an awful noise. The yogi looked up and silenced the bird dead, and he was filled with his own power. He said, "Wow, look what my practice has done for me!" He went off on his alms rounds and came to a little town where he usually went. He knocked and called in through the open door. A woman called out and said, "Can I help you?"

He said, "Yes, I am a yogi and on my alms rounds."

"Just a moment, please."

He waited about ten minutes and was getting quite irritated. He had just had this remarkable experience, a sign of his deep universal power, and this woman wasn't giving him his due.

She delayed again and again. When she came out after a half-hour, he was pretty irritated. She said, "You are irritated because you silenced that bird and think you are such a great yogi."

"How did you know that? Are you a yogi?"

"No, I am the mother of five children."

There are some mothers of five children, particularly some of the black mothers I have seen down South, who are greater yogis and know more about common courtesy than some of the people whose books we read—because that is what it is all about, common courtesy.

16

TONI PACKER

In order to interview Toni Packer, I drove from Wisconsin to New York. It was snowing heavily, and the drifts were high when I arrived. I plowed through them with my car, hoping I wouldn't get stuck.

Toni Packer's interview was a tremendously transformative process for me. She did not answer my questions; instead, she went past them, and together we reflected on the state of the questioner. She helped me get to the heart of the matter by seeing what was behind all the information I had accumulated while doing these interviews and ultimately who or what was behind my search. I edited this interview as little as possible so that the power and struggle of the interaction would remain intact.

During the interview, the questioner in me was confounded by Toni Packer's replies. This so unnerved me that my perception of the room became altered. It was as though the thoughts that had organized my mind until then had splintered and were searching for something solid, a concrete idea perhaps—anything to keep them afloat. At that point, I couldn't think; I was totally confused. I recall mumbling something to Toni Packer about the fact that the cup on the table was looking kind of funny. She assured me it was a regular cup—but that wasn't the point. The point was that everything was looking different, because in the midst of my self-confined chaos, there was a moment when something else was able to make itself known...

The pain of not knowing was the beginning of my search; could it be that the acceptance of not knowing was the end?

I knew more about myself, about the world both spiritual and concrete, but the most important thing I learned, the thing that remained with me, was the mystery.

It seemed ridiculous that this was the culmination of my search so far. The years of searching and agonizing emptiness had led to this: Seeing a pebble in the middle of the road, I pick it up.

Toni Packer disturbed me the way Chokyi Nyima had. They were both direct, and they focused in on the questioner rather than the question. Since I could not hide behind my questions, I felt naked.

Chokyi Nyima was a Tibetan lama I met while in Nepal in 1985. I interviewed him for the University of Wisconsin fieldwork project titled "A Philosophical and Dialectical Inquiry into the Major Religions of Nepal." This fieldwork was really a cover for my true intention, which was to find the meaning of life.

Chokyi Nyima's monastery was large and located on a small hill. He was much younger than I expected, with a small, oblong-shaped head and eyes spaced far apart. He smiled as I asked him about the purpose of life.

"You mean, what is the reason?"

"Yes, what is the reason?"

"No reason."

"No reason?" I asked.

"If you say 'No reason,' I say reason."

I was silent for a moment while I searched for a new strategy. "I'm trying to ask you . . ."

"Why am I here?"

"Yes."

"Why not!"

He was obviously playing with me. Then he pointed to his nose and asked me why he had a nose like that.

"To smell with, I guess."

"No," he asked seriously, "why shaped like this?"

I thought for a second, and then I devilishly smiled to myself. "Why not?" I said to Chokyi Nyima. I laughed at my own cleverness. Now the lama had some of his own medicine. But the look on his face told me he didn't think I was funny.

"No," he said, leaning forward on the edge of his chair, "Why like this? Why?"

I didn't understand what the big deal was, but I said the first thing that came to mind. "Maybe that's the way it is."

"Okay," he said, as he leaned back in his chair, seemingly satisfied with the answer he elicited.

The rest of the interview went smoothly. He answered the remaining questions as expected. Afterward, I was quite satisfied with myself. After all, I had another good interview under my belt. The sun shined through the monastery window, and the lama sat across from me, beaming. I basked in our mutual understanding.

He offered me a cup of tea, and I accepted. When the tea arrived, the lama looked at me.

"Do you want me to grow hair on your head?" Chokyi Nyima asked, referring to my balding head.

I jumped. The teacup shook in my hand. I didn't quite understand what he was doing.

"Because I could grow hair on your head if you wanted me to, you know."

A friend once described the uncomfortable surprise of a child who had pocketed an unfinished jelly sandwich, only to reach back into that coat pocket one day and Yuck!—there it was. That day I was in that pocket, drowning in jelly sandwiches, while the lama just smiled.

"Uh, I don't know . . ." I mumbled.

"Are you sure? I really can."

My mind was swimming; my spiritual demeanor had been destabilized.

"It's okay," he said compassionately. "Really. Everything is all right. Don't worry. You're okay."

I settled down, and he smiled at me. I was shaken and hadn't quite figured out what just took place. There was no judgment or malice in his face.

I was just beginning to breathe more easily when he leaned forward in his chair.

"You think you're a smart guy, don't you?" he said accusingly.

I jumped again.

"A real smart guy," he repeated. I shook again.

I once read a story in a paper about a pet store owner who sold little ducklings that danced in his front window. People thought it was cute because the ducklings danced to music. But then they found out that the ducklings were dancing because they were standing on a hot plate.

"You're right," I said, as I stopped shaking and gave in. "I do think I'm a smart guy. And I think that's one of my problems."

"Don't worry. You are a smart guy. And remember, you need me—and I need you." Then Chokyi Nyima smiled and put his hand on my shoulder. "You can call me Yoda."

Toni Packer has been the resident teacher of Genesee Valley Zen Center since 1982. She is a spiritual oddity. After being chosen as the successor to her teacher, an honor most spiritual seekers would have embraced, she declined and followed what she perceived as truth.

In 1967 she became a student of Roshi Philip Kapleau at the Rochester Zen Center and was later asked to assume some teaching duties. In 1981 the entire teaching responsibility for the Rochester Zen Center was transferred to her, but her encounter with the work of Jiddhu Krishnamurti reinforced and clarified a deep questioning of all established forms and traditions. It became clear to her that she could no longer work within the boundaries of a traditional Buddhist organization. She left Rochester Zen Center at the end of 1981 and opened the Genesee Valley Zen Center.

On what beliefs do you base your life?

I don't base my life on any belief.

If you had a friend who felt the need for some beliefs to base life on, what would you tell the friend?

I would wonder if my friend was interested in finding out why this need to have a belief exists, whether there is fear or insecurity. Why not be in touch with this fear and insecurity and see if one can get to the root of that, rather than escape into these beliefs? There is no belief system in my life.

Look out there. [She points out the window.] The sun is about to set. Do you have to believe that? The wind is blowing; the snow is swirling. Do you have to believe that? If you see something is so, it is so. If you don't see it, you are afraid, and then you have to believe. I feel having ideals is a very dangerous thing for human beings. We have ideals because we have lost the ability to see directly. Ideals conflict. Your ideals might be different from my ideals, and therefore we are at odds with each other. Let's find out what the truth is and not indulge in speculating about our ideals. Watch the mind. Do we have an awareness of the processes? What is an ideal? It is thought. It is conditioning and is taken from others. But what is the truth? That is what interests me, not ideals. Can there be listening without ideals, without beliefs, without the separation of me and what I'm listening to? Just simple, open listening? It can't be put into words. Words are very limiting.

Do you think there is a purpose to life?

"What is the purpose of life?" is not a meaningful question—although this was a question that was driving me tremendously during the war years and prewar years in Hitler Germany. I saw how meaninglessly and senselessly human beings were living, with constant antagonism, conflict, and struggle. They were persecuting and killing each other, and I had to resolve for myself the question of the meaning of life.

But the one who asks this question feels separate from life: "me" and "my life." Because of this separation there is this haunting question, What is the meaning of life? When there is no feeling of separation, then there is just living. There is just life. No one is standing outside of life and therefore worrying about whether this is pointed toward something else. Everything is what it is; it doesn't point toward something else.

You seem to be refuting the questions I am asking. It makes me feel as though the questions are ridiculous.

That is quite all right. As you said in the beginning, these questions are the questions we ask.

What would you say is the greatest obstacle to truth?

Truth has no obstacles. You mean the perception of truth and understanding. The greatest obstacle is this deeply ingrained sense of self, of me—the deeply ingrained sense that I am a separate individual, separate from everyone else, and all that goes with that sense of separation.

We believe we are separate because we are deceived by our thoughts, images, ideas, ideals, and our own sensations. Do you believe it? We must believe it because it feels that way, doesn't it? Are you interested in finding out what makes for this strong feeling and belief that there is a separate self? If that question grabs you, then you will begin to observe what makes for that feeling of separation, the thoughts that come up, the feelings and emotions in that relationship.

We have an image of what I am, what I was, what I could be, and what I should be. What people think of me and what I want them to see in me has a tremendously strong hold on the mind and the body. All ideas and images are made up and come out of memory, which is connected with deep emotions and sensations. This in turn affects our perception of people and things.

Suffering is connected with this sense of self. There is suffering because we are sufferers or because we feel victimized. It has to do with the sense of me and what is happening to me. If that sense of self isn't there, then pain is pain and sorrow is sorrow, and we are not the sufferer of that. But this doesn't mean no depth of feeling. We can feel feeling for the sorrow of humankind, but it is not pity or self-pity with us but seeing what we do to ourselves and each other.

At one time you were a Zen Buddhist...

Yes, but now I don't consider myself anything.

Do you have any ideas about enlightenment?

Enlightenment is not an idea. If an idea about enlightenment is carried around, it affects our action. We want it and will do anything to get it. We will submit to any kind of discipline or system to get that enlightenment; in the process of trying to get the enlightenment, we will not be in touch with what is actually going on. For instance, there is wanting, lacking, having a goal, striving, and competition—all because of wanting enlightenment. So what I am concerned with is what is going on right now in the human being. Can there be an open, free awareness of this? That is not the case if one postpones being in touch with it now for the sake of getting something in the future.

The thought of enlightenment can be highly inspirational and can give one rushes or gushes of energy in thinking "I can get it." But it is just an idea and thought. Does one understand what is going on when this thought of enlightenment starts fueling desire and reaction? Can that come into simple awareness—in other words, shedding light on how we live? how we think? how we act?

What do you think about death?

That is what we do: We think about death and scare ourselves. The thought that is trying to capture what-death-is is continuously thinking. It is trying to think what-is-death. I want to know about it; I want to have an attitude about it or a comforting thought about it. It is all thinking. Thinking that after death I may go to heaven or to hell—that is thought. Thinking I will be born again or reincarnated or live future lives—why do I think that? Is it because I am afraid of the thought of death? As long as thought is trying to capture this thing called death, it is continuously active; thought is actively thinking. But dying is not the activity of thought; dying is the ending of thought.

So, is it possible that thought ends? That there is just listening without knowing? Listening inwardly, outwardly without reference to the me, myself? We want to continue as a self, and because we want to continue as a self, we are afraid of dying. So, can there be dying to the thought of self? To the me: my image, my future, and my past? Can there be dying to that thought? With simple awareness and simple listening? Not, "I am listening; what do I get out of it?" or, "Will I be enlightened if I listen?" That is simply a continuation of the concept of me. Can there be an ending of the concept of me? That has to be found out.

Death is at the end of life. I haven't died yet. We all will die, and I'm not afraid of it. I don't know how I would feel if the airplane was hijacked and somebody was threatening me with a gun or the plane was going down. How can I tell? Sitting here right now, there is no fear of dying. My concern is not what will happen to me when this life ends. My concern is, can there be a dying to resentments and grudges? What he did or what she did to me—can we die to that? Be done with it? Maybe there was anger a moment ago. Can that anger end, be finished and not carried over in the mind? Can we die to each moment so there is a freshness of living that is not possible if we keep carrying around everything that has happened?

I'm not concerned with what happens after death. That is idle speculation used to cover one's fear of death. I remember becoming in touch with Buddhism and joining a Buddhist place. How nice it was thinking of these future places, thinking of having a better, more developed life. But what is crucial for us human beings is for us to be alive now. All these ideas of what will happen later or what I will become are not as important. Can we be in touch with what is true now?

What about teachers who wear robes and say there are certain practices one can do to attain enlightenment?

That is what we human beings do. We are attached to things. Just because we are the teacher doesn't mean we are not attached to our system.

Do you think there is any worth to certain practices that give one gradual steps to truth?

There are no gradual steps to truth.

I read that truth is spontaneous, but things leading up to it are gradual.

I know the teaching that things leading up to enlightenment are worth doing: practices like rituals, bowing, and incense burning. But these things don't lead to truth. They comfort us. They give us a feeling of refuge and belonging. We love being able to do something. We are conditioned to feel good if we are doing something, and this is what these things are very well suited for. These practices have nothing to do with understanding; they don't even shed light upon the practices themselves. One is not encouraged to question these practices, either. One has to have insight into what one is doing when performing a ritual, but performing the ritual itself doesn't shed light; it just gives inspiration or a good feeling or energy.

If we think certain practices can arouse energy, of course they can. We can arouse energy in all kinds of ways, but why do we want to arouse energy? For what? Wanting is involved, self-centered motives and a goal are involved, in order to become something—to become enlightened, to become a better person. I want to have this. I want to do this in order to get that, so I do things as a means to an end, which means I'm not really with it. I'm just doing them to get something else. Why do I perform the practices in the first place? Can I get to the bottom or root of what motivates my actions? What is the source of it?

Even when a person meditates, why is the person meditating? Is the person sitting in order to attain something? Is the person sitting because he or she has found out that by sitting, the system calms down, the heartbeat slows down, and the person feels a little bit more at ease, a little bit more relaxed? Well, then, if the person sits for that purpose, that is why one sits. If one sits down because one wants to find out what is going on, right now, then can the mind open up to listen to what is going on?

Do you feel there is a practice that a person can do to open the mind?

No, I don't think so. If the mind opens up, it isn't due to a cause. Every teacher will tell you, "I have The Way to open up the mind. I have the means. Come into my group or tradition or church and learn the practices, and you will get what you desire: an open mind or enlightenment." But one has to find out for oneself.

I don't know how a mind opens up. I couldn't tell you. It is either open or closed. When it is closed, we perform all kinds of practices to get it open. When it is open, we don't know how it happened! We may deduce or think this led to that. If I practice focusing my mind on certain parts of the body, it causes energy in those spots. We can do all kinds of things with practices. Things happen when we color in a coloring book. I have a grandson, and we color together. It is a very soothing thing, putting things in between lines. I once heard about a woman in a psychiatric ward. She had very erratic brain waves. They had electrodes hooked to her brain, and the brain waves became very steady while she was adding numbers, but when the sums were added and the task was over, the brain waves were erratic again.

Do you feel that all religions lead to the same place?

We haven't defined what we mean by *religion*. If religion is the church and the organization, I think organization breeds division and conflict, not just among its own members, but with different organizations.

I don't want to be disrespectful, but where do religions lead to? Where have all religions led to? To perpetuating themselves, getting followers, adherents, believers? Do religions lead to finding the truth? I cannot answer that. Think of all the religions that have existed and perpetuated themselves throughout history and the wars that have been fought in the name of religions—religious wars.

Feelings identified with religion, no matter what the religion is, lead to conflict. No matter what one calls the religion, there is always the feeling that my religion is better than yours. I heard a spiritual teacher once say, "You wouldn't belong to this religion if you didn't think it was the best." What happens in our minds, in our relationship, when I have the best and you have the second-best? Either I try to convince you, or I think you don't have what I have. If I think you have a better religion, I may leave mine to join yours, or, at worst, we find each other and kill each other.

There are no paths in finding truth, just energy gathering to wonder, to look, and to be silent. If there is clarity of seeing what is true, what is so, that is not Christian truth or Buddhist truth or Muslim truth. Truth has no qualities about it, no names or labels or tradition. Truth has no tradition. Tradition is man-made and woman-made. It is the product of thought and the accumulation coming out of that thought and action. Does that sound upsetting?

Disturbing.

Disturbing is the right word. Don't we need to be shaken out of our molds? We just continue so happily ever after in what we believe, and we say that every religion leads to the same truth. These are all nice thoughts and philosophical attitudes, but what is actually happening? Let us look at what is actually happening and get out of our ideal setups! But maybe that's not exciting enough.

What makes you happy in life?

That question has "me" in it and "my" happiness and "my" life—all these different elements. As long as there is this sense of me and my life and "Am I happy or not?" there is no happiness. I prefer to use the word *joy*. *Happiness* has a certain ring to it that doesn't go very deep for my personal taste in words. But there is joy if there is walking through the woods and watching the snow trickling from the branches. The little creek down the road is all frozen over, but underneath it is sputtering and gurgling. This morning the sun rose with a clear sky. Just after the moon had set, there were crows cawing from one tree to another. The beauty of it all, the stillness of it, the freshness of the morning—there's a joy in that. Or being with another human being when there is no sense of division or competition or wanting something from each other. Is that joy? The word doesn't capture it.

What makes you sad?

When I see how little children, those so full of wonder and innocence, become conditioned, I get sad. I don't mean conditioned to behave politely—I'm referring to the whole process of child raising, the deadness of it, the deadening of the curiosity of children. Also, the lack of love among parents, lack of love among human beings. Maybe we could say there is evil, because there is no love; because when there is love, there is no evil.

I get sad when we do things so compulsively yet so ignorantly, so darkly, hurting each other and hurting children and hurting each other without realizing what we are doing, justifying it or defending it or just ignoring it.

Sometimes anger wells up. At what? If one isn't understood rightly, anger wells up and wants to set something right, but it doesn't last.

What do you feel is the most important thing you have learned from living?

Everything is important.

Some people think that personal relationships like marriage get in the way of a person's spiritual growth. What do you think about that?

Does it then follow that if there is no relationship and no marriage, there will be no impediment to spiritual growth? This is all such convoluted thinking. I once read about a monk, a man in his older age, who said there was a man who left his wife at a certain age to free the energies for his spiritual search, and in retrospect, the man said he spent more energy suppressing his sexual desire and thoughts than when he was with his wife.

It all depends. How are we related? We can be self-centered without being married; we can be self-centered regarding the idea of our enlightenment. We want something for ourselves, so we are not going to indulge in this or that because we want to be enlightened.

In married life or in living together, we make each other over in our image, but we also find out about ourselves in each other—spaciously, freely. Learn from each other and about each other through relationship, because relationship brings up hosts of conditioning that we may not see if we are in a cloister or hermitage. We may feel quite calm, but let somebody knock on the door and offend us, then where is the tranquility?

What was the most significant event that ever happened to you?

Coming upon the teachings of Krishnamurti ten years ago. I realized that while I thought a certain degree of freedom and insight had been attained, one really was attached—hung up on a system, a method, and spiritual advancement. One needs really to open the eyes to all that had been ignored, even though one felt well advanced in a tradition.

I could so easily put it into words and it would sound like Zen training, but it was different from Zen. Zen professes and says the same thing, but in practice, in fact, it isn't so. There are certain things that are not looked at, not examined and questioned. One doesn't question things; one continues with the whole format of it—the belief system, rituals, and ceremonies. The position of the teacher and the whole teacher/student relationship is not examined. It is sanctioned. Whatever the teacher does, bow and serve. I could go on and on. What came to mind when you asked this question was, "Don't believe, but find out. Look for yourself."

Do you think a person can be truly free and still fall into traps?

The moment there is no awareness, we are in a trap. We cannot assume we have attained freedom for the rest of our life. We cannot assume anything. We have to look and be aware. When there is no awareness and there is attachment to anything, then there is no freedom.

Can a person have a constant perception of truth?

That has to be found out by each person. The instant there is no awareness, something else clicks in, and that is the conditioned mind. There can be partial awareness of the conditioned mind, yet with a continuing of conditioning. If the awareness is full, then the conditioning leaves. If you ask, will this last forever?—find out. Why do we want this guarantee? It is theoretical or speculative.

Are there teachers who are totally free?

Look what is happening among teachers. Very often it is explained as the teaching methods of the teacher. If there is a questioning of it, students may be told that this is their ego being judgmental of the teacher. That is one thing demanded of students by their teachers: an almost unconditional turning of oneself over to the teacher. In Zen teaching I was told the teacher sits in the Buddha's place. When I started teaching, I was told, "You are sitting in the Buddha's place." Can you imagine what happens to the mind when one is being told that, and then the students start coming and prostrating to the teacher?

What made you approach life this way? Was there something that was happening that made you look for the truth?

The traumatic happenings during the years of my childhood in Germany: the persecution of Jews; the War; the disappearance of people I knew and those who did not come back from the front; the air raids; the incessant news of destruction and killing; fear for one's own life, either through being taken to a concentration camp or being burned in an air raid shelter. Just a deep questioning of what the sense of it all was. What was the sense of this senseless life? Did it make any sense? And yet, never giving up on it and always wondering about it gave me no peace. I asked the usual questions: What is the meaning of this? Why are we here? These questions were accompanied by very depressing feelings.

Do you feel there is something life still has to teach you?

Every moment, life is teaching. I don't consider learning to be stashing things away in the memory bank and accumulating and drawing on that. That kind of learning has its place in mathematics or making shelves. There can be learning every moment because every moment is new. The Buddha's last words were, "Be a lamp unto yourself." See for yourself; find out for yourself. Most people want advice so they don't have to look for themselves.

17

RABBI ZALMAN SCHACHTER-SHALOMI

My interview with Zalman Schachter-Shalomi did not start very well. After I arrived at his office, I reached into my bag and realized I had forgotten to bring a tape for the recorder. After getting over this initial embarrassment, I was able to buy a cassette from his assistant. I self-consciously put the tape into the recorder, but the nightmare continued: the tape recorder didn't work. So Zalman Schachter-Shalomi had to run upstairs to get his tape recorder. I could hear him rummaging around in his closets. Fifteen minutes later he returned, but by then I had discovered that the problem with my recorder was that the pause button was on.

Rabbi Zalman Schachter-Shalomi has kind eyes and a laugh like a ten-year-old's. Sometimes he's the wise old man; other times he acts like a rascal. I found him very easy to be around, and his wisdom left me feeling very solid. Sometimes after an interview, I leave feeling spaced out. But Zalman is earthy.

After the interview, I had an urge to eat cheesecake. I asked Zalman where I could find some good cheesecake, the real creamy kind. He gave me very specific directions, and the cheesecake I found was excellent. I decided to make a gift of half the cheesecake, so I returned to his office. But Zalman had already left to pick up his grandson, so I left the cheesecake with his secretary.

As I drove away, Zalman pulled up in his car. He didn't see me, but I saw him, and in a different light. No longer the spiritual teacher or rabbi, he was now just a grandfather. As I watched him with his arm around his grandson, the two talking and smiling intimately, I wished that Zalman had been my grandfather, too.

Like that of Pir Vilayat Khan, Rabbi Zalman Schachter-Shalomi's office was filled with computers. It was a busy-looking office. In my life, I've struggled with being too busy, because doing seems to be in antithesis to being.

While I was in Nepal and India, and even before that, I was taught by different spiritual teachers to be as aware as possible of what I was doing at all times—to get in touch with "being" and not just "doing." One of the spiritual practices for becoming more aware is to walk very slowly so that a person is aware of the movement and the mental elements that accompany the activity of walking. When I returned to the United States, some friends expressed frustration with how slowly I was moving. "C'mon, hurry up," I can still hear one friend screaming, "or I'll leave without you!"

I handled the situation by labeling her and other doers as "neurotically doing" and being out-of-touch with their being. Meanwhile, she labeled me as a bum who didn't have to hurry because I had nothing important to do anyway.

The first thing a foreigner notices in India is the harsh conditions under which people live. The second thing one notices is the acceptance of these conditions by the Indian people. This acceptance of their state or being allows them to enjoy a life Westerners wouldn't accept. The "being" aspect of Indian philosophy seems to have been emphasized in order to deal with the harsh way of Indian life, perhaps because if a person focuses on what needs changing in India, it is overwhelming. So acceptance of the present condition is a spiritual discipline, but it is also a strategic way to survive. Because of this, it is true that India is more in touch with their being. There is a spirituality in the air that one doesn't find in the West. This is the positive side of their philosophy.

The negative manifestation of this philosophy is the passive reluctance to do anything about the conditions. Consequently, there's so much to be fixed in India, from diseases that we in the West eradicated years ago to malnutrition, which millions of people suffer from. India and a misguided spirituality can play havoc with the ability to act in the world. But India taught me to slow down and to be. I got comfortable with being and with accepting the present condition.

When I returned to India years later in order to finish this book, I was different. I had interviews and time obligations. I had to do; there were things that had to be done. Once, when I expressed my frustration at the inefficiency of the Indian way of doing things to an Indian travel agent, she said, "Sir, in India, all things take time."

Back in the United States, I realized there were a lot of things I wanted to do in life, but this put me in a bind. In the West, we change anything outside of us that needs changing, the sooner, the better. We "do" things now; doing is our ideal. Consequently, we have many materialistically successful people and our society often looks great, but as Jean Houston said, "People today don't know who they are; they're severely wounded and haunted by despair." Or as Mother Teresa said, "People in the East starve for food; in the West, they are starving for love."

Whenever I was doing, I seemed to get tense and feel uncomfortable. I lost the comfort and bliss of being; and I was so focused while doing that I forgot to appreciate life and the people around me, to take time to smell the roses along the way.

So these two aspects were in conflict. To be or to do?—that was the question. When I saw Zalman's office crammed with computers and saw how he was running around with a thousand things to do yet seemingly in touch with his being, I seized the opportunity.

"You seem busy," I said.

"Thank *God* for that," Zalman replied, succinctly and simply.

Rabbi Zalman Schachter-Shalomi was born in Poland in 1924 and raised in Vienna. He fled the Nazi advance and settled in New York City in 1941. He taught religion at Temple University and currently is directing the work of spiritual eldering—the opportunity to expand our awareness to match our extended lifespan. His books include *Fragments of Future Scroll: Hasidism Here and Now, Paradigm Shift* (1994), *Spiritual Eldering* (1995).

On what beliefs do you base your life?

That there is a living God and that earth is alive. We are theotropic beings who grow toward God, and we have the help of revelation and tradition in our process of growing toward God.

There's the Infinite, and *there's* the God—where the Infinite exists. The Infinite is. Nothing else is. We are absorbed in that. We don't quite exist. Where we exist, our connection with the Infinite is made via a root metaphor, a name—*God*. So when we speak of the name *God*, the word *God*, the being God, that's not the Infinite. God is an interface that becomes transparent *to* the Infinite, who connects us finite beings, caught in time and in space, *with* the Infinite. I believe in the God, worship the God, adore the God, and call on God's help, but when I say *God* I don't quite mean the Infinite.

Meister Eckhardt would speak of the Infinite as the Godhead and of the other as God. So when someone says, "Do you have a personal God?" the personal God is that interface, that root metaphor. When I say, "God is a Father," then I'm a child. When I say "God is a Mother," I'm a child. When I say "God is a Judge," then I'm the one who's up for being judged. When I say "God is a King," then I'm a subject. Each one of these is a facet of the God. None of these are facets of the Godhead of the Infinite because the Infinite is not *this* and not *that*. There is a Part that connects us to the Infinite, of whom I can say, "Yes, God is the nurturing, nourishing, revealing, caring Being."

People generally want God to be the God of the good. They don't realize that the same Source that is the Source of what we call good is the Source of evil. The Source of what we call the beautiful is the same Source of the ugly. In fact, it is the Source of Allness. When we start picking and saying we like "this" better and "that" less, we are making the division between good and evil.

One of the problems about resisting any negativity is that, in resisting the negativity, we become negative ourselves. But when we come into contact with evil, there is a witnessing there. That is what Aikido and the other martial arts keep pointing out: If we get to that place, we can sidestep it and let its impetus cause it to fall. That's much better than trying to resist it with the same energy it comes at us with, because then we have to use the methods that that energy, the opposing or evil energy, uses. So, antiterrorism is terroristic! It doesn't work either.

That's the biggest issue of how to deal with crime. If the cop shoots indiscriminately, it's a bad situation. Because he has a badge doesn't mean that his shooting is good and the other shooting is evil. Gotta watch that! It's not so clear-cut as to who is good and who is evil in that situation. On the other hand, we know what is socially enhancing of life and integration, and we would say that

that's good. Whatever breaks life down and terrorizes it and makes it violent we would call evil. I don't have any problem with that. The problems begin when we start looking about for an ideology and saying, "This is a good one; that is an evil one." When we move that which belongs in the realm of attitudes into the realm of ideas, we are going to get problems.

What is the purpose of life?

That depends on which level of observation you are on. On the level of an atom, the answer would be to become a part of a molecule! If you ask a molecule, the molecule would say, "To become part of the cell." If you ask a cell, the cell would say, "To become part of an organ." If you ask an organ, the organ would say, "To become part of the organism." If you ask an organism, a human organism, the answer would be to become part of a larger social organism, ultimately the organism of this planet. That is how it is on this plane.

On other planes of existence, the purpose can be defined differently. For example, each time we become flesh, we become incarnated. In mystical Judaism, we believe in reincarnation. It's called *gilgul*. We believe each time we incarnate, we move a step forward. Coming down one time prepares me for the task I have to do the next time. Whatever I conclude in this lifetime, if I come back again, I can take up from where I left off—not with the same memory, mind you, but with the same traces and vibrations and merit and clarity and God-connection that I had. Then I can go farther in the next incarnation to provide more input. If I learned a lot this time around, I get to teach the next time around! If I did wrong this time, I may get a chance to fix some of the wrong I did.

There are other levels of spirit, higher levels, where the purpose of life is to become permeable while in the body to the highest spiritual stages available. Up to now, people have not achieved that, by and large. There are only a few holy geniuses who have achieved a kind of cosmic consciousness while being involved in everyday stuff.

What do you think is the highest ideal a person can reach?

There is no general statement one can make, because if I say "X or Y is the highest ideal," then we think everybody has to achieve that. But if you achieve what I have to achieve and I achieve what you have to achieve, then I haven't gotten my realization and you haven't gotten your realization. There are individual differences. The Universe is made up of so many individual bits. Each one has to achieve what it is meant to achieve. For someone who is a dancer, the ideal may be the ideal leap. For another person, it may be the ideal meditation. For another, the ideal act of love, kindness, or charity. If I were to say that the greatest philosophical understanding is the Ideal, then Mother Teresa hasn't reached it. If I say the greatest amount of unselfish caring is the Ideal, then Einstein hasn't reached it. I have to give them both credit for genius in their specialty. But a person doesn't have to specialize, because if a person has to be a generalist, he must "specialize" in being a generalist. You have to specialize in your own thing. One Hasidic Master said it very beautifully: "I'm not afraid that God will ask me, 'Zusha, why have you not become an Abraham, Isaac, or Jacob?' But I am afraid that God will ask me, 'Zusha, why have you not become what Zusha was intended to be?'"

The method, up to now, has been called Spiritual Direction Literature. There is Eastern Spiritual Direction Literature; there is Western Spiritual Direction Literature. The trouble is, the literature alone can't show one how to achieve attunement. For instance, if I have a symphony and I show it to you through the literature, you will still not be able to tune your violin by it. I have to present a tuned sound by which you can tune your violin. That's why we're always looking for a school where spirituality is being done. We're looking for a Master, someone who has mastered the art and gained that knowledge. And we begin to attune. After a while, we learn how to pray. When we learn how to pray, we learn not just how to recite words, but how to open the heart. It's like biofeedback: When we are with a person who is opening the heart, we can feel attuned to it. "Ah, now it feels right in my heart!" But if somebody says, "Open your heart," and you've never had that "thing," how do you know you've done it correctly? If you're in a larger group where all the people are doing this and there is a liturgy being celebrated, you get to feel at one with the people who are in this elated place. That's how you attune to it.

The spiritual direction people have gotten is on that level. Some people do overtly religious things; other people do martial arts or make pottery. It doesn't make any difference how one attunes because total realization can happen anywhere. It can happen spontaneously, and it can happen under direction. Very often, even that which is under direction requires the moment of grace, of spontaneity. But there are people who can achieve attunement in synagogue and church but not in the marketplace, for instance.

Most disciplines have something to do with the body, the way in which one interacts with the body, so that the body is under a kind of control. I don't mean a rigid control, but I mean that the body is open to interact. Then the next level is the feeling place. There are four levels: the yoga of body, the yoga of feeling, the yoga of mind, and the yoga of being and intuition. Our prayer book operates on those four levels. Every day there are things to take from level to level to level, and then back down again. The spiritual practices have those four levels involved. Some people concentrate more on one level than another, but somehow all four contribute something. Some people are personally gifted on one level but not on other levels. Some people like to do the stuff they're gifted in and ignore the other levels. That catches up with them; it's no good. The issue is wholeness, roundness—holistic spirituality.

How does one attain this ideal?

First of all, if one needs to be more grounded, just simply be "you." Feel the earth beneath you; feel the chair; feel how gravity upholds you. Gravity is the way earth loves us and attracts us. We should allow ourselves to be supported by that. Second, do one thing at a time; be totally in that thing you're doing. That's a way to be grounded! The next way to be grounded is to realize that there is stuff above that the groundedness has to support. The point isn't just to be flat on the ground. The point is to be firm enough on the ground so that the rest of you can go up.

What is the greatest obstacle to obtaining new levels?

"The sin that is the hardest to atone for is habit." That is the biggest obstacle to reaching new levels, as one rabbi put it. The more we're in a habitual state, the more unlikely it is that we'll go beyond. We won't be in the moment; we won't be in the here and now. We will hear the routine rather than the challenge that comes at this moment.

Will all people eventually reach this ideal?

I believe that all people will reach what they have to reach. I'm a universalist, in that sense. That they will reach the same state is not likely. It is enough for a toe to be the toe of a realized person. If I could be the toe, as it were, of realized humanity, that's fine. Not everybody is going to be the brain cell that fires off a great realization. Still, we'll all be organically connected with that, and the organic connection is what fires, just as an organism has a connection with the toe. So the final enlightenment will have a connection with that concept. It's not likely that there is going to be a final enlightenment. I don't like the word *final,* either, because enlightenment continues to the next level and the next level, and it's infinite in God. We no longer have the temple in Jerusalem, but when it existed, the holiest person on the holiest day at the holiest time in the holiest place would pronounce the holiest word. There would be a kind of implosion of all the Onenesses. That name *is* a connection, and each year on Yom Kippur, the old connection goes away and the new connection starts coming in. Sins interfere, spoil and ruin the old connection.

Will all people be given another chance until they make it?

Sooner or later, but the way in which you're raising the question implies that everyone on the human level is going to do it. You forget that when we are on the human level, we're already talking about molecular, cellular, organic, organismic, and social levels. It may just be that my connection with you and your connection with other people and finally with a book is all we need to do to participate in the process of that enlightenment. And having done that, it's enough. That's our contribution to "it." It's very hard to say that everybody's going to graduate. We graduate if we have done the task that was ours to do. Then, when all of us graduate, that is like saying, When the whole of me graduates, my toe will graduate, also.

There are some things we won't know until we get there. There is the Divine potential of the Infinite. The more it gets realized, actualized in all the realms—not only the material realms, but the spiritual, astral, intuitive, and divine realms—the more the Universe becomes the Divine. The Universe, which begins as a potential for being divine, becomes in actuality the Divine. That Infinite is like an hourglass. One can't really speak about this in finite terms, but in finite terms it's as if all the stuff from one side has poured itself into the other side, and then it turns around again. We are now in a phase of making the whole globe, the whole planet, conscious. This is what some people have called the Divinization of the planet.

Choice is available even on earlier levels than the human. That's what, to some extent, the Heisenberg Principle of Uncertainty is about. We can predict the statistics, but we can't predict the specificity of it—which electron is going to jump off and when—and that is like an element of choice. On the other hand, I reject the whole notion of either-or-ness in terms of choice and determinism, because I think that's sort of a mental trap. We are not 100 percent free, and we are not 100 percent determined. It goes between 99 percent on one side to 99 percent on the other side, and the pendulum swings. There are times when there are such moments of high confluence between choice and determinism that we call it synchronicity. What I'm doing and intending is so together with that flow of things, it doesn't feel as if we're fighting at all.

Now one of the purposes, if I speak from our Judaic mystical tradition, goes like this: Prior to this cycle of world creation, there were other cycles of world creation. Holy sparks from those other cycles of world creation, when they were broken, lodged here. Our task is to find those sparks, gather them and bring them together, and restore the balance in the cosmos—to enthrone God again. The Divine Crown, as it were, has gems missing, and in each physical act, we pick up a spark here, a spark there, and bring them together. When all sparks have been gathered, our tradition speaks about the coming of the Messiah. To me, this means something like global oneness—peace and harmony on the globe when we reach the next level of integration.

When we become more conscious of the physical and at the same time aware of the highest spirituality, we'll have what I would call the Resurrection of the Dead. This resurrection happens together on a physical and spiritual level. The physical plane is our plane of observation, though everything that happens on a physical plane is not open to our observing. What's happening between atoms we don't quite see with our eyes, but if we were on the atomic level we would say, "Ah, this oxygen atom got married to two hydrogen atoms, and they made a water molecule!" But we don't operate on that level of awareness. When I put a pot of water on the stove to cook, a lot of weddings take place between the oxygen from the air and the hydrogen that's in the gas, so water gets created. That's a level of observation, the submolecular level, that we don't see.

Now in our personal drama, on another level of observation, higher things are happening. Ultimately it takes a meditative leap into other dimensions to be able to see. There is a Latin word that's translated "under the aspect of eternity." It means to look down, to see what is happening in the temporal realm. Then we begin to see what Earth is about, what the planet is about, and what history is about from a much higher level. I believe we are just learning the beginnings of the holy psychotechnology, a spiritual psychotechnology that will allow us to get to such places as observing fine moments—or larger ones. Some people have had the larger experiences. Geniuses have had profound mountaintop experiences before. I would say, "If they can see the Infinite, they can see the infinitesimal also, because awareness is up and down the scale." By and large, people haven't bothered to look at the infinitesimal. Now, with nanotechnologies becoming important, people are beginning to concentrate on those things.

What about death and what happens after death?

I do believe that death is only part of the connection between the physical and the inner. It's like pulling the plug. Most people know enough to get their inner out of the way. Let's say you drive in your car and it's rattling; it's in bad shape. Finally, it's all over. You drive it to the junkyard. You get out of the car, and then a crusher comes and crushes it down. You'd be a fool to sit in it after the car is dead. I have the same attitude toward the body. Bodies wear out, and it's a wonderful thing that they wear out. They get recycled, which gives the passenger a chance to get out and pick another car, another vehicle . . . or to decide not to walk the earth for awhile.

Our tradition teaches that a whole series of things happens after death. A soul has to go through purification because of the contamination of being on this level and the habits that are acquired on this level. After purification (which is what *Purgatory* means: one gets purged), then come other things that are delightful, ecstatic, and marvelous. Some of them have to do with the realm of feeling. That is one Heaven. Others have to do with the realm of knowing. That's another Heaven. Then there is the Heaven in which we know intuitively and are known by God; we are identical with That. There's a higher level still. Sometimes one just stays there, because it's wonderful. Sometimes one is needed back down here and gets called.

In Judaism after people die we say the Kaddish, the memorial prayer, and we do acts of charity for the souls of the deceased. This allows us to help people advance their process now and to help in their purification if they haven't been able to do it in their lifetime.

If you see yourself bounded by your skin, then you would ask, "How would something I do help the deceased?" When you recognize that half of your chromosomes are your father's, half are your mother's, and a quarter of them are your grandfather's, you realize that your grandfather is still alive in you, in a quarter of your chromosomes. So if you say a prayer, it is almost as if a portion of him is still available to help that other part of him that is beyond. That's why the disciples of a Master get together at the anniversary of his death to celebrate. There is a feeling that there is so much more of the Master available at that moment.

Why is there suffering in the world?

That's a question that gets us into trouble! Every time I've figured it out, I have to learn another level of the same thing. One could say the greatest education we get is through suffering. Consciousness is being raised through deprivation. I will never know what it means to give people food when they're hungry unless I have experienced hunger myself. I will not know how to help somebody who is in pain unless I have experienced pain myself. One could say suffering is the school for empathy. It creates that, but that's only one element of suffering.

Sometimes suffering exists in order to bring us to our senses. Sometimes suffering exists in order to show us that there are tragedies we can't overcome with our childish omnipotence in the world. We begin to see that every choice we make has its consequences. Suffering is the way in which we learn, after the fact, the consequences of our moves. Then there are some people who suffer and can't identify this reason or that reason. It's just one of those things. "Why do bad things happen to good people?" is the question behind all that, and I haven't yet found a convincing answer. Sometimes no matter what we do, we get clobbered! On a lower level of preparation and understanding we would say, "If we do only the good and the true all the time, we're going to be okay." On a higher level being good doesn't help. The biggest ethical questions are based on just that point.

Do you feel that all religions or spiritual paths do lead to the same place at the same...

All is a big word. If I want to honor all religions, I would say yes. There is such a thing as what Matthew Fox called "the deep Ecumenism" or what I call the generic religion, which is a no-frills religion. Behind the brand names, there's a no-frills religion. Sometimes in the supermarket we buy generic products rather than brand names. It's cheaper that way. The active ingredients, whatever works, are there. The frills of packaging, of extra flavor, of this or that are left out. Each religion has frills. Each has an ethnic component. The Roman Catholicism of Haiti wouldn't do very well in Ireland. It's hard to separate religions from one another. Each religion is a living, organic thing. If it helps its people and has the basic ingredients—that is, if the no-frills religion stuff is there—then I would say it works.

There are some religions or some cults that take people off the path and lead them to some negative things. Maybe the people in Jonestown when they took the Kool Aid had last-minute enlightenment and sanctification. Maybe they did, but I doubt it. I wouldn't equate a religion like the one in Jonestown with, say, Hasidic Judaism or Trappist Catholicism or Tibetan Buddhism. It's not in the same league. So I just don't want to say all are the same.

If you could meet anyone throughout history, whom would you want to meet and what would you ask that person?

I would like to meet myself at the moment after enlightenment. Then I would like to ask, "How did you do it?" All the other people would just satisfy a kind of curiosity, but it wouldn't help me in my stuff, so I wouldn't want to go into the past so much as into the future. But you want me to name somebody in the past I would want to connect with. There are many Hasidic Masters, but I would like to go the founder of the Hasidic movement, Ba'al Shem Tov, and just be with him and not ask him any questions. I would want to look at him, to have him look at me, and then to pray in such a way that I could learn something from him. I would want to attune to his spirituality. That's all. It's not words I would want.

What is the most significant thing that ever happened to you, and what did it teach you?

It doesn't work that way, because there are moments when one thing is significant and moments when something else is significant. For a man to be present at the birth of a child is an overwhelming thing. I've been present at the birth of my children, and it's really amazing. I think that's the greatest, deepest miracle, because all other things have their space . . . Yet when I look back, every once in a while I make a kind of rosary of high moments and start saying, "There were moments of love; there were moments of insight; there were moments of prayer." There were even moments of terror, almost like facing death, that made me say, "Aha! Now I understand what it's all about." But I'm still learning about spiritual and holy eldering. Most people don't know how to live the holy life after retirement. You see, popes have remained in the saddle and rabbis have remained in the saddle until they die. I would like to learn how to withdraw gradually from the active life and to spend the last years furthering my solitude with God. That's what I feel life has to teach me. I'm learning to let go of things that are not in my hands to change, learning to live with what, otherwise, would be increasing frustration when I get older.

Life is my teacher. Artificial intelligence is trying to do what natural intelligence is doing. Natural intelligence means that a naturally intelligent organism continues to learn throughout life. Each situation provides a deeper learning, greater learning, a more profound learning. We're all going through a learning, so if I had to pick out one learning as the most significant, I'd say, "I can't; it's constant. The learning that is happening in life is constant because life is a teaching machine." From whom did I learn about life? I learned from life about life, by living life.

What is your core practice?

All the Judaic forms are connected with how my life goes. Judaism's form is important to me. This is why, for instance, I wear the fringes underneath my shirt: so It touches every aspect of my life. The kind of food I eat, when I work, when I don't work—it governs the year, governs the life cycle. That's my practice in general. Three times a day there are prayer times. That's important. The practice that nourishes me most these days is quiet prayer of the heart. Just sitting very quietly and opening the heart and letting God in. Some people call it Centering Prayer. In Hasidism it's called *Dvekut* or *Shivithi*.

What makes you happy? sad? angry?

I'm happy when I have contentment and moments of no conflict. I'm happy when I feel love coming and going from my heart to those who are around me, when I feel integrated with the Universe and at peace with God. The opposite makes me sad. To see people suffering and not to be able to help makes me sad. The child has an earache, and there's nothing at this point that can be done. I can hold a child, but it's not going to make the earache go away. To be powerless over pain that others experience is sad. What makes me angry is willful, malicious obstruction of the common good.

Some people say that getting married and having relationships get in the way of spiritual progress, especially some religions where monkhood is the ideal. What do you think about that?

I've seen and heard of people, in history and also during my lifetime, who have become recognizable as saints. When I start looking, I see that the development of their saintly characteristics was at the expense of other parts of their beings. In the past, one might view somebody who lived on a pillar, like Simon, and say, "Oh, he's such a saint!" whereas today we'd say, "He's off!"

Who is a saint? Today's saint is the holistic person who manages to carry on and stay centered and loving and caring, who is clear as can be. I don't see any single quality that makes a person saintly. There is more than one way to be a saint.

Look, for instance, at what happens with a child or parent. Situations between them stir up many things. Often there are people whom you'd call saintly and holy, but if their mother starts messing with them and calling them to clean up their room, all of a sudden they're little kids again. They lose "it." Or the dad wants to meditate but the kids bug him at that time, and he doesn't know how to create a situation that can embrace both the child and meditation. People who have done it without being in the world have done wonderful things, but a few of them might be spiritual idiot savants. In one area they're wonderfully developed, but in other areas . . . So I trust saints who are householders more than I trust celibates.

There is another element. If saints would marry one another, they could have good kids. What has happened in some religions is that the most wonderful genetic stock did not get reproduced. St. John of the Cross didn't marry Teresa of Avila, and so they didn't have any kids; or St. Francis and St. Claire didn't have any kids. That means that it was the genetic end of the line for the stock of saints. I'm much more for the householder's way.

What is most important to you?

Can't say. It varies and changes. If I can't take a breath of air, then the most important thing is to take another breath of air. Imagine: I'm diving underwater and can't get to the surface. How important a breath of air is then! When I have the breath of air, then what's important is how I reach the shore. I don't believe these things are static. There is a dynamic element that's always before us. Right now what I want is to finish the week and to clean up as much of that as I can. Then, to come to a Sabbath rest is the most important thing. It will keep changing all the time.

I do what I do out of concern. My sense is that the more life, the better education, and the more tools that are made available for people to manage their physical and spiritual life, the better off the planet is going to be. And that's what I'm most concerned about.

What are the greatest problems in life?

The main problems in life are making a living, making a loving, and making a dying. Making a living is a big problem for many, many people. When that's together, then there's the question of making a loving—how to have good relationships and to receive and to give love. People who don't have that can have all the money in the world, but it's no good! For people who've had a good life and a good loving and a good living, when the time comes to leave that life, the problem is how to do that gently and gratefully.

Do you think there's a basic difference between men and women besides their physiology?

That's not a "besides," because the physiology alone determines so much. Look at what it means for a woman to go through menopause, for instance. I can understand what's going on with people who are on drugs. Then I think, how much more is going on with people on drugs that the body produces at a given time? A teenager getting hot on sex presents the same situation. Something is happening in the body that is very strong stuff and often not understood. Things happening to males and females are of such a nature that we haven't begun to learn the vocabulary of what they're all about. I believe men and women have a different way of looking at the universe, maybe based on physiology. Men by and large look at the universe in discrete detail, like particles in particle physics, everything boom, boom, boom, boom, boom, boom. I believe women see the universe as a lot more connected, like waves. Whether or not this difference is due to physiology is, at this point, a moot issue. Maybe the viewpoint happened in their soul, and they chose a female or a male body.

18

PIR VILAYAT KHAN

Pir Vilayat lives at the Abode in New Lebanon, New York. The Abode sits on top of a hill, perhaps a mile from the center of town. I stayed in town that night at a rooming house where the owner talked about the nice people with "weird names" who lived on the hill. She recalled fondly how Pir Vilayat had walked into town one day, wearing flowing robes, while his students followed closely behind in single file on their way to the ice cream shop.

The following day, I walked up to the Abode. I was chauffeured the rest of the way along a winding road to Pir Vilayat's hut. Before I entered his hut, I did what I did before every interview. I went inside myself and got in touch with my motivations for writing the book. Only then did I venture in to meet Pir Vilayat. I sat down across a table from him and promptly assured him that my motives for writing this book and interviewing him were sincere.

"Yes," he said, "I could see that as soon as you walked in the door."

Pir Vilayat's hut is more of a high-tech tepee than a hut. He likes to wear robes, which contrast noticeably with his computers in his high-tech tepee.

This interview, more than any other, tested my ability to move between two worlds: the world of conceptual thought and the world beyond concepts. I was forced to stretch myself between these worlds until they became one.

I had a devil of a time forcing Pir Vilayat to speak in ways that could be commonly understood. I minimally edited the beginning of our dialogue because it's amusing to follow my pursuit of Pir Vilayat's philosophy. In hindsight, it probably says more about me than it does about Pir Vilayat. With a mind like that of a sensitive scientist, Pir Vilayat took me on a tour of his internal world with great gentleness. It was a world developed from over fifty years' contemplation, and I naively attempted to follow his experience of this world in one hour. It was difficult. At times, my mind was overwhelmed by all the information I was given. It was fortunate that I had written most of my questions down beforehand, because during our visit, I was often left without the ability to form questions, or the need to ask them.

After our meeting, I read and listened to the interview many times in an effort to understand everything that was said. His language when describing mystical realms is often scientifically based, which is Pir Vilayat's way of presenting timeless mysticism in modern language.

After our talk, Pir Vilayat gave a talk at the Abode's lecture hall, while I sat outside underneath a tree. When the lecture ended, a queer thing happened. Pir Vilayat exited the hall and walked in my direction until he passed right by me. For a second, he glanced at me, and I had the odd feeling that he was wondering where he had seen me before.

Pir Vilayat Khan was chosen by his father, Hazrat Inayat Khan, to succeed him as head of the Sufi Order in the West. In turn, Pir Vilayat has given the role of successor to his son. This lineage of wisdom is handed down from one person to another in order to preserve its authenticity.

There is another lineage of sorts, and in a sense we all belong to it. We are connected to this lineage, whether we like it or not. I discovered it in the back room of a bookstore one summer afternoon. I had nothing to do that day, so I walked over to a used bookstore. Once inside, I went over to the religious, spiritual, and psychological section. There were stacks and stacks of books that had just arrived. Hundreds and hundreds of books, all on the subjects that I loved. I was a kid in a candy store.

As I piled up the books I wanted to buy, I noticed that the same name was written in black marker along the binding of each book. RON COHEN the writing said in BIG letters. I paused for a second and looked at the wall of books. It was a mountain! And all of them had the same name on them: Ron Cohen.

When I brought the books over to the counter, I asked the guy who Ron Cohen was. "Oh, him," he said, "he's dead. He was a religious studies teacher at Illinois State. He taught for forty years, and his family brought them in after he died."

The rest of the day I thought about that. Here was a man who read all those books. Having lived a long life, he brought all that knowledge into an understanding, and he must have conveyed that unique understanding in his teachings. Having come together in him, this understanding has now dispersed, like a river returning to its source, without a trace or track. All that was left was a pile of books—that I now own. And one day, someone else will own them.

Pir Vilayat Khan is a meditation teacher and head of the Sufi Order in the West, which was founded by his father, Hazrat Inayat Khan. He has led retreats and workshops for over thirty years. His books include *Introducing Spirituality into Counseling and Therapy, The Call of the Dervish,* and *The Message in Our Time.*

On what beliefs do you base your life?

A belief is a construct, and with many people, it is based upon the authority of some person or a book, whereas I go by *faith* rather than by *belief*. Faith is a kind of realization that one has, an insight one has that might challenge one's mind and way of thinking and therefore could easily be confused with belief, but for me, it is a very different thing from belief. One has to—as my father says— destroy, to shatter one's ideal on the rock of truth. One also needs to be able to shatter one's belief in the strength of one's faith.

The ultimate belief is a belief in God. I see in that belief a lot of people's psychological projections. My father once said very clearly, and very rightly of course, that we confuse our image of God with God. They're substituted.

Much of what I'm doing is done in admiration of what my father said. It's based on many of the things that he said, but I am sure he would say many more things today than he did before. I would love to meet my father again. He had a wonderful combination of tremendously high attunement and, at the same time, the wisdom and clarity that enabled him to express himself in words.

I continue to rethink, refurbish, replace, and reprogram my beliefs. I'm using an updated language that is the language of our time. I understand that most spiritual teachers are still using the old language, so I'm using words like *meaningfulness*. There's meaningfulness and intelligence behind the Universe, and the Universe is the way in which that meaningfulness becomes being. I think of God as the Universe just like something that is totally at an abstract level. Like the level of realization, it becomes material; it becomes tangible. So for me, the physical Universe is the Body of God. When I say the Universe, I don't mean only the physical Universe, but all levels of reality—angelic spheres and so on. It's all the Body of God.

The beliefs you have are beyond conception and then you bring them into conception?

Yes. Let's say the conception is the underpinning, the infrastructure, which is giving it some cohesion so that it can be communicated to people. The reality, however, is far beyond the conceptual level.

When people come out of the place that is beyond conception and into conception, what are the beliefs you would recommend in order to help them get back to the place that is beyond conception?

First, we have to distinguish between information processing and the concepts we have created, which are the constructs we make based on our experience of information. They are actually the interpretation of our experience by our middle-range mind. If we act creatively, then our thinking is not limited to concepts, so what we are affirming is our grasp of meaningfulness. I think that is the meaning of realization: it is meaningfulness that cannot be limited by the concepts we make from the world of experience.

A second belief is that the purpose of our lives is indeed to make God a reality, and that means to make our highest ideals tangible in our behavior and also in our personality. Therefore, I use the word *splendor,* which becomes *excellence.* It doesn't only manifest; it becomes excellence. Our highest ideals become a reality in excellence. For example, a carpenter or even a businessman makes something beautifully. Whatever we do, if it is done with excellence, that is the way we give reality to the world of splendor.

A third belief is that if indeed everything is—I'm trying to avoid the word *created* because Buddhists wouldn't like that—if everything is the actuation of incredible Intelligence, then death (as most people imagine it being the end of a life) is totally incongruous with the tremendous Intelligence behind all things. Therefore, death is again a concept, our way of interpreting something that we understand even less than life. In this belief about death, I would follow the precepts of Buddha: "Never say something you don't know." What do we know about death? Of course, there are similes, parallels that we draw. For example, we hear of statements of people who have gone through a clinical death, and if one has done astral travel, one realizes that one can continue to experience without a body. But that's no proof of life after death because there's still the "silver cord," or whatever it is. For me, the continuity behind change is the thread behind it all.

I think in terms of negentropy instead of entropy, which means that information is built upon matter. I'm thinking twice before using the word *matter,* but let's say that software is built on hardware, although it was the opposite in the beginning. A symphony of Beethoven would have a reality even if it weren't played anymore, even if all the scores were burnt. What has been acquired has a reality at a higher level, which one might call the world of metaphor. For me, that constitutes something that would give us a clue as to what death means.

When I say that I believe, what I mean is I have faith. It's beyond my understanding; it's in a continuity beyond change or subliminal to change. I see in Buddhism a kind of despair because of the changeability of those things that are passing without our really grasping the continuity behind change, which is the important factor.

When Buddhists say "Life is suffering," it's almost as if a belief becomes a dogma. Suffering, for me, is frustration, because somehow we have need to be creative. In fact, the purpose of our life is being creative. The building blocks with which we create are us. To be creative, we need to create the world as us. In fact, that's the whole purpose of life. The Universe becomes created in each individual, so it's a holistic view of the Universe. Therefore, we base our construction of ourselves upon the building blocks that we get from the Universe. When those building blocks are taken away, we suffer frustration because we don't know how to transmute the elements with which we build our being from external building blocks to an internal pattern. Once we understand that, then we don't mourn a loss because, while the object has disappeared, its meaningfulness can never be taken away from us. It's part of ourselves. For example, in the case of a person to whom one was attached but who has left, what that person meant is part of one's being. That's what it was all about.

Some people think personal relationships interfere with spiritual growth...

Of course there's constraint in a relationship. There's an involvement, which is always at the cost of one's freedom. On the other hand, we have to distinguish between circumstantial constraint and constraint in one's way of thinking and in one's emotion. One needs to understand how to accept an external form of constraint while maintaining freedom in the higher areas of one's being and one's way of thinking and feeling.

Sometimes the challenge of dealing with social constraint applies also to a personal relationship and can be used to foster one's growth. A lot of people think, "As long as I have to live with this person, I'll never be able to develop certain qualities in myself." Sometimes it's the other way around. It is because one is being challenged in this particular situation that the qualities one might develop would be really adamant, would be really strong. Otherwise, one might develop them in isolation and find that one can't maintain them when facing the impact of the outside worlds.

It's just like the Indian raga. There are constraints. You can use certain notes and other notes, and the consequence is that the kinds of melodies that come out of that constraint are much more clearly defined than if you have a chromatic scale where you can use any note anytime, and then the style of the music becomes amorphous. It's just like language. If every word meant everything, then there would be no language. So there has to be what is called redundance, which is limitation, in order to develop creativity.

What about the Christian idea of hell?

Different people have different motivations. In some cases hell embodies a sense of hatred for a person, a kind of unavowed wish that the person will suffer the flames of hell. Of course, metaphysically I believe that ignorance is not understanding why things happen the way they do. When I say that, I don't mean understanding

197

with one's conceptual mind. Ignorance is the hell for anybody who has a desperate need to understand.

My sister landed in Nazi-occupied France as a radio operator and was tortured at Dachau. Robbing one's freedom, even just the freedom of speech, is a hell. I think of hell as constraint, as opposed to our ultimate wish, which is for freedom.

What are your beliefs about how the Universe came to be?

Everything is continually coming into being, so we mustn't think of the Universe as having happened in the past. And it is coming into being in each one of us. What is more, we are making it come into being because our thinking is isomorphic with the thinking of the Universe. We think the way the Universe thinks, except that the thinking of the Universe gets funneled in our thinking and gets distorted in our thinking. Not only that, but the emotion of the Universe gets funneled in our emotion and distorted in our emotion sometimes.

The whole process is one in which the software becomes hardware. It becomes actuated in the hardware; it remains and gets more and more complex, more and more rich. The Mind of God gets enriched by the physical aspect of the Universe in each of us. I'm also saying that we have a personal contribution toward the thinking of the Universe; that means the thinking of God, which is a modern way of thinking, I think. It means not thinking of ourselves as the instruments through which God thinks; we are the Divine thinking. Something is gained by this multiplication of centers, each one having some influence on the others. That's how evolution takes place. When there's a mutation that takes place in one animal in a species or one plant, if it is successful, it tends to have the effect of spurring others into the same mutation.

Understanding is not enough to bring about change. One also needs energy. This is what they call, in science, homeostasis, which is a tendency to maintain the constancy of a system, but then it becomes sclerose; it never progresses. That is, of course, what one feels in Fundamentalism. People are threatened by other beliefs; they don't want to venture beyond their beliefs because there's some safety in them.

One must be progressive and be prepared to question one's beliefs and let the system get, as a physicist in Belgium says, away from equilibrium because of its dissipative structure. That is true of our personality. Sometimes there's a breakdown in our personality; that is a sign that things are beginning to move. Otherwise, we become sclerotic in the way we are. If the breakdown is carried a little bit further from equilibrium, then we can't come back to where we were, and so we have to bring about a change, though people will resist change. One finds resistance everywhere. That's homeostasis. On the other hand, the creative people are those who promote change, which is called heterostasis. I'm very much for that, of course. I'm always promoting change.

The purpose of life is to make God a reality. That means for people to construct the Universe as themselves, or partake in that act whereby the Macrocosm becomes constructed in each fragment of Itself, where the particular idiosyncrasies of that Microcosm, which is derived from the Macrocosm, have an influence on the whole Macrocosm. To do things beautifully, to handle ugly problems beautifully, with a deep regard for the sacredness of the human status—that is the Divinity in each of us. That means, for example, loving people whom one dislikes, which is unconditional love. That's how one is able to overcome the limitations of one's judgmentalism. It means having the courage to stand by one's ideal, particularly of truth, when one is being threatened or frightened or cast upon by people; building a beautiful world, of beautiful people, even when circumstances around one are ugly. I don't say that one will have immediate success, but doing things beautifully has the ultimate value, and so eventually it will carry success with it.

Making God a reality is the counterpart of one's realization, which means that awakening is overcoming the limitation of one's personal vantage point. It's extraordinary to what extent people get stuck in their vantage point. There's a reason for it, because consciousness functioning in a human being is focalized into what one calls the personal consciousness. It is really the Consciousness of the Universe, but it is functioning as though it were focalized, and consequently one is judging things from that vantage point. Awakening is being able to change one's perspective from the personal vantage point and being able to see what is being enacted beyond the appearance of things.

This objective needs to be counterweighed by making God Reality, so that it's not just all in one's realization, but in one's action, particularly in service. I think that just being an end to oneself is not good enough; in fact, it's counterproductive. I would say enlightenment plus service; I would say those two together, not just enlightenment at the cost of service. That is the reason the Sufis say, "Renounce the world and then renounce yourself and then renounce renunciation out of love." There is a kind of selfishness in seeking illumination or awakening for oneself. That is, of course, the idea of the Bodhisattva, who will relinquish awakening until everybody else is awakened, but what I see is something beyond even that, which is not for the sake of awakening, but because of love.

Having the freedom to give up your freedom once you've attained it?

Yes. That's it. You've got it.

If you were a psychotherapist and were consulting people, you'd see how people have gotten stuck in their ways of thinking about who they are. The only way to help another person is to be awake, that is, to see where they are stuck.

Liberation and awakening are connected. They aren't the same thing, though they're very close, because liberation is liberation from the personal vantage point and also from the personal emotions. The liberation from this vantage point is still negative, not yet positive. It's like "Neti, neti": This is not this, it's not that, but it's not yet, "Well, how are things?" That is very positive. That's where, after going through the dark night of the soul when one has given up one's judgment, there is that sudden breakthrough where one not only sees all things very clearly, but one is just full of love. One comes back to the world and one gets beaten up by people and one still loves them because one has just made that hurdle.

Would it be difficult to identify with people who aren't awakened?

No! That's when one really does identify. In fact, incidentally, in order to develop intuition, one needs to revert to a different mode than the subject of its relationship. Intuition is based on affinity rather than otherness. It's the I-Thou relationship that Martin Buber speaks about, so that one can read into another being only because one discovers in oneself the same thing that is to be found in that being by resonance, you see, based upon affinity.

There's no end to the Universe, so there isn't a point at which there is a Day of Judgment when everything is fulfilled. In our finite minds, we think of an idyllic state in which this would happen, but, of course, time is endless; it's all in infinite regress. One can never say that one has attained liberation. It's again our finite minds that think in terms of an end, of a point that has been reached, that has now been acquired. People do have moments of illumination, and that means that they, as beings, are illuminated.

If you could meet anyone in history, whom would you meet and what would you ask that person?

I would have loved to speak to Johann Sebastian Bach, but then, he already forestalled my question when he said that the purpose of his music was to build a pattern for a social commonwealth, and music was the means whereby he was building that model. He said the theme for each instrument should not despotically dominate the themes of the others, but each theme should participate in the richness of the whole and each limit its prerogatives in the interest of the whole. He ended by saying, "Such is the symphony of the spheres." What he was saying is that his music is expressive of his way of understanding. It expresses how the creativity of the Universe is fostered by the respect for freedom, so that there can be innovation, and how each one contributes toward that elaboration. But there was to be some kind of discipline; otherwise, it's a free-for-all, and each one's activity is at the expense of the activity of the others. There was a very deep philosophical motivation behind what Bach was doing. I consider him to be a very great spiritual Master.

I would have had less success talking with Beethoven, who was rather irascible, but the slow movement of the fourth Piano Concerto tells me he really knew what he was doing. He has given us a lesson in how to place a buffer between the challenge of the world and ourselves so that we can consult with our deeper selves and use some of the resourcefulness in our beings. If we jump into action without doing that, then of course we get into trouble and we're less creative.

When I was younger, I was on the guru hunt in the Himalayas. The curious thing is that I would ask questions of a number of saddhus, but those who were able to give me the most were Hunis, people who were not speaking. Meeting with them was more enriching than meeting with those who spoke. What they were communicating was attunement, therefore beyond all concepts. In turn, it is hard for me to give up my concepts of being a Rishi (a meditative hermit) in the Himalayas.

Why do you think there is suffering?

I don't want to entertain theories about causality. If you ask why, you're assuming that there is some cause, and that evidences the limited manner of middle-range thinking, of trying to reduce events to things in that place in time, one causing another. That's the old-fashioned theory in physics. There are new ways. In Newtonian physics, for example, quantum has knocked causality off its feet. We have to account for purposefulness rather than causality.

If we're asking the question why, what we're asking is whether there is a purpose in it, not only a cause, but there's even more than just cause and purpose. There's a visible cause, and there's a transcendental cause that is not the cause in time but the cause that goes from transcendence down to transience. Science, of course, has concentration of causes, like synchronicity, but the finite mind can never account for why things happen.

We're frustrated by the fact that the elements with which we construct the Universe as ourselves get taken away from us. We have to be able to realize that the construct is not a construct of stone but is a pattern in which the sublime manifests as beauty.

19

ALBERT ELLIS

On the plane to New York, where I was to interview Albert Ellis, I sat next to a man who lived there. I showed him the addresses of the places I had to go and asked him for directions.

"You're going there?" he said. "That's a bad place."

"A bad place?"

"What time are you going?"

"About two in the afternoon."

"It's still light then. You should be okay. But don't leave anything in the car."

"I'll park in a ramp," I assured him.

"Well, put everything in the trunk and don't give the attendant the trunk key, then." I was beginning to get a little paranoid about New York. "Promise me," he continued, "that when you get to this intersection, you'll make a left and not a right."

"Why is that?"

"Just promise," he said with a look of knowing danger, "you'll go left."

"Okay. I'll go left."

I arrived in New York City, and after parking my car, I walked to Albert Ellis's office. During my walk, I noticed that just about every parked car had a cardboard sign in the window that said "NO RADIO." Car radio theft is so prevalent, I was told, that people have given up the idea of having a radio in their cars. The sign apparently saves the criminal the time and effort of breaking into a car, provided he can read. People also leave their glove compartments open, showing that there is nothing inside, again deterring potential crime. What is weird is that this way of life is considered normal by the local population. On the ten o'clock news, there was a story about some police who arrested a gang of purse snatchers. When the sergeant was asked about the thefts, he said, "It was victim negligence." He said it was the victims' fault because they did not take the proper precautions and protect their purses well enough. What kind of craziness is this? When I walked down the streets of New York City and smiled at people in my friendly Midwestern manner, people either ignored me or quickly scurried away as though I wanted something from them. New York is the only city where people are threatened more by smiles than by guns.

I arrived at Albert Ellis's building safely and rang the doorbell several times. Finally, a man came to the door and looked through the window.

"What do you want?" he asked, peering intently through the iron bars that separated us.

"I'm here to interview Albert Ellis."

"Who are you?"

"I'm Bill Elliott."

"Oh," he said, opening the door, "I thought the interview was going to be done on the phone. Wait here. I wasn't expecting you, and I have to clean up."

Albert Ellis then went upstairs. After ten minutes he returned and told me to follow him to his study. He taped the interview at the same time I did—"to prevent misquotes." The whole time we talked (well over an hour), he never looked at me. Instead, he constantly rubbed his forehead with his right hand and looked downward with his eyes shut. I was nervous during the interview because I felt he might at any moment look up and say, "Interview's over!" It must have been the abrasive tone of his voice, as though he were irritated at something, that gave me this feeling. But in the end, I had to hand it to him. He answered every question I asked and gave me more information than I needed. I enjoyed his way of answering my questions, because he didn't worry about editing his comments and seemed to enjoy provoking people with them. One of the first things he said to me was, "Practically all humans are out of their minds."

I won't argue with his assessment, but in my job as a counselor for the elderly mentally ill I work with people who by society's standards are considered out of their minds. Even though they might be diagnosed as schizophrenic, they have a deep insight into life.

I work the graveyard shift, and usually the residents sleep all night, but on occasion there may be one or two who have trouble sleeping. One morning at three A.M., a resident named Sam got up. It was only my second night at the home, and I was still a little uneasy about the job. I was watching television when he walked into the room. He was quite a sight. He's eighty-two years old and eighty pounds overweight, and he looks just like Winston Churchill. The only thing he was wearing was his boxer shorts.

"Time for breakfast yet?" he asked.

"Sam," I said, "it's only three in the morning."

"Oh, I thought it was time for breakfast."

He turned and shuffled with his walker back to his room. After a few minutes, I could hear him talking to himself. I wondered what kinds of things he might be saying, so I went by his door and listened.

"The first look," he said, "and they start criticizing."

Dr. Albert Ellis is the founder of the Institute for Rational Emotive Behavior Therapy, which now has branches throughout the United States and around the world. He is author of more than forty-five books, including *A New Guide to Rational Living* (with Robert A. Harper, Ph.D.), *Sex without Guilt,* and *Sex and the Liberated Man.*

On what beliefs do you base your life?

That the Universe is meaningless and that there are no supernatural beings in the world. It is foolish to be afraid of being dead. Death is exactly the same state as before we were conceived: zero, nothing. We didn't exist at all then. We had no feeling, no thoughts, and no behaviors before we were conceived. The day before we were conceived, we were zero. The day after we're dead, we are equally zero, and therefore there is nothing to fear about death. We have only this one life, and therefore we'd better make our own meaning and enjoy ourselves as much as we can without needlessly harming other humans.

I don't believe in God. There is equal probability that there are gods, fairy godmothers, gnomes, and fairies, and I don't believe in *any of them.*

There is no purpose to life. We make a purpose to life. There is no purpose, no cosmic purposes, as Victor Frankl foolishly says there is. (He cops out with that.) No, there isn't any meaning, purpose, goals, or values. We *give life* meaning, purpose, goals, and values. And we'd better, because otherwise we would lead a relatively dull existence. If I create meaning for myself, I'm more likely to enjoy life. I give various meanings to life; there's no one meaning. I like to live, I like to learn, and I like to find enjoyable things to do. The biggest meaning I've given to life for a good many years now is to find ways of helping people not to seriously upset themselves about anything, which is the topic of one of my books. Because people stubbornly refuse to upset themselves about anything, they are more able to find what they think is enjoyable and to avoid what they consider unenjoyable.

Since 1955, when I first formulated Rational Emotive Behavior Therapy (REBT), my big purpose or goal or meaning in life has been to promote and teach its principles and practice to as many people as possible—not just in individual psychotherapy, because it would reach very few people then, but also in talks, workshops, cassettes, articles, and books. I try to teach it to as many people as will accept and use its principles and practices.

The highest ideal for each individual is not to seriously upset himself or herself, but to feel healthily sorry and regretful when things go wrong, as they very frequently do. Feeling frustrated and annoyed at the injustices of the world is healthy, but don't whine and scream about these injustices, which the vast majority of people do for most of their lives. Most people are whiners and screamers, and that's the essence of neurosis.

What is the highest ideal a person can reach? What are the obstacles to this ideal?

The highest ideal is not to whine and scream very much. As Reinhold Niebuhr said, "Change what you can change, accept what you can't change, and have the wisdom to know the difference between the two."

Absolutistic musts, shoulds, oughts, commands, and demands are the obstacles to this ideal. Humans take their preferences, desires, wishes, wants, and likes (almost all of which are fairly legitimate), and they foolishly change them into Jehovistic commands, demands, shoulds, oughts, and wants, which really don't exist in the universe—because they invented them. So they upset themselves needlessly, make themselves depressed, angry, horrified, and anxious, and panic themselves. They hate and pity themselves, which interferes with their going after what they want and avoiding what they don't want in this, their only life. Try to change whatever is against your interest and try to accelerate and abet whatever is in your interest, but don't *demand* that the things you like exist or that because you dislike something it *must not* exist. These Jehovistic commands and demands constitute the core of human neurosis.

What do you think about family life . . . ?

Family life is one of the many forms of bigotry that exist in the universe. It is a necessary form because without it, maybe the human race wouldn't have survived. Just about every species has some kind of a family, and humans are usually raised in a family. There are groups of other animals where just the mother raises the child, but in humans that usually never exists. So the family, up until recently, has been necessary for human survival and therefore good, but it creates prejudice. Just like "My country right or wrong," which is really a fascist view, the family view is "My family right or wrong." We're very prejudiced in favor of our family members, especially in favor of our children. We care for them much more than for other people's children, which one might say is unethical and immoral, to some degree.

The family has many good aspects since it fosters humans and teaches us to care for each other, but it has many pernicious points, especially prejudice and bigotry. The family teaches us bigoted ideas and teaches us to hate Jews or Catholics or blacks or strangers. If your family is Republican, they almost always raise you Republican; if they are Democrat, they raise you Democrat; if they're Jewish, they raise you Jewish. This is really unfair to the child. There preferably should be a law against indoctrinating little children with dogmas. Unfortunately, they will make up their own. Children are easily drawn to other people's dogmas, and have a strong innate tendency to create their own bigotries.

There's no question there's a thing called "love." Poets say "love makes the world go 'round." Love means caring and being vitally absorbed in having affection for people or things. Some people love a cause or love to watch baseball.

Humans are born with the tendency to love. They usually love their parents, caretakers, brothers, and sisters. They also fall in love romantically with other people. But love can be obsessive, compulsive, sick love, and it can be superunrealistic romantic love. Love is unrealistic when we think we have to be madly in love with and happily married to one single person forever. Intense romantic love almost always fades—especially in marriage!

Why do you think there is suffering or evil in the world?

Because there is. It's obvious that there is and that humans are born with a tendency to suffer. Suffering has two aspects. One aspect is frustration, annoyance, pain, sorrow, and regret, which is healthy suffering, because when people don't get what they want, we hope they're not happy. And when they're happy, I hope, they're not just calm and serene, as some of the Asian philosophies would try to get them to be.

When we don't get what we want and we do get what we don't want, then we suffer some pain. Therefore, we are motivated to correct that by getting more of what we want and less of what we don't want. Suffering is therefore a kind of healthy pain. It's okay to be stressed, to suffer in order to change ourselves, our actions, our thoughts, and our feelings.

The other kind of suffering—feelings of rage, panic, anxiety, depression, self-pity, and whining—is needless suffering. Rational Emotive Behavior Therapy teaches people to minimize needless suffering. This kind of suffering is pathetic because it's needless. Humans are born easily disturbable. They're born with a very strong tendency to demand and command that bad things not exist in the world and that only good things exist. When people demand and command in the Jehovistic fashion, then they needlessly create a foolish, neurotic kind of suffering. Not everyone will stop being whiners and screamers. Some are too dull to do so. Many are too ignorant and have to be taught to do so. But it's possible for most people of average or above-average intelligence to stop whining.

There are, however, some severely disturbed people—biologically disturbed people such as psychotic or organically impaired individuals—who would have great trouble doing or who are limited and cannot do as much as the merely neurotic population can do. In my estimation, practically all humans have strong neurotic tendencies. A minority of them have severe personality disorders, so they're not quite the same as the nice neurotics who can change and stop their whining without too much trouble. Personality disordered people have much more trouble changing.

Evil means something, like AIDS, that is against the human condition, against human happiness, against pleasure, against goal-seeking, and against healthy motivation. Why does disease exist? Because it exists. There's no cosmic reason.

Good things are things like creativity that abet human happiness. Good and bad things both exist because they exist, but we can minimize the bad things and maximize the good things if we think and act sensibly and rationally. I cannot exactly conceive of a world where there is no evil. Life might even be a bore if there were no evil and no badness.

Very few of us would like to be hermits, so when we go after our desires for money, for sex, for love, we have to compete with other humans because they want the same things.

Sometimes the things we desire are limited; therefore, there's no way we can live in a social group and not harm other humans at times. My getting to the finish line first or the food first prevents somebody else from getting the prize. But there are ways in which we can stop ourselves from needlessly harming others. If there is food only for one and there are two of us, and I get there first and take it, that harms the other. If there is one job and twenty people apply for it and I get the job, I harm the other nineteen—I take satisfaction away from them. But when I go out of my way to lie, to steal, needlessly to harm other humans when I don't have to, and could live satisfactorily without doing so, that is immorality in the social group.

I'm not sure how we could ever get rid of all the evil in the world. That would be utopia, and utopia is a silly romantic concept that, in all probability, will never exist. There are problems in life. Love and work, and our interpersonal relations in business and love, are two of the biggest problems in life. Another problem is unconditionally accepting ourselves, not because we do well or because we're bright or because we're attractive or because people love us, but accepting ourselves because we're alive and because we exist. Very few people achieve this. We hope they will achieve it in Rational Emotive Behavior Therapy.

If you were on your deathbed, what advice would you give to your son or daughter?

I would give them the same advice I give to everybody: "There are many bad things in the world, especially at the present time. There's the atomic bomb, wars, fascism, bigotry, and racial prejudice. There are many evils and much frustration. But if you're wise you'll follow the principles of Rational Emotive Behavior Therapy: Make yourself feel sorry, sad, disappointed, regretful, frustrated, and annoyed, but stubbornly refuse to make yourself miserable by making yourself panicked, horrified, depressed, and enraged."

If you could meet anyone throughout history, whom would you want to meet and what would you ask that person?

I would like to meet all the great philosophers and thinkers and discuss their theories and particularly our disagreements. I would like to meet Immanuel Kant, who wrote *The Critique of Pure Reason.* It influenced me when I was a youngster. When I was nineteen, I started to translate it from English into simple English because it was so abstruse. Kant influenced me in terms of the potency of thinking. He said that absolute truth didn't really exist and that if it did one could never achieve it. There's no way that humans with limited abilities could achieve it. But then Kant stupidly wrote another book, *The Critique of Practical Reason,* in which he said, rightly, that there's no absolute truth, but he also said there's no way to have morality without believing in God and religion. I would ask Immanuel Kant if he really believed that crap or whether he wrote it for political or other reasons.

I would ask Spinoza the same thing. As far as I can see, he was an atheist but without the courage of his conviction, and perhaps rightly so because the bigots of his day might have killed him. So he resorted to pantheism, where God is Nature. It's silly to call nature God, and I would ask Spinoza whether he really did believe in any gods or if he copped out to save his own life.

Karl Marx said, "Religion is the opiate of the people." He was correct, but it depends on what we define as religion. If by religion we mean some absolute dogma—that there was a Jesus, that he was the Son of God, and that he, if we pray to him, will save us or, for that matter, destroy us, then religion is an opiate. That kind of dogma, that absolutism in religion, is pernicious and is a source of much human disturbance. Not the belief that there *may be* a God, but that there *inevitably is*, that He is the only God, and that those who don't believe in Him should be damned and killed—that is bigotry and absolutism and is a disturbance.

What was the most significant thing that ever happened to you, and what did it teach you?

I was madly in love with a woman when I was twenty-four years of age, and she was very erratic. She loved me one minute and the next neglected me and didn't show up for appointments and meetings. She kept telling me she loved me, but she didn't act that way. I would write her long letters—twenty, thirty, forty pages long—questioning, "Do you really love me?"

That was not the first time I had ever been in love, because I had often been in love since the age of five, but this was the first time I was really relating to a woman with whom I was in love. So I went for a walk in the Bronx Botanical Garden by the lake. That was in the old days when one could walk in the parks at midnight; now, I would never do it—I'd get mugged! I realized that I not only wanted her but I absolutely *needed* her, and that this *need* was foolish and self-defeating. When we don't have what we absolutely "need," we're depressed and miserable; when we do have it, we worry about having it tomorrow. We can't win with necessities, needs, musts, absolutistic shoulds, and oughts.

At that time, I was not a psychologist; I had a B.A. in business administration. I was trying to be a writer and not a psychologist, and I read tons of books on psychology and philosophy. I knew from philosophy that need wasn't a good idea, but this time it really hit me that I was direly needy and that this need was going to screw me—that I would be miserable with a woman who was hot-and-cold. So I decided to give up need. I had a long talk with myself in which I gave up needing. Afterward, whenever I needed anything (or thought I did) I would fight it like hell and get rid of it. That night I gave up my need for her and was able to go back to her the next night and tell her that I still *wanted* but no longer *needed* her.

That's mental health: not giving up your feelings, your emotions, and your desires, even being passionate in your desires, but never transmuting those desires into "necessities."

Eventually, I got around to giving up psychoanalysis, which I found to be largely full of crap from beginning to end. Analysts have no real idea what emotional disturbance is nor how to reduce it. Then I got into Rational Emotive Behavior Therapy and the concepts of neediness and anti-neediness. I have taught people ever since that time that if they *desire* to do anything, then they should do it very strongly and passionately but never *need* what they want. My experience was significant because I used this kind of therapy on myself, and I am a great example that it works because I am no longer needy.

What do you feel is something life still has to teach you?

I still have to learn to make myself even less upsettable. I still get angry a little too often. And there are times I get too sure of myself, because I think my theories are better and more efficient than other theories. I forget Rational Emotive Behavior Therapy's weaknesses, and I could certainly teach myself to be less arrogant. I like problem-solving: taking complicated things that don't have a good answer and figuring out the answer to them, putting "solutions" together and taking them apart. To arrive at Rational Emotive Behavior Therapy includes a great deal of problem-solving. It looks at what people are thinking and how they can correct this dysfunctional thinking and lead themselves into less disturbed and happier lives.

What makes you sad? angry?

I get sad sometimes about politics and corruption, but not depressed because I just accept the reality of things that I cannot change. We often have the wrong men as presidents in the United States. We have nuclear fission, war, racism, and stupid fashions. We don't spend adequate money on health care. I'm sad about innumerable immoralities, un-niceties, hassles, and stupidities in the world, but I'm not so upset about them that I interfere with trying to fight them. Nor do I allow them to interfere with my pleasures. I haven't been depressed and can't recall any panic on my part during the last fifty years. I don't get depressed, but I frequently get sad about these trials and tribulations in the world.

Practically nothing makes me angry anymore. I just get displeased, sad, and sorry about stupidities. Anger is the Jehovistic command that because this bad thing exists, it should not and must not exist. Once in a while I get angry, but only very briefly, as I sometimes do at my Friday night workshops. When I get somebody up on stage to talk about a problem, I ask the other people, "Please be quiet because the walls reverberate and your neighbor would rather hear us than you, so shut up right now!" Then some people will start speaking up and I'll look at them sternly and say, "That means you," and they shut up. But some continue talking, so once in a while I say, "Now, look, shut your big mouth. Get back in the john and go masturbate if you're not going to shut up." I'm angry and not merely displeased at their behavior. Then I immediately say to myself that being angry at them is foolish, because I'm telling myself they *shouldn't* be the way they undoubtedly are. Anger is that Jehovistic command. Then I forcefully tell myself, "Too bad! That's unfortunately the way they are!" I immediately get rid of my anger. In the old days I used to be angry at practically all kinds of human stupidity and un-nicety, but now I accept what I can't change and fight what I can, but I very rarely get enraged at anything.

What is important to you?

It's important that I continue to live, enjoy, and have good health. I like teaching, persuading people, and talking about my ideas; and I am very enthusiastic about sex and love. I've been in love with one woman or another since the age of five. I've had a number of close relationships, and my present relationship has gone on for thirty years now with the same woman. I love music and have a talent for composing. I've never studied music, but I compose it. I've loved writing since the age of twelve. I was determined to be a writer, and I'm still writing after publishing over fifty books and more than seven hundred articles. I love giving workshops and talking to my clients. It's my nature to get very absorbed in things; that sense of absorption is really a form of love.

It's important to me that humans stop upsetting themselves needlessly, foolishly enraging themselves, making themselves panicked.

They can stop doing themselves in and learn to accept themselves fully, unconditionally. "I'm okay because I do well and because you love me" is a sickness called self-esteem.

I always accept myself. I never damn myself, no matter what I do. Nor do I rate myself as a noble, godlike person. I am a person who does good and bad things. So let me try to do better and enjoy myself more. When I was very young, I was sick with kidney trouble and almost died once. I had headaches from the kidney trouble, so I decided that life is a hassle. How could I figure out ways to enjoy life and not upset myself about it? I had a little more adversity than others, but I tried to figure out ways of not upsetting myself. I inherited a good intellect, and I got into trying to help the rest of the world preserve itself and enjoy itself more.

Whenever I tend to feel upset about anything, I immediately say, "Now look at what I am doing to upset myself, to screw myself. I don't *have* to succeed, but I *prefer* to succeed. I'd *like to* be approved but there is no reason why I *must* be." I look at what *I'm* thinking when I feel upset or *defeat* my own desires and values and refuse to blame others, the world, God, the devil, or anything else. By taking responsibility for my own screwups, I can much more easily deal with them and minimize them in the future.

20

JACK KORNFIELD

Sometimes before an interview, I experience an uneasiness over whether I will appear "spiritual enough" for the people I interview. What's more, I wonder how "spiritual" they will appear.

About a year ago, I did a ten-day Vipassana meditation retreat. Vipassana is a meditation practice that teaches awareness of oneself and one's surroundings. At this retreat, I meditated eleven hours a day and didn't talk at all for ten days. Even when I went to sleep, I was supposed to sleep "aware." Aware, aware, and aware—everything was this whole idea of being aware. When the retreat was over, I said good-bye to everyone with awareness, and then I drove off with awareness. On my way home, I discovered I had forgotten my bags.

So before my interview with Jack Kornfield, who is a well-known Vipassana meditation teacher, I was concerned about not appearing as an unaware slob who didn't have it together.

I was pleasantly surprised when I arrived at Jack Kornfield's house and found that his home was not spotless and totally together. It was more like the house where I grew up. His kid's toys were all over the floor. I was aware once again of the preconceived ideas I had about spiritual teachers and about what it means to live a spiritual life. When I saw the toys on the floor, I relaxed the ideals I had set for myself. It was okay if I wasn't perfect. And who knows? Maybe toys on the floor is perfection.

I interviewed Jack Kornfield in his meditation room. His atmosphere was that of an experienced meditator. He was relaxed and centered. After thirty minutes, he looked at his watch and jumped up, saying, "I gotta go pick up my kids." We said a quick good-bye, and then he ran to his car.

Jack Kornfield is the cofounder of the Insight Meditation Society, a major teaching center for Vipassana meditation in the West. He has taught at the Naropa Institute, Esalen Institute, and other centers worldwide. He spent six years in Asia studying and practicing as both a layman and a monk in the Theravada Buddhist tradition. Upon his return he completed a Ph.D. degree in clinical psychology. His published works include *A Path with Heart, Living Buddhist Masters,* and *The Heart of Wisdom* with Joseph Goldstein.

On what beliefs or truths do you base your life?

I was drawn to spiritual practice from a young age. Partly I had suffered; partly I was intellectually curious; partly I was inspired by some people; partly there are reasons I don't understand. But there was a sense that there was something great and grand and wonderful that was possible for human beings.

I base my life on a few truths learned after many years of Buddhist practice and probably a lot of beliefs, some of which may not be correct. One truth is that all things are impermanent. Everything that is born dies, and there are natural cycles to all things, beginnings and endings. I believe in a reality that is called "the way things are." It is also called the Dharma, which means the laws that govern nature, the universal laws. I believe in the Ultimate Reality of the pregnant void—which can be experienced—the timeless space out of which all things come, and I believe in the laws that govern this creation. It's called the Dharma. One could call it God, I suppose, or the Tao. It's an experience as much as a belief.

The second truth is that there's a mixture of pleasure and pain, light and dark, sweet and sour, and that's the way it is. I've not met a single being or seen a single circumstance that has only one half of that, so I accept this truth as best I can or try to accept it and live in accord with it.

The third truth is that, basically, I can't or don't possess anything. In the end I don't even possess my own body, not to speak of my thoughts or feelings, which tend to be quite autonomous most of the time. So I try to relate not so much from possession as from honoring or loving or understanding. I've learned that it's not how much I get that matters but how much I'm able to let go or give or share. And I've learned that everything changes, so I can't possess anything.

The other truth is the truth of karma. What I do or how I act or how everyone acts shapes the future. If I act by practicing hatred and aggression, after a while it becomes automatic to me, and it creates a response from the world around me that's hateful or aggressive in the long term. If I sow the seeds of kindness, awareness, and love, after a while that shapes my own heart and character, develops it, and it affects the world around me.

What is the purpose of life?

I don't have any idea. I could make a guess, and I've felt different things at times, but I don't relate to life in terms of its purpose. I'd say sometimes it seems like a school to learn from, sometimes it seems like a big mistake, maybe a strong delusion, sometimes it seems like creative play and the divine.

Sometimes it seems that to ask that question is useless. There's a very different question I ask, which is not so much why, since that seems impossible to answer in words, but how. Given that we're here, given that there is this life and it is as it is—how can we live in it? How can I live in it in a way that maximizes, that fulfills the capacity for wakefulness, love, freedom, liberation of the human heart?

There are a lot of words for that. I used to think of the purpose of life in terms of freedom: liberation from fear and greed and prejudice and delusion, or more simply freedom from the sense of self as a separate entity, from that illusion. Now I express it more positively in terms of universal compassion or love. It's the melting of the illusion of separateness and the living in oneness with love or compassion for all beings all our lives.

Another way to see the purpose of life is that we let go of our fears and our illusions and our separateness and come to that reality that is already true. There are many good paths: Christian, Buddhist, Hindu, Sufi. I prefer brand names—the great traditions—because they've been tried by one or two hundred million people and they have the kinks worked out. I know that the freedom or liberation

I spoke of can be found in a number of the great religious spiritual traditions. There is a common spirit in many of the great traditions.

I've seen that people are nourished by compassion and great freedom, just as plants in the garden are nourished by sunshine and rain and fertilizing and proper seeds. I also believe that as humans we each have the capacity to express extraordinary compassion and great freedom. It is done through understanding and faith, as well as some systematic path of practice that involves surrender and wakefulness and living truthfully and compassionately more and more from day to day. That places it in time. In truth, it's already present. My basic spiritual practice is Vipassana practice. It's the practice of mindful awareness or of surrender and receiving what is true, seeing it clearly, and developing a wakeful and loving, compassionate relationship to all of life as it shows itself. Vipassana practice is a practice of learning to be here now, to live in the moment, wakefully and with compassion.

What is the greatest obstacle to obtaining this ideal?

Carlos Castaneda was told by Don Juan, "The trouble with you is you think you have time." We often put off what we know, thinking our lives will last forever or very long. Very long is not forever. Then all of a sudden we find someone near us die or we get sick and realize, Whoa, I better live in ways that I haven't because I thought I had time. Understanding this brevity and the preciousness of life is one of the important obstacles and the freedom from that.

If you could meet anyone throughout history, whom would you meet and what would you ask that person?

I would like to have met the Buddha, followed by Jesus or Lao-tzu. I wouldn't ask anything at all. I would just want to be around them and hang out and listen.

Why is there suffering?

Ultimately, asking about suffering is like asking what the purpose of life is. I have no idea why suffering exists, but I know that pain is inevitable, just like light and dark and up and down. Pleasure and pain are part of the duality that creates existence. But I also know that suffering is optional. Our human suffering is based on misunderstanding or ignorance that causes prejudice, separation, fear, grasping, delusion. It's possible to see through that illusion and not suffer.

Why is there evil?

I don't know. Ramakrishna said, "To thicken the plot." From one point of view, I wouldn't even say there is evil. There is ignorance, very deep ignorance.

What do you think about death?

It happens to everything. One day, I will be on my deathbed, no ifs, ands, or buts about it. And on my deathbed, I'll remind my children to love well.

Death seems appropriate. An endless life would probably be a disaster. Change is part of the nature of things. To live with an appreciation of change makes life more beautiful and full.

When I first did my spiritual practice, I did not believe in rebirth at all. I just believed this was it and the rest was fantasy. All those stories that spoke about death from day to day and hour to hour as we change each part of our lives were really poetry. The child dies and the adolescent is born. But some very deep experiences in my meditation and visions have led me to the opposite conclusion. First, I didn't believe in anything—not death or other beings or other planes. Now, I'm inclined to believe in everything.

The mind creates everything. It has an incredible creative potential. Just as it can create an earth and a sun, animals of a billion varieties, it can create heavens and other realms. And death and consciousness and life are a play, and it continues. That's what I believe. When we die, there is not the same person, any more than an apple on a tree is the same apple as the one from the seed that planted it. But there is a pattern or process that continues changing and evolving.

If you could change anything in life, what would you change?

Myself.

Some people think personal relationships interfere with spiritual growth. What do you think?

The Buddha also said that at times. I don't believe it. I see people who are serious who are monks and nuns (whether Buddhist or Christian), and I see people who are very devoted to spiritual life who are lay people. I also know many monks and nuns who have no interest, or almost no interest, in real spiritual practice and who are monastic for a variety of other reasons, who are as unspiritual as the most worldly person, and vice versa. It's not the form, but the heart that matters. I'm married and have children—extraordinary! They teach me very deep things about surrender and love.

Do you feel there is a basic difference between maleness and femaleness, besides the body?

If you have a son and a daughter, you learn very quickly that men and women are different species, different energies, and different patterns. We're all created in patterns. The archetypal feminine and masculine are in each of us, but one tends to predominate in women and one tends to predominate in men. These archetypal patterns are apparent in ways of thinking, ways of feeling, and ways of perceiving. There's a difference, although it's hard for me to articulate it. I work in a preschool with my four-year-old daughter, and the little boys I see there are very different from the little girls. They start that way. It's not just a cultural conditioning.

How would hypnosis and trance states tie into the Eastern idea of enlightenment and awareness?

Hypnosis is based on surrender and on concentration, making the mind deeply concentrated. Those are elements that are found in meditation as well. Most meditation includes concentration; often it involves surrender. It also involves many other things like awareness and learning and investigation that are not always present with hypnosis. Hypnosis is generally used to direct someone in a certain way. Meditation can be used for that, but for much more, including the discovery of many realms, the deepening understanding of oneself, or the practice of letting go and freeing the heart and the mind of fear, greed, and so forth.

Erickson said we go from one trance state to another; we're always in a trance. To be enlightened is to wake up from the trance of separateness.

What is important to you?

I believe in taking care of other beings as if they were really a part of myself. I really believe in caring for children and in education.

If I were to die now, I would be most concerned with whether I loved well—the people I know, my family, my friends, the work I do, the earth, the trees, and all creatures, life. That question informs my life a lot: Have I loved well?

What makes you happy?

Loving and being loved make me happy. Being, discovering freedom, feeling that freedom in my life and seeing it for other beings, serving others, creativity, feeling the joy of touching the earth, the joy of painting, of walking, of designing, of playing music, the expression of life.

What makes you sad? angry?

When I get caught in my own headiness, fears, or delusion. When I see other people harm each other out of their fears and delusion and pettiness or hurt each other because of the way they've been mistreated. When I see unnecessary suffering, people going hungry, people without medicine—and knowing that there's help for them that isn't reaching them. When I see the grief and sorrow that some humans carry and don't know how to release in their hearts, how to find compassion and a freedom that releases their sorrows. Lots of things make me angry, but very few of them justified. I get angry at injustice; I get angry at being hurt personally. I'm trying to learn to bring a great strength to helping in situations of injustice, but to do it out of a place of caring, as Gandhi taught, rather than of anger.

What do you feel is something life still has to teach you?

I'm a beginner. I still have to learn every spiritual truth in a deeper way, and a whole lot of worldly things besides, from sex

221

and money to rock 'n' roll on down. Being born taught me about having a body and eyes and ears. I had a wonderful spiritual teacher named Achaan Chaa, who lived with great humor, delight, joy, and freedom of spirit—and taught me that possibility. I hope I can follow his example.

21

S W A M I
SATCHIDANANDA

In the 1960s and 1970s, Eastern philosophy flourished in the West. One of the Eastern spiritual teachers who came to the West was Swami Satchidananda. I first saw him on television, and the thing I remembered most about him was that his eyes twinkled. Years later, when I first made my way into a spiritual bookstore, I recognized the eyes, though I had forgotten his name.

I drove to Virginia in order to meet with Swami Satchidananda. Along the way, I got lost, so I stopped at a gas station. There were two men talking. One was spitting tobacco as I approached.

"Can you tell me how to get to Buckingham, Virginia?" I asked.

"Where in Buckingham do you want to go?" I could sense him sizing me up, while his buddy just stared.

"A place called Yogaville."

"Yogaville?" he said with a drawl. For a second I half-expected him to call me "boy."

"What the hell you want in Yogaville?" he said as he looked at his partner, ridiculing a place he'd never been to and anyone associated with it. They looked at me with their arms folded across their chests, with a what-have-we-got-here expression on their faces.

"Just some swami that's there," I said in a tone that emphasized to them my lack of interest or connection with my destination.

"A swami?" the man replied with a smirk. They both laughed again. I found myself smiling with them in order to be accepted as one of them. We laughed together, and I no longer had to worry, because they could see I shared their joke with them.

I walked back to my car with directions, but I felt guilty. It was as though I had betrayed a friend. Although it wasn't as grand as Peter's denial of Jesus, there was a similarity. I had always wondered how Peter could have pretended he had nothing to do with Jesus after having known him, but now I understood.

I finally arrived at Yogaville—two hours late. It was too late for a personal interview, but I was told that since it was Saturday night in Yogaville, there was something special planned. Swami Satchidananda was going to answer my questions at tonight's lecture.

I was led into a gigantic hall. There was a stage framed by thirty-foot high curtains at the front of the hall. On the stage was a big chair that resembled a throne. I was suddenly afraid I was going to have to interview the swami up on stage in front of hundreds of people.

"Come this way, Mr. Elliott."

I was led to the VIP section. On my left was a tiny nun from India, on my right a brother from a hermitage. I sat between them: nun on the left; monk on the right; me, the guy from Madison, in the middle.

Suddenly a man walked out on stage and grabbed the microphone. "Tonight we have three special guests!" the loudspeaker said. I cringed at the thought that I was one of the three special guests.

"We have Sister Indira," the speaker continued. "She's from India and works with lepers! Please stand up, Sister!" She promptly stood up as the crowd clapped.

"And Brother Joseph is here from the monastery... You remember Brother Joseph!" The brother stood up and everyone clapped again.

"And last..." (not me, not me, I silently prayed to myself) "...Bill Elliott from Madison, Wisconsin, who is..." (the speaker struggled to find my credentials) "...writing some kind of book!" The crowd applauded, and I reluctantly stood up and waved to the audience. I stood there holding my tape recorder with a nun who works with lepers and a brother who meditates in a monastery. I felt overdressed for the occasion.

To make a long story short, Swami Satchidananda read my questions from a sheet of paper and answered them up on stage. Afterward, he descended and walked down the aisle between two rows of his students. He walked past me without saying a word. I thought he had forgotten me, but then he stopped and turned around. "Did you get the answers you needed?" he asked, looking at me kindly.

I was about to answer, when I realized there were hundreds of eyes and ears gathered around us, anxiously awaiting my reply. It was quiet, and people were waiting to hear how their teacher ranked on my list. They wanted to know if this Bill Elliott fellow, who sat in the VIP section and who traveled all over the world for answers, had found his answers with their teacher.

Up to that time, I had felt I had found some answers—not particularly from Swami Satchidananda—but more from the whole journey I had undertaken. Yet as I looked around me, his followers seemed to need reassurance about his wisdom, so I quickly searched for a way to reassure them without undermining my own integrity. "Yes," I answered, "I got what I needed."

The swami smiled and continued on his way, while his students breathed a sigh of relief.

I packed up my belongings and walked to the door. Many of his students stopped and thanked me for asking such profound questions. I was touched that people had finally noticed how important the questions were. After all, without good questions, there can be no good answers. And there can be no wise men or wise women without the perfect fool.

One nun, dressed in robes, introduced herself. She was the person who had arranged my visit. I was grateful to her and reached out to give her a hug, but she pulled away and said, "I'm sorry, but we're not supposed to hug members of the opposite sex here." I stepped back and awkwardly smiled at my faux pas.

Returning to my car, it saddened me to think that human beings can be so lost that they have to refrain from human contact in order to find themselves and happiness.

Before getting into my car, I stopped to enjoy the atmosphere of Yogaville one last time. There was serenity at Yogaville, but it wasn't my style. There was a part of me that wanted to be a regular person and experience the life that Zorba the Greek lovingly called "the whole catastrophe." Sure, I wanted serenity and peace, but not while sacrificing the experience of the world. This was quite a change for me, since there was a time when I suffered deeply and my goal was to find that which did not suffer. I had believed that enlightenment or my search for God would give me that—a place without suffering. And there were times when I thought I found that place of no-suffering. But I have come to believe that this place of no-suffering is a place for angels, not human beings. Although I still try to minimize the suffering

I inflict on myself and others, I realize that suffering seems to be an indivisible part of life. Although I am reluctant to experience suffering, I am still drawn into the experience of life, with both its joys and its sufferings.

Swami Satchidananda was born in India. He came to the United states in 1966. He is the founder of the Integral Yoga Institute, the Satchidananda Ashram, and the Light of Truth Universal Shrine, which celebrates the Universal Truth in all religions, in Buckingham, Yogaville, Virginia. He is author of *Integral Yoga Hatha* and *To Know Yourself.*

On what beliefs or truths do you base your life?

The main belief is that I always want to be super happy because I feel that is the experience of God. When one experiences God, one is supremely happy. Everybody is looking for that happiness, whether a person is a believer or a nonbeliever, is religious or not. Even animals and plants, everything that is created, visible or invisible—they all look for this one thing, happiness. If I put a plant in a dark corner, it doesn't seem to be happy there. It strains its neck toward the window to get a little light. Everything wants to be happy, and we human beings will do anything just to be happy. Ask somebody who robs a bank, "Why are you doing this?" The robber will reply, "I want to get some money." "Why?" "To be happy." Ask the FBI, "Why are you looking for the culprit?" "We want to make money and be happy." The thieves, as well as the police, want to be happy. Everybody wants to make money—to be happy.

If you ask me to give a name to God, I would say Mr. Happy or Ms. Happy. That is the reason all Hindu monks have their name ending in *ananda*, which means supreme happiness and bliss. Ultimate Reality is a condition where one is in supreme bliss. One may call it God or *samadhi* or *satori*; it doesn't matter, because God is an experience. Remember that. God is not a person. If you say God is a person, then God is limited. Then God cannot be omnipresent. Anything that is infinite, omnipresent cannot have a form. For communion's sake, we see the formless through form. It doesn't mean God is limited by our form. We use a form to know the formless. So the formless God is an experience. When we have that experience, we are peaceful; we are joyful. That is the Ultimate Reality.

What is the highest ideal that a person can reach?

I would like to use my famous triplet: healthy, happy, and useful.

First, always be useful and not useless. Sacrifice is the law of life. Life's purpose is to serve others. Everybody is created in this universe not for oneself, but to serve others. That's what we see in Nature. Everything—grass, fruit trees, sun, moon, stone, metal— they're all there to serve others. Human beings are not exceptions to that. We are not here just for our own sake; we are here for others' sake, to serve others.

Second, always be healthy; never have to look for a doctor or pills. There is a country where the doctors are paid as long as the citizens are healthy. The moment somebody falls sick, they stop payment to the doctors. That means the function of the doctors is to make citizens healthy and free from disease.

Last, always be peaceful and happy.

When we have a healthy, happy, and useful life, our enlightenment comes. Enlightenment means knowing our true nature, experiencing that always. By experiencing that true nature in us and as us, we are able to see everybody and everything made of the same spirit. First we know our self as the spirit, then we are able to see the same spirit everywhere because we see others according to our image.

A man was lying in the road. A drunkard saw that fellow as another drunkard, while a saint saw that fellow as somebody sitting or lying down in *samadhi*. So if we want to see God in everything and everybody, we should have God's eye. That means our perception begins with God. As God, we see God in everybody. If we don't experience that God in us, we will never see God in anyone else because we have no eye to see. With physical eye, we see the physical body. With intellectual eye, we see the intellectual side of the person. If you were to come across a nice musician, he would immediately ask, "Are you a musician?" He would want to see everybody as a musician. He will talk that language. A carpenter would say, "Are you a good carpenter?" because he sees others from his eye. Likewise, a saint will see everybody as a saint. God will see as God. So that is the foremost duty: to know our true nature, know our self.

To attain this ideal, first know thyself. Then see thyself in your neighbor. And then love your neighbor as you would love yourself. To me, heaven is where we are. If we can see heaven, we can see heaven even if we are in hell. It is in our perception. If we don't have that heavenly experience in us, even a heaven will be a hell to us. So heaven is what we see, what we feel, what we experience.

Accumulating things makes us heavy. When we accumulate too much fat, we become heavy. When we accumulate too many things, we become heavy. When we give up everything, when we drop all the pounds and dollars, we become light. That's what enlightenment is. Losing pounds will make us light. Although it sounds like the physical side, it's also the spiritual side. Spirit is always light. Experiencing the spirit in you, as you, is what you call enlightenment. You are experiencing the light *in* you, and I emphasize "*in* you," because you are no different from the light in you. You are that light, the spirit. It is all self-realization. Who am I? I am that pure spirit. I am the image of God, according to the Bible. Anything else is ignorance.

Sacrifice your littleness, your limited, finite self. The minute you sacrifice this, you realize the supreme self in you. That's why sacrifice is the law of life. Stop this *I, me, mine.*

We often think sacrificing means sacrificing things. "Oh, I've given up my home." "I've given up money." That's not sacrifice. Sometimes I come across someone who has sacrificed his palatial home in the city, who comes all the way to the ashrams and says, "Swamiji, I've renounced everything. I want to become a swami." I'll say, "That's wonderful," and tell him to stay for a while; let us see. In two days, he'll be at the post office waiting for a letter from his home. Or sometimes he goes into a cave, sits there, and if anybody comes to pick up his begging bowl, he says, "Oh, that was given to me by my guru." He has sacrificed the whole palace, but here he is attached to his begging bowl. It's not running away from the world, throwing things away, that will make you a monk, a renouncer, a person who sacrifices everything. Sacrifice your attachment to the *I, me, mine.* The minute that happens, you become enlightened.

After Abraham begged and requested for years, through God's will he got a beautiful boy. But Abraham had to remember that it was really God's boy. After a certain age, he had to give it back to God. He had sacrificed everything except his attachment to that little boy. He forgot that the boy was given to him; it was not originally his child. God named Abraham's son *Isaac* because the "I" has to be sacrificed. Once the "I" gets sacrificed, the person who sacrificed the "I" becomes Abraham. It's an Indian name. *Brahmin* means supreme God. They just deviated a little and called him Abraham—a-Brahmim—a super Brahmin.

God insisted, "No, even that little attachment to your own beautiful son, who is not really your son, has to be given up. Give the boy to me." When Abraham was ready to give the boy back to God, God said, "Okay, I'm not interested in your son; I just wanted to see how much of an attachment you have to that boy. Now you don't have an attachment, fine; you don't have to sacrifice him." That is the secret. A monastery, an ashram, or a spiritual seeker's place means that is where one learns to sacrifice. In every religion the sacrifice or a sacrificial altar is an important part, because without that sacrifice there's no real peace, real happiness. There's no enlightenment.

Attachment is the biggest obstacle. I, me, mine is the biggest obstacle. "Mine" is the most dangerous obstacle because if you put it around you, it explodes. So don't throw "mine" around you and make it into a battlefield filled with mines. Renounce the mines.

What makes you happy? sad? angry?

Nothing makes me happy. If things make me happy, then when I lose them, I will become unhappy. I am happy always because I don't need anything to make me happy. If things make me happy, then the same things will make me sad. Then I'll find an excuse, a scapegoat for losing that, and I'll be angry. One follows the other. Be happy yourself. You don't need things to make you happy.

What do you think about death?

Death is only to the body. Death means we just discard the body. Death is like discarding an old shirt, but it also means buying a new shirt. We get to be a new shirt. Just as a little bird cracks open the shell and flies out, we fly out of this shell, the shell of the body. We call that death, but strictly speaking, death is nothing but a change of form. Material dies to become a robe. Wood dies to become furniture. Clay dies to become brick. Brick dies to become wall and building. Death is just transformation from one form to another form. The previous form is dead; the new form is born.

Literally, there's nothing that is destroyed. There is a saying in English, "Nothing is lost when a candle burns." A candle burns and melts. It completely disappears after some time, but nothing is lost. Why? Because the wax became vapor, went away. You don't see the candle, but it still exists in the form of vapor somewhere. The spirit of life force, the energy, that is within the body, making the body move, goes away. Just as when a switch is turned off and the fan stops, so the spirit is the one that uses the body to function. If we want electricity to function, we have to have gadgets. Without gadgets, what good is it to have wire all over the house? You have wire in the house, you have electricity in the house, but you don't have light, a moving fan, television, or radio. Why? Because the gadgets are not there.

Why is there suffering? evil?

There is no suffering, no evil. If there is a cause for suffering and evil, it is ignorance. Out of ignorance, we call it suffering or evil, but in reality they are helpers. Pain, yes. My master used to say, "Pain is my friend. If the pain is not there, you will not know where the problem is." Suffering is a process of cleaning. The dirty linen goes through suffering in order to get cleansed. Would you call this suffering undesirable? Of course not. It has to go through this process in order to get clean. So those who are interested in getting cleaned should look for suffering. To burn. To purify.

There's no such thing as evil. I know that some religions are built upon that. If you live life in the wrong direction, it becomes evil: l-i-v-e becomes e-v-i-l.

What is evil? Evil is a right thing in the wrong place. Things become evil if we don't know how to use them. A knife that would cut a fruit is good; a knife that would cut a throat is evil. So evil is something we make. It's a label we put on something when we don't know how to use that thing. Like "killer whale." Who kills the whale? Whale killers, not killer whales. Cobra poison—if you know how to use this deadly poison, you can save lives. Doctors use it as medicine. If you don't know, even nectar can kill you. So our not knowing is the worst evil. If there is an evil, ignorance is the evil. God has never created evil. How can all-merciful God create an evil? Beautifying processes, testing processes. God created Adam, and then he created Eve. Why? God wanted to test Adam. To Adam, Eve was probably evil. She is the one who tempted him to do that. But God created Eve in order to test him, so that he would know his capacity, his understanding. The student in school will see the examiner as evil. He will want to copy the book, but the evil man is constantly watching him. That's the way we make evil.

Do all religions lead to the same place?

All religions, even all actions, will ultimately lead one to the same place. The purpose of the world is to go toward that goal, knowingly or unknowingly. Even if one doesn't want to become a religious person, one will be forced to become a religious person one day. The suffering in life makes one remember God. After all, what is religion? *Religion* means to get back to the source. So all the paths lead to the same place. One may or may not call it religion, but to me everything is religion because everything helps one get back.

We label religion as religion because we have conceptions. The moment we have conceptions, we conceive ideas, and the moment we conceive, then we have to go through labor pain. Conception means labor will be there; then there's pain. Normally, we think religion means to go to church or the temple and to do this or that, practice meditation, pray, and contemplate. If you don't do that, are you not religious? Well, not necessarily.

This reminds me of a beautiful young lady in Russia who said, "I'm a nonbeliever. Don't talk God to me."

I asked her, "What do you mean by nonbeliever? Could you tell me what it is that you do not believe in?"

She didn't expect that question. She was searching for an answer. I added, "Maybe you don't believe in going to your church or in reading the Bible? You don't believe in any of the rituals?" In these, she didn't believe.

Then I asked her, "Don't you believe in love? Don't you have a boy?"

"Sure, I believe in love."

"Don't you believe in friendship?"

"Yes, I have friends. I believe in friendship."

I threw another question: "Don't you believe in comradeship?" The Communist Party assigned her to us as a translator while I was talking to some Russian orthodox monks. So naturally, she believed in comradeship. I said, "Okay, loving everybody, being friends with everybody, looking for comradery is what you call religion. If you don't have any of these things and you call yourself a religious person, you are not a religious person. All the religious practices are there to help you find this universal brotherhood, unconditional love. And you seem to have it; you seem to believe in that. So you are the real religious person."

Unless somebody comes and asks me if there's a better way to live, I won't bother to tell that person anything. Why? His dirty life will make him come to me one day because it won't always make him happy. That's the world. Its purpose is to give us knocks and bumps. Every time we make a mistake, it will give us a big knock. Then we will wake up: "I think this is not the way. I've tried all these kinds of things. I am sick and tired of all this." The moment we begin to say "I am sick and tired," we're not going to be running after the world anymore. Then what else should we be doing? We'll be seeking for that permanent happiness. That's why I say that we sometimes become sicker first, then a seeker later. Sick and tired, then seek and be happy. The world helps us become sick and tired. Even if we don't want to worry about God or religion and we don't want enlightenment, the world is not going to spare us. It's certainly going to make us seek one day; it's only a matter of time. If we cooperate, it'll be a little faster.

Mother Nature is going to wash us thoroughly, whether we like it or not. She'll put us in the tub, smear the soap. That's why I say the world is a frying pot with a holy ladle, and we are hot oil. Take fritters. In the beginning, a fritter is all moist, a lot of wet moisture there. We don't want to go into the hot oil. We make a big fuss; we want to jump out. Then the Mother Superior puts the holy ladle on top of us and keeps us there. If we jump out, where will we go? Into the fire. So we better stay there. Very soon the noise stops. We change color. Everybody is being fried. But we should not be afraid of being fried. When everything is fried well and all the moisture has gone away, then we are happy in the same oil. It is still hot oil, but we don't want to jump out, we don't make noise, and we begin to float around in the oil. So those who are well-fried will find heaven in the same world, and they'll be moving around comfortably without making noise. They'll be totally silent. The world becomes a monastery for them.

That's why we say that all paths and roads lead to the same truths. I was asked once in the Vatican why I said "Truth is one part of many." I didn't answer the priest directly. I said, "Father, living in Rome, you should not be asking that."

"What do you mean?"

"Haven't you heard? All roads lead to Rome." And Rome has so many roads, so all religions lead to the same place.

If you were on your deathbed, what advice would you give to your son or daughter?

I'd say, "See you later, because you are going where I am going. Don't think I'm the only one dying. You will follow me."

Once, a saddhu, a spiritual seeker, was wandering. He was tired, and he found a small veranda outside of a house, where he just lay down. At that time, there was an old lady and her young grandson talking in the house. Just then, a funeral procession passed by, a dead body going to its salt. (It's always the salt site where the crematorium is built.) The grandma called to the child, "Son, find out who that is and where he's going."

The saddhu thought to himself, everybody knows he goes to a crematorium. Within ten minutes, the grandson returned. "Grandma, Grandma, he is going to heaven." The saddhu wondered how the boy knew that, but before he could knock at the door to ask the question, another body was going by. The grandma said, "Tell me where he is going." After ten minutes the boy returned. "He is going to hell."

This poor saddhu couldn't resist anymore. He barged into the house. "You have a great boy. How does he know where the soul goes, whether to hell or heaven? Could you please tell me how he found out?"

"Swami, don't you know that? It's very simple," said the boy.

"Please, boy, tell me. I don't know."

"Well, I go to the funeral procession and listen to what the people who are following the body talk about. In the first case, they were saying, 'Oh, what a nice man. He was really useful, really helpful, a loving, wonderful person. I don't think we'll be able to see a person like him anymore. We lost a good friend.' Everybody was very sympathetic and appreciative of his life, so where else will he go?"

"Well, what about the second case?" asked the saddhu.

"That was terrible. They were saying, 'Now we can all sleep comfortably. Oh, what a big relief. One day I got ten dollars from that guy and he was pestering me to give him that money and another ten dollars within a month. What a stingy man. He used to fight with everybody. Now the whole village can sleep comfortably.' So tell me, where will he go?"

Probably if I have time enough to advise my son or daughter, I'll say, "Imagine that you are dying now and find out what others will say about you. Don't let them say, 'Oh, what a big relief.' Lead a useful life, a loving life."

Some people think personal relationships interfere with spiritual growth. What do you think?

A personal relationship will interfere because it is personal. It limits us. Impersonal relationships are okay. Universal relationships, okay. But very personal means we are splitting our lives. We begin to see the people we have personal relationships with as different from the others, which creates division in life. That is one of the reasons a monk doesn't have any personal relationships, nothing personal. Even within his own person he doesn't have a personal; he's not a person at all. He becomes totally universal. The scriptures say that even with God, we should not have a personal relationship. That means we are limiting. So any kind of personal relationship limits us.

Spiritual means we see the whole, not the little. If we see the whole and experience the whole, then if we have a personal relationship, it doesn't affect us. You say I belong to Yogaville. I have to have a personal address so that the mailman can bring my mail, but I don't have to get stuck with that personal address. Wherever I go, that becomes my home. The mailman doesn't know that, however, so for his sake I have to have one address—but that's what I call a personal relationship. We should not get caught in that.

We should lead a totally dedicated life, rise above these little limitations, because we are minute particles in the entire cosmos. We are part of the whole. We are not just separate individuals.

What do you feel is something life still has to teach you?

I still have more to learn. That's why I'm still alive. If I had finished learning, I would have left this college long ago, so the fact that I am still in this college means I still have to learn something. But I don't know what it is. When it comes, I will learn. I don't even worry about the future. *I* am not doing anything. I've been *made* to do, so you better ask the guy who makes me do. I don't question. Mother Nature made me approach life this way. The very life that guides me throughout gently moves me along. It's not that I decided to be like this or to do this.

I'm not simply answering philosophically; I'm answering from my heart. I have no goal in life. I don't have to approach anywhere, do anything. Every minute I feel the unseen hand. Wherever he puts me, I'm there. Whatever he makes me do, I do. That keeps me always free from any kind of stress, always happy, peaceful.

All these people call me founder—Director Swami Satchidananda. That's all their labels. They have to have something. I don't know what the labels are for. I just move; the divine wind moves me. I am nothing but a dry leaf fallen from the tree. Every time the wind blows, it goes this way and that way. I don't even question, Why are you making me do this? Why are you are pushing me here and there? I have no problem with that.

People come; people go. Organizations come; organizations go. Anything that comes will go. Last night we gave a farewell party for somebody and a welcome party for somebody else—the same party. Cut the same cake for both. Life is like that. Accept it. I am not here to reform the world, but to reform myself. When I have changed myself, then I have changed the world.

22

FRANCES
VAUGHAN

Frances Vaughan's idea of personal growth is that there is no one way to be. At one time, my idea of a wise person had been very specific. Namely, it was just that: my idea, or what I thought a spiritual person looked like or did.

I have a friend with whom I always enjoy talking about life and its mysteries. Since his wife never seemed interested in these talks, I assumed she wasn't as wise as we were. One day when I visited them, my friend knocked over a planter, spilling the contents everywhere. His wife came over and proceeded to put the poor plant back together while we just watched.

For a rare moment I could see out of my usual way of looking at things. I saw my friend's wife with great care and loving awareness placing the plant back into its pot. I realized this mattered to her. She held and mixed the dirt and handled the plant in a way that I couldn't do. She possessed a knowledge or wisdom I did not have, a love for something I could not see or feel. She cared about the plant in the same way I cared about other things. Suddenly, the difference in the things we each cared for no longer mattered. What mattered was that we both cared. And it was no longer her caring or my caring—it was our caring.

I had been lulled into a sleep in which the dream revolved around me. That day I felt as though I had reached out, past the foggy boundaries of my dream, toward someone else's dream, and into our world.

Frances Vaughan, Ph.D., is a psychologist in private practice in Mill Valley, California. A student of cross-cultural mysticism, she has worked with *A Course in Miracles* and has practiced yoga and Buddhist meditation for many years. She is author of *Awakening Intuition* and *The Inward Arc* and coeditor with Roger Walsh, M.D., of *Beyond Ego, Accept this Gift,* and *A Gift of Healing.* She is on the clinical faculty of the University of California Medical School and is former President of the Association for Transpersonal Psychology.

On what beliefs do you base your life?

I see life as a journey of learning and the evolution of consciousness. I believe consciousness is evolving, and we participate in the process, with or without awareness. Evolution, however, is only part of the process. Simultaneously there is a process of involution that sustains life. Life is essentially a journey of awakening to the reality of who and what we are.

The purpose of life has something to do with learning to love and becoming wiser in the way we relate to each other. Very simply, the purpose of life is discovered in learning and loving. This seems to give meaning to our lives.

In the process of learning to love, we often find that we have to remove some psychological obstacles to the awareness of love's presence in our lives. Love is more than a feeling or an emotion. That is only one aspect of love. The experience of love may also be associated with a feeling of ultimate belonging and the experience of bliss, joy, and peace. The words "being-consciousness-bliss" may be used to describe that experience. Universal love is different from personal love or emotional addiction to another person. Different traditions have different ways of defining love. There are always subdivisions, as in the distinction between *eros* and *agape.* We are familiar with romantic love, brotherly love, love between parents and children, love of friendship, and love between spiritual masters and disciples. There are many different forms of love, yet essentially love is one.

Love is the power that heals us. We become whole through learning to love ourselves and to love each other. And the process of awakening to love's presence involves letting go of fear, guilt, and anger. Much of the work in psychotherapy involves letting go of fear, guilt, and anger—letting go of the past—and recognizing our capacity for love and learning in the present.

Do you believe in a God or Ultimate Reality? What is It like?

The term *God* can be problematical because people mean different things when they speak of God. My own feeling is that many people have an experience of an underlying reality that they call God. Others who have similar experiences use different words to express it. If you are a theist—a Christian, for example—you might say it is possible to have an experience of God or an intuition of God. On the other hand, if you are not a theist—a Buddhist, for example—you might argue that there is no thing that can be called God. Depending on your point of view, you may or may not find the concept helpful. Whether you think of the great mystery in theistic or nontheistic terms, an experience of the unitive reality that mystics from many traditions have accessed has a profound influence on human life.

What is the highest ideal a person can reach?

Wholeness, rather than perfection, is the highest ideal from a psychological point of view. Many spiritual disciplines suggest that a state of perfection is possible. For example, the ideal of the Arahat in Theravadin Buddhism is one that some practitioners aspire to. From a psychological perspective, there is no endstate to be attained. It is not a matter of living up to an ideal image, but a process of the unfolding of awareness and continuing growth toward wholeness. Being awake can be an ideal in either spiritual disciplines or in psychotherapy. To see things as they are, free from self-deception and distortion, is the aim of many practices.

The journey to wholeness can be facilitated through many different methods designed for self-awareness. Paying close attention to experience, telling the truth about experience, communicating, teaching, and learning all contribute to waking up and becoming whole. One may become a student of life and explore many different paths. They all seem to involve a process of self-discovery and eventually, self-transcendence.

The paradox is that as you go deeper into your own experience, you find that it opens up into the collective. We may discover that our personal dramas are a microcosm of the human experience. Many times the deeper we go into our inner work, the more connected we feel to humanity and the rest of the world. Although the process of self-exploration is sometimes perceived as narcissism—whether in psychotherapy or spiritual practice—it seems that the more open we are to ourselves, the more open and connected we are to other people.

The psychotherapeutic relationship provides a safe space for telling the truth about our experience. We learn to listen better to ourselves and to others. As we do that, we enhance our capacity for learning, for seeing things as they are, for loving, and for making a more significant contribution to the well-being of the world. The quality of life does change as we do these practices, both in terms of increased inner peace and in terms of our capacity to deepen our relatedness to each other.

Will all people reach the goal of wholeness and self-transcendence?

Perhaps. It depends on how you define a person. Not if you are thinking of the individual personality. Who you think you are doesn't reach transcendence. If you talk about the soul, it depends on how you define *soul*. Even belief in reincarnation assumes a continuing separate self. If reality is one consciousness that manifests as multiplicity, then it depends how we perceive ourselves in relation to the One. Is the drop of water that falls into the ocean the same drop of water that went through the cycle of evaporation and condensation, returning to the ocean as rain? Is it the same drop or a different drop? I think the analogy of the drop of water in the ocean is one of the best analogies of the separate self in relation to the Absolute. If we regard the phenomenal realm as illusion, then reincarnation is also illusory insofar as it exists in time, and time is illusion from that perspective. However, in our everyday experience, time, separation, and duality seem very real.

Sometimes there is a confusion of levels when we try to talk about these things. When we speak of the level of perception where consciousness is one, it is not the level of perception where most of us live most of the time. Here and now we have preferences. We see things and people as better and worse. There is suffering and relief from suffering. There are joy and sorrow, love and fear, and many other polarities. And what we choose makes a difference.

Part of what we seem to be learning at this stage of our evolutionary journey is that, from a global perspective, we are all interdependent beings and that, in many respects, humanity is one. Our very existence is totally dependent on the welfare of the earth itself. We are increasingly aware that we are a part of the earth. Despite the problems and critical issues that we are facing today, one of the most heartening developments is the fact that it is now impossible not to know that we are in crisis. We are much more aware of the state of the earth and the necessity for recognizing that our actions have consequences than we were even twenty years ago. In a sense, humanity is at an existential crossroads. We can choose to live together consciously as brothers and sisters, or we will destroy ourselves.

What is the greatest obstacle to achieving this goal?

Fear is one of our greatest obstacles. Evil seems to be a product of our fear, greed, and delusion. What humans do to humans seems to be the primary source of evil in the world. People seem to create evil in the world out of ignorance. One cannot say that the people who perpetrate evil in the world have not suffered. On the contrary, their suffering may be very great. The violence that we abhor is often a reaction to oppression. If you empathize, you can understand it. And to understand all is to forgive all.

Violence may also be a reaction to physical abuse. Hitler, for example, was a badly abused child. It would seem that turning an infant into a torturer would require a great deal of painful conditioning. I don't believe that anybody is inherently evil. Given the appropriate loving and nurturing and caring environment, a person can usually grow up to be a healthy, contributing member of society.

People who perpetrate evil in the world generally have been victims of much suffering and abuse. The main thing is that their feelings have been turned off. That can happen very early; they learn not to feel their own pain and not to empathize with others. Then there is an increasing degree of separation and alienation from others. I don't think people want to harm others if they have not endured suffering and shut down feelings in the process.

Basically, ignorance is the problem. Greed, hatred, delusion, fear, guilt, and anger—those seem to be the major obstacles to peace. And of course they are interrelated. Anger and hatred are two sides of one coin, and fear is the root of greed. Delusion is in all of them. Guilt, fear, and anger are all forms of illusion. Fear is essentially based on fantasies about the future. And greed is based on the idea that I won't have enough. If I'm fearful about the future, I may try to accumulate things for security. It may be greed for power, for money, for experiences, or anything that will add to my false sense of security. Unfortunately, it doesn't work. Fear persists, no matter how much we accumulate. Anger and hatred are rooted in fear. We feel angry when we feel threatened, or when we feel somebody is potentially harmful to themselves or others. We may feel righteous anger when we perceive other people as life threatening. And we often get angry with people who fail to live up to our expectations.

Some people say suffering is necessary in order for people to learn and grow.

I don't agree with that. Suffering is inherent in the experience of separation. Being a separate self means suffering is inevitable. Relief from suffering comes from reconnecting to ourselves, to nature, to each other, and to Spirit. Healing occurs when we feel loved, when we join with another without defenses, in defenselessness. I don't think that suffering is necessary for anything; it just is. I think we make a mistake in turning a description (of suffering) into a prescription (for suffering) when we say it is good for you. There is suffering in the world, and we all witness it in various ways. And we can learn how to heal and relieve it.

How does psychotherapy help enlightenment?

The idea of enlightenment is something we intuit as a possible state of being long before we actualize it in daily life. And yet enlightenment is a recognition rather than a change. It is also a state of mind that people aspire to. The problem is that when we seek it or aspire to it, we separate ourselves from it rather than opening to it from wherever we are.

Many people consider the process of psychotherapy remedial. The most common view of psychotherapy is based on a medical model that aims at curing mental illness. However, my orientation in psychotherapy has always been growth-oriented. This suggests that you don't have to be sick to get better. You can always grow and deepen your capacity for love and learning. This is closely related to spiritual growth and self-awareness. Self-awareness is involved both in psychotherapy and spiritual disciplines. Certainly inner work in psychotherapy can sometimes help people who are on a path of enlightenment to recognize it.

The problem with comparing the search for enlightenment with psychotherapy is that in both areas we tend to speak only in generalizations. There are many paths by which people seek enlightenment, and there are many different forms of psychotherapy. It is difficult to say anything definitive about either one if we lump together a variety of different disciplines and approaches. Nonetheless, we might say that both aim to relieve suffering, both try to improve the human condition and access greater wisdom.

In psychotherapy we learn to be aware of feelings. We know it doesn't work to suppress, repress, or avoid them. This can be one of the traps of taking up a spiritual path that does not allow for communication of feelings. The challenge in psychotherapy is how to express a feeling and communicate it without attack, without doing harm to yourself or another person. It needs to be brought to light, because if you try to push it away or hide it, it usually gets worse.

Self-observation that is taught in Vipassana meditation can be very useful in working with emotions such as anger, fear, grief, or any negative emotion. In practicing meditation, you become much more aware of how feelings arise in your experience. Also in meditation we learn something about how the mind works. In psychotherapy we are also working with the mind. Many people see it as a process of healing for the mind. I think both psychotherapy and meditation can contribute to healing the mind and healing the heart.

Do you think all religions lead to the same place?

To say that all religions lead to the same place is rather superficial because religions offer different paths that lead to different experiences. I would say that all religions ultimately address the basic human experience of life and death and our relationship to the cosmos. In that sense they are all, as Carl Jung said, "therapies for the soul." That does not mean that they are all the same. There are significant differences between religions, yet they all address the deep issues of meaning and values in human life.

Do you think that relationships can get in the way of spiritual growth?

No, not necessarily. They *can,* but they can also contribute to spiritual growth. They can be an integral part of a path of spiritual growth. I think that as we progress along a wholesome spiritual path our relationships improve. We learn a lot about who and what we are in relationships. They are very much a part of human experience and recognizing our relatedness, not only to each other, but also to all life and to the earth itself is part of our spiritual awakening.

Do you feel there is a basic difference between maleness and femaleness, besides the body?

There are important biological differences between men and women. However, the more conscious and evolved people are, the less differences there seem to be between men and women. In other words, we all have within us both masculine and feminine characteristics. The more we grow toward wholeness, the more we become aware of both masculine and feminine aspects of the psyche. Sometimes we think of it in terms of dynamic and receptive energy. We all need both. The more well-developed all of our faculties are—for example our capacities for thinking, feeling, sensing, and intuiting—the less marked the differences between the sexes. Of course there are always differences between individuals.

How does the idea that we move from one trance state to another relate to being aware and to what we call enlightenment?

There are degrees of being awake or asleep. In practicing dream yoga, I have worked on recognizing that I am dreaming when I am asleep and also when I am awake. The next step is to realize that we are dreaming all the time. According to Tibetan teachings, if awareness can be maintained twenty-four hours every day, it may continue after death.

What do you think of death?

Since I have not died yet, I cannot speak from experience. However, from all the accounts of near-death experience I have heard about, it seems that death is not something to be afraid of. Part of being enlightened means realizing that there is nothing to fear. It may well be that our beliefs will affect what happens to us at death. It may be that for some people death is the end, and for some it is not. Coming to terms with death as an integral part of life is one of the challenges on the spiritual path. Acknowledging the fact that sooner or later we are all going to die enhances our appreciation of life. Perhaps enlightenment means being fully awake to all of life and death.

23

BROTHER DAVID
STEINDL-RAST

There was a similarity among many of the people I interviewed. It was the eyes. In most people as they get older, their bodies seem less energetic. They look older. The people I interviewed were different. The energy seemed to have left their bodies and gone to their eyes, making them brighter and more loving. Brother David's eyes were like that.

I expected the monastery, where I met Brother David, to be disciplined and solemn. At some retreat centers, the food line is often quiet and the movements are measured. Here, it was different. There was a feeling of festivity in the air.

It was a joy meeting Brother David. Now I know why the monks call themselves Brothers. He acted and felt as though he were my brother. As we talked and looked down at the ocean from his monastic hilltop, his brotherly arm always seemed to be on my shoulder. I felt as if he considered us old friends.

Whenever I am around what I consider to be a healthy expression of Christianity, I remember the hypocrisy and repression I was taught as a child being raised a Christian.

When I was young, I attended a Catholic high school. Once I went on a retreat, and the priest who led the retreat was named Father Boyle. "In the army we said confession face to face," he growled. "There was no partition between us. We'll do it the same way here so that I can see you man to man." If John Wayne had been a priest, he would have been Father Boyle.

Father Boyle had no teeth. In college he blocked a punt to win the game, and the punter's foot came up and kicked him in the mouth, knocking out his teeth. He seemed to revel in toughness. "I remember one teammate in particular," he told us. "In the middle of a game he thought he had a stick up his nose, so he pulled it out with pliers—it turned out to be his nose cartilage."

On the last night of the retreat before our last confession, Father Boyle brought the seven retreatants together. "Boys," he said, "during World War II, I was the company's chaplain. One weekend the sergeant gave all the men weekend passes and told them to go out and find women—to commit adultery. It was in Germany, so the men went out and found themselves German women. When the weekend was over, only half the men came back."

Father Boyle then looked at each of us, sending his fear into our transfixed eyes. "The men who didn't come back were found dead in bed with knives in their backs. These men had been stabbed by the women while in the act. Now, boys, I don't know if these men went to hell for what they did—but they could have." As Father Boyle paused, my soul seemed to teeter on the edge of eternal damnation. "And boys," he added, "it's time for confession."

Meeting Brother David now, I can see the life-affirming spirit of Christianity. Where were the Brother Davids then? Why aren't there more of them?

Brother David Steindl-Rast, O.S.B., has written several books on contemplative life. Born in Vienna, he studied art, anthropology, and psychology there, holding degrees from the Vienna Academy of Fine Arts and the University of Vienna. In 1953 he joined the Benedictine Monastery of Mount Savior in Elmira, N.Y. He has been involved in the monastic renewal in the United States and in the dialogue of Oriental and Western spirituality.

On what beliefs or truths do you base your life?

As a Benedictine monk, I stand in the Christian tradition, its catholic form, which I would spell with a small c. *Catholic* means "all-embracing."

I believe in the human heart. I believe in Common Sense (capital *C*, capital *S*), which is the deepest insight we have in the depths of our hearts and is common to all of us. It is quite different from just reasonableness or conventionalities. It's a very deep personal thing, yet it unites each of us with all of us.

Ultimately, when the heart is cultivated, wisdom and compassion result in the direction of the human "other." The human heart has something like a built-in compass needle. It always points due north. Those who use the term *God,* if they use it correctly, use it for that direction in which the human heart points. It's more a direction than anything else, as far as we know.

Do you believe in a God or Ultimate Reality? What is It like?

I don't believe in "a God." I believe in God, which is quite a different thing. Christians do not believe in A GOD; they believe in GOD.

The lowest common denominator for God is the direction of the human heart or the direction of our belonging. God is the reference point to our belonging. In our best moments, we experience that we belong. We are not orphaned in the world; we are at home here. The ultimate reference point is what I call God.

Not every human being who is open and dedicated to the quest of the human heart makes all these discoveries. Not all traditions have made them. But any individual can make the discovery of that belonging that is our lowest common denominator. We can make the discovery that this belonging is always mutual. Whenever we belong, even with things that belong to us, to a certain extent we belong to them. It can even get to the point where we are enslaved by them. Plants have certain claims on us when they belong to us. If you have a plant, you have to water it, do certain things for it. Animals are even more so. Human beings can't even tell anymore who belongs to whom. Which friend belongs to which? Both belong to one another; it's mutual. Then we can extrapolate and see that the Ultimate Reference Point of our belonging must be the One who belongs to us. All of a sudden, we have a personal element introduced here. We believe not in God as a person (Christians do not believe that God is "a person"), but God has all the *perfection* of personhood and none of the limitations. Because I am a person, I cannot be you. That doesn't bother me right now, but if we were

247

in love, it would bother me very much. I would want to *be* you; I'd want to *become* you. That's a limitation of being a person. We see that God has all the perfections and none of the limitations of being a person. God can be you and can be me; God can be every plant and every animal and every thing that's around.

I believe in heaven! But I don't believe in heaven as a place somewhere else. Heaven is everything transfigured by God's presence. Therefore, for many people heaven starts here, and for many people, hell starts here. Life that is transfigured by love and compassion and wisdom is heaven. It's not complete heaven, but it's a beginning.

We have all experienced heaven and hell. In our best moments, in what Abraham Maslow calls the "peak experience," we have experienced heaven. This taste of heaven is a moment in and out of time. It is not really in time. In a peak experience, it may just be a split second and seem like a long time, or it may be an hour and seem like a split second. We are in the present at that moment. Most of the time, half of us are hanging onto the past, and the other half are stretching out to the future. There's nothing left for the present moment. But in our peak experiences, we are really there, and this is *now*. That is where we experience heaven.

When my time is up, when I die, time is up. I do not believe that time goes on for me. That's not death. There may be all sorts of surprises in store for me, but then that wasn't what I call death. There may be some other life after this life, but there's not much evidence for that, either. That's sort of an interpretation of other things. The way I see it, when I die my time is up, and I don't have to worry anymore about anything after. That's a great relief to me. If I had to worry about things going on and on and on, that would not be particularly helpful to me, for my peace of mind. But I have a measured time, and then my time is up.

When I am free from time, which is the one thing that always pulls me out of the now, the past continuously eating up the future, when time is up, then I have now. And the now doesn't pass away because the now isn't in time. Then I have all these heavenly moments all at once. Do you see what I mean? Of course, we don't know too much about it. This is just an awkward way of speaking about it, but it seems to be a contemporary way to speak about what heaven could be like. For me, this conversation that we have now is a wonderful thing! If I were still more alive, I would see it

248

still more glowingly, but certainly either it's part of my heaven or too bad! The joke is on me! It ought to be.

We have all experienced hell, as well. By hell, I mean alienation. The essence of all that is positive is belonging, mutual belonging. Love is that Yes! to our ultimate belonging. The opposite is No to belonging; it's alienation. It is being cut off from everything—from ourselves, from all others, from God, Ultimate Reality, from everything. Even as little children we have already experienced hell. For instance, we are sulking somewhere. Everybody else is having a good time at our own birthday party, and maybe we are standing in the corner stamping our foot and we've completely forgotten why we are there. We want nothing more than to get out, and yet we *don't* want to get out. We are in this bind. We have caught ourselves in that. That's what they call hell. We have cut ourselves off, and we're too proud to come out of it. We can lock ourselves in there, but in life, we experience over and over and over again that God brings us out of our hell. Because God is the ultimate cause of everything, through all sorts of intermediated causes, He brings us out of that—over and over again. Something may happen at this party—somebody falls off a chair or a dog comes in and everybody starts laughing, and we start laughing too. We have forgotten why we're in this corner, and everything's fine again and we snap out of this hell. When we are grown up, it is sometimes a little more difficult to come out of hell, but again and again something helps us come out of it.

We stay in this hell, however, when we lose our way, when we lose ourselves. In adult life, often an obstacle gets in the way. One of these obstacles is attachment. In hell, everybody hangs onto something or other. Experientially we know that. Often we see that our friends hang onto some ideal, idea, or grudge about themselves. The hanging on is the problem.

Impatience is another obstacle. I can't wait, can't wait. Can't really be here, always itchy, always running. People who are in hell are not just the depressed ones sitting there, but some of those who are zooming around from this appointment to that appointment, running around and around, always doing something.

Laziness is a third obstacle. I couldn't care less. I just feel blah; nothing interests me. This is because we don't take little things gratefully. *Gratefulness* is my key word for everything. We can learn gratefulness. It's the only appropriate attitude toward life. If you learn gratefulness, everything makes sense. We are no longer lazy. We are no longer attached. We are no longer impatient. We begin to love—we *are* loving because gratefulness implies that Yes to belonging, and there we are!

What do you think the purpose of life is?

You have all these casual questions! Life in my experience has meaning more than purpose. It's like a dance or play. A dance has no particular purpose. The main thing about a dance or play is that you give yourself to it and that it has meaning. You dance not in order to get somewhere; you sing not in order to get finished as soon as possible. But you sing in order to sing; you dance because it's meaningful to you. There are many purposes in life, but for me, purpose doesn't seem to apply. For me, there's meaning.

God is the source of meaning. The human heart is restless until it finds meaning. Purpose is not enough for us. No amount of purpose is enough. We want meaning, which is quite a different thing. Meaning is something that's given to us. Although we make a great effort to find meaning, we always receive it as a gift. It's always a given. The whole world is a given world. We can think of God as the Ultimate Giver, as the Ultimate Source of meaning and the Giver of Meaning.

The Universe exists out of love. This is the Christian answer to purpose. What is love? Fullness of being that's overflowing. Fullness of life that's overflowing. If we think of God as being personal, then God loves. And God is fullness of being. Therefore, God is love, self-giving, overflowing of being with everything that's around, because God's love gives it to us. God gives it. When we look at something and really see it, that's what we see in it. When we see the love aspect of it, it makes sense; it has meaning. When we don't see the love aspect, it doesn't make sense. So, in all natural things we find that love aspect. Christians speak about it as everything being the "word of God." God speaks to us through everything there is.

There are ways of dealing with Ultimate Reality called *via negativa* and *via positiva,* and they are mutually complementary. In the Buddhist tradition, there is largely what we call *via negativa* with a bit of the *via positiva*. Christianity is mostly *via positiva* and very little *via negativa*. The more we get into the mystical core of a tradition—even in Christianity—the more we get of the

250

via negativa. However, that doesn't mean that it's better—more mystical or more elevated. *Both* are valid.

In the Christian tradition this is expressed in the mystery of the Blessed Trinity. What we call the Father is the Godhead, the Abyss of Silence, the Ineffable. The second person of the trinity—with "person" very carefully used—is God completely *expressing* all that God is and the eternal good. The third is the understanding, the Holy Spirit. Understanding is our own understanding of the divine reality that comes by realizing that the *via negativa* is the *via positiva* and the *via positiva* is the *via negativa.* Before one realizes that, one doesn't have understanding. *Understanding* ties the two together.

What is the highest ideal a person can reach? How is it attained?

Finding fulfillment is different from one person to another. I don't see it as a competition for a particular ideal; rather, I think in terms of reaching personal fulfillment.

We are very different from one another in many, many ways. In the human heart, we are united, but from there on, we are very different from one another. I affirm these differences. I enjoy them, or sometimes I don't enjoy them but make an effort to enjoy and affirm them because it takes this great variety to create this higher unity. If each one of us becomes what we are meant to be, then all of us together will be what we as humans, and what the whole universe, are meant to be.

A person can reach this ideal through obedience, but obedience, in this sense, means something quite different from doing what somebody else tells us to do, like a dog in an obedience school. That's not what I'm talking about. The obedience that I'm talking about is a deep listening with the heart.

Obedience in a monastic form or religion is a *method* and has the goal and purpose to teach us the virtue of obedience. Properly pursued, it can lead us to deep listening. The goal of this obedience training is no longer to have to be told what to do and what not to do, but to have learned, moment by moment, to listen to the present moment. The present moment will tell us what it is time to do and what is right not to do. It's not only a matter of dos and don'ts. Actually, obedience goes much further than that: to finding meaning in life. When we listen to the bird, the bird doesn't tell us what to do, but I call that obedience, too. We are listening with our whole heart, and we find the meaning that comes to us only through having listened to the bird singing. That is the method.

Will all people eventually reach the ideal?

Though it is very difficult to find evidence for it, I believe in my heart of hearts that if one believes in God and believes God is love and is almighty, then God is powerful enough to bring everyone to self-fulfillment, because that's what people are created for. So I trust in it, even though the evidence is sometimes against it.

There are three obstacles we have to overcome. Each one of us has all three of them, but sometimes one is in the foreground, sometimes another. In our younger years, one may be in the foreground, and in our older age, a different one may be in the foreground.

The goal is to listen to what it is time to do, what is right and appropriate in this present moment, but we can miss the present moment in three ways.

One is attachment. It's clinging to something that in itself may be very good but is not the thing for the present moment. We have to let it go in order to be free and responsive in the present moment.

The second is impatience. We're always ahead of ourselves, preoccupied with what might come, what should come, or what we wish would come.

A person may think, If I have neither impatience nor attachment, then everything is fine and I am in the present moment. But there's a third obstacle. We can be in the present moment, but not awake. We're asleep, lazy. So even though we are not attached and not impatient, we may be too lazy to rise to the occasion.

We counteract these three obstacles with love or compassion. If we are really loving or compassionate in the right sense of loving, we are *not attached*. We are lovingly upholding the other, and we are not clinging to the other. If we really have this loving attitude, this life-affirming, compassionate, wise attitude, we will counteract attachment by detachment. But immediately we have to be very careful, because detachment can be cold detachment, and that's not loving. It would have to be a paradoxical thing, namely, affectionate detachment. It doesn't sound right, but that's exactly it: affectionate detachment.

When we are in love, we are also alive and alert. We're *not asleep*. We are *not impatient,* because genuine love is very patient with the other. To counter impatience, there is of course patience, but there's a kind of patience that couldn't care less, and there's no difficulty being patient in that way. That kind of patience is not the loving kind of patience. I would say the correct attitude is a fervent patience or passionate patience, not a wishy-washy, blah, couldn't-care-less patience.

Regarding laziness, the opposite is of course fervor—zeal, fervor, aliveness. That, too, could be either impatient or attached, however. It has to incorporate the best quality of fervor. There is a very beautiful quality to laziness if you look at a cat that's lazing around. It's relaxed in the sense of not being tense, so the opposite of bad laziness must be fervor, but a relaxed fervor, a very easygoing fervor.

What's so nice about lazy people is that they're easygoing, so fervor has to be easygoing. And what's so nice about attached people is that they're really caring. Therefore, the detachment must be really caring. What's so nice about impatient people is that they're really fervent, so real patience should incorporate what's nicest about impatient people, which is fervor. It should be fervent patience.

We all know what it feels like to be in love, but one very quickly falls out of love and then one falls in love and then one falls out of love again. So this "falling in love" is only a kind of trick that life, or God, or whatever, plays on us to show us what it's like. We must *rise* in love—not just *fall* in love, but *rise* to love. We know what love is like; we know how wonderful it is; we know how it transforms the world. Now let's do it—and not wait until it happens! Passionate patience and caring detachment and easygoing fervor are the ways.

What do you think about death?

When I listen to what other people have to say about death—not only Christians but people from other religions, too—I feel they are not taking death seriously enough. For me, death is not a sleep where we wake up on some other side. There's nothing that indicates that, and I wouldn't even personally desire it. My heart of hearts does not desire to wake up somewhere else. This "now" is plenty for me.

This measured time, whatever it could be—sixty or seventy or eighty years or whatever—is plenty. I'm now sixty-three, and I feel that even at my age I've had all that I can possibly ask of life. If I die today, I will be very grateful. I don't need to wake up anywhere else because when time is out, I *have* all this. I cannot lose it. I have my best moments that happened thirty years ago. I have them as much as time permits in the sense that time always gnaws on them and sort of clouds them, but I have them now. I possess them. I can remember them, and in this memory they *are*.

"All is always now," as T. S. Eliot says in the Four Quartets. When I enter into this *now*, which happens when time is up, that's what I call death. Death is that in which afterward, there is nothing. As I understand, it's the end point of time. Anything else seems to be a little soft pedaling and a little too tame. It *is* the end, so I better make good use of the time that I have.

Death is that after which there is nothing, because there's no time after it. I do believe in beyond life, however, but most people who say that they believe in afterlife mean the same thing as life now.

Why do you think there is suffering?

Suffering, as I see it, is a consequence of our human freedom for self expression. We can *willingly* unfold in harmony with the inner workings of reality, but we can also *willfully* express what is not our true self and so clash with reality. This clash is suffering. All the more so at the edges, where willfulness rubs against willfulness making one another suffer.

This is suffering from a bird's eye view, but when we speak from the side of the sufferer, then it seems very important for me to distinguish between two kinds of suffering. One is *with* the grain, and one is *against* the grain. The suffering *against* the grain springs from attachment, laziness, and impatience. The suffering *with* the grain is the patient suffering; it is a zealous and detached suffering that is creative and life-giving.

In the whole biblical tradition, both Hebrew and Christian, wherever there is talk about suffering (and there's a lot of talk about suffering), the image used is always that of birth pains. Positive suffering is birth-giving. It gives birth to the child within us. It gives our life for the world, as a mother gives her life for the child. It's always life-giving.

In that sense, there is no real difference between the Christian view of suffering and the Buddhist view of suffering. There can be a Christian misunderstanding of what suffering is, which clashes with either a Buddhist understanding or a Buddhist misunderstanding of what suffering is. But if we take the correct Buddhist understanding and the correct Christian understanding, both reject the suffering *against* the grain, and both affirm the suffering *with* the grain.

It's very significant that Buddhists as well as Christians affirm suffering *with* the grain. I was once at a small group interview with the Dalai Lama, and someone asked, "Your Holiness, what do you have to say to the view that Christians wallow in suffering while Buddhists have this wonderful way of overcoming suffering?"

The Dalai Lama immediately saw what was wrong in the question and corrected it. "Do not think that suffering is overcome by leaving pain behind. That would be a mistake. According to Buddhist teaching, suffering is overcome by bearing pain for the sake of others."

That's the bodhisattva ideal, and there's no better Christian statement than that. Suffering is overcome—because everybody wants to overcome suffering, Christians just as much as everybody else—by bearing pain for the sake of others. So we have Christ, who corresponds to the bodhisattva, and every Christian who does that sort of thing corresponds to the Buddhist ideal, like Christ.

Why is there evil?

Evil is inseparable from freedom of choice. Without freedom of choice there could be no love, which is our highest good. That we have freedom of choice cannot be denied. For even those who deny our freedom take credit in their heart of hearts when they make life-affirming choices. Freedom of choice does not consist in choosing between alternatives: it is the opportunity to choose reality, to go with the flow. Its opposite is to close ourselves off to this flow. Thus, evil is merely negative: our resistance to go with the flow of love. Evil is our self-destructive refusal of the opportunity to love. In my trust, in my faith (I equate faith and trust; it's the same for me, this ultimate trust), I trust even sometimes against the apparent evidence that ultimately even the freedom that has been abused and has gone astray is caught up in a greater meaning. It ultimately has meaning, ultimately makes sense, and is ultimately redeemed.

Do the major religions all lead to the same place?

That's one way of putting it, but it seems a little too narrow to me. I affirm what stands behind your question, but I don't like the imagery. Baker Roshi says that the different religious traditions don't converge by climbing up the same peak and meeting there, as though they each come up different sides, shake hands, and raise a common flag. Rather, they all explore the same territory and lose themselves in it. That's a much better image. If we use the other image in which they all come to the same point, then they would have to agree in the end and in everything, because from that same point everything appears alike. If, on the other hand, we allow them to explore this infinite territory, what theists would call the God-space, then we can allow for the possibility that each one discovers a completely different country and it's still the same space. They never meet, but they all explore the same space. In the end, they will meet, because they have already met in their depth. They all explore the same territory, namely the territory toward which that compass of the human heart points, that territory of the God-realm or Ultimate Reality or whatever you want to call it.

I've had many wonderful opportunities to talk with representatives of other spiritual traditions, and the best proof to your question is that the highly achieved Buddhists (by Buddhist standards) get along wonderfully with the highly achieved Christians (by Christian standards). One could parallel that with any other tradition. People who have really made it in their own tradition are at home in the other traditions. They may not have been exposed to or may not know the other traditions, but once they meet—when the saints meet—they all get along fine.

I'm a Benedictine monk, and I've had opportunities to spend time with other traditions. I've spent quite a bit of time with Zen Buddhists, a little bit with Tibetan Buddhists, a little bit with yoga people. When I'm with people from other traditions, I enjoy, but I don't mix practices.

When I am in the Benedictine monastery, my practice is the Jesus prayer. It's basically the repetition of the name of Jesus as a mindfulness exercise. It is a kind of mantra or prayer. I use a short form. It is just, "Lord Jesus, Mercy, Lord Jesus, Mercy." Sometimes I use the beads and say it in rhythm with my breathing. I breathe in "Lord Jesus" and breathe out "mercy." One focuses oneself in that way. I use the rosary as a pneumatic device. It helps to train me so that every time I move a bead, I say this mantra (or internally say this mantra), even if I am talking with someone or doing something else. I have this inner motion, like a light that clicks on and off. It's there, and I do not lose sight of it completely. Or sometimes I do, but the training is toward not losing sight of it, even when I talk with you and do other things. It repeats itself, and I don't lose sight of it.

The sound of the Jesus prayer has not been particularly stressed, but there is some sort of an inner sound. It is not a thought; it is an inner sound. I suppose if we chanted it (as some Christians do), that might be more helpful, because it would be like a song that we can't get out of our head. It comes over and over again. But it is a little bit like that anyway, even without the music. The whole environment and daily life in the monastery is set up to foster mindfulness, so everything we do in a monastery is designed to help us be more mindful, which means more grateful, more loving, more compassionate.

If you could meet anyone throughout history, whom would you like to meet and what would you ask that person?

The German poet, Essendorff. I like his poetry very much. He's a nineteenth-century poet, a late Romantic poet. As far as I know, he's never been skiing, so I've often thought I'd like to meet Essendorff and go skiing with him, because he has all these wonderful experiences of nature and he's never been on skis. I thought that might be a nice thing to do.

Maybe I would like to meet Jesus, but I meet Jesus all the time. That is, I'd like to meet the historical Jesus Christ, because there is quite a difference between the historical Jesus and his historical message, on the one hand, and the message the different Christian traditions have handed down, on the other. I am very interested in the historical Jesus—what he really taught and what he was really like. Also, what is the relevance of the message of Jesus to us today? Not the message about Jesus, but the message of Jesus, the message this man brought and promoted. I read about it, write about it, think about it, and talk about it.

The Austrian Maria Theresa was empress from 1740 to 1780, and she was the ruler, a real peacemaker and a real mother of the country. I dream of her quite frequently, about as often as I think of my grandmother. I would like to meet her and kiss her hand.

If you could change anything in life, what would you want to change?

I would set up a world court, or I would give power to the world court that already exists by revamping the United Nations so that they were really a federal government of the world—a world government. Any problems that threaten our lives, like nuclear extinction, poverty, hunger, exploitation, oppression, or environmental abuse, will require order. This international Wild West, international anarchy, where whoever has the bigger gun shoots the other one down, doesn't work. Order can be reached only by world federation, and I hope that it will come within my lifetime.

The biggest problem in life is survival. It is against all statistical probability we haven't destroyed ourselves and the planet already. If we want to talk about any other problem, it is on the presumption of being around. So if we want to be around, we have to do something about order. The key to survival seems to be a confederation of nations, a world government that has power and can enforce law on the world, a law to which the nations freely submit.

The second greatest problem is that two-thirds of the human family go to bed hungry. It's completely within our power to give everybody enough to eat. This could be achieved through world government. Before people have enough to eat, there's not much point in talking about anything else.

The next thing would be to help people find fulfilled lives. Just because people have enough to eat doesn't mean that they have fulfilled lives. There are many people in the United States who have enough to eat, and more than enough, but have anything but fulfilled lives. We have to raise the level of human dignity and wisdom.

Some people think that personal relationships interfere with spiritual growth. What do you think?

It used to be a Christian bias that if one really wanted to be a good Christian, one had better become a monk or a nun. This is no longer generally held to be true, and people in general are more enlightened about it now. I've been a monk for thirty-five years, and I appreciate it because it is a tremendous help for the kind of person I am. I have met many people inside and outside the monastery, however, for whom monasticism is no help at all. It would be a tremendous hindrance, in every respect, to their becoming fully who they are; it would be a hindrance in their religious life. All that matters is that we become ourselves. We don't get *away* from relationships in the monastery. We have relationships in and outside the monastery. All relationships are the material by which we become who we are. We don't become ourselves in a vacuum. Relationships might be more selective in the monastery, but then they often have more intensity. Even wrong relationships show us what we have to learn. Somehow, we learn it by working the relationship out.

Do you think there's a basic difference between men and women besides the physical difference?

Yes. In my experience there's quite a difference between the two. These differences are very charming and necessary, but they can also be very painful and upsetting.

I experience the working together between men and women as often problematic. I have been privileged to know extremely fine women and extremely fine men, and I have no disrespect for women, but precisely because of my respect, I see that the cooperation between men and women is an extremely difficult thing. The reason seems to be that women think globally and men think linearly (although this is a cliché to a certain extent). I would not want women to think primarily linearly, and I would not want men to think primarily globally, but the difficulty is in pooling these two ways of thinking.

This is a difficulty that one should not underestimate. It is very hard for someone who thinks linearly to appropriate what is best in global thinking; it is very hard for someone who thinks globally to appropriate the linear thinking. For instance, I get quite impatient when I listen to lectures by women, even women I respect and admire, because they're real women and they think globally. Their way of presenting stuff drives me up the wall. But then I turn this around and imagine what they must think of my linear way of presenting things. We may have to make a great effort to bridge this gap between linear and global thinking.

Of course, the finest thinkers among men also think globally, and the finest women have the capacity of thinking linearly, but for most men and women, cooperating effectively is a very difficult task that hasn't been sufficiently seen in its dimensions.

What in life makes you happy? sad? angry?

Children make me happy. Animals make me happy. I love cats, music, singing, hiking, beautiful landscapes, the ocean, the mountains.

Almost everything that is in newspapers makes me sad. I'm saddened by exploitation, oppression, lies, destruction of our environment, unnecessary suffering, big promises with nothing behind them. In history, there are big gaps between the ideas and teachings of Christ and what the church is doing. It always was, and unfortunately always will be, that way.

Lies make me angry. It makes me angry when, in a democratic country like the United States, only about 50 percent go to the polls at election time. People close their eyes to what our government is doing. I have had the privilege of traveling, and if we open our eyes, we can see that what America stands for in the world is not peace; it's not positive. It's destructive. It's just terrible. That makes me angry because I'm powerless. (I have one vote among two hundred million.) Anger is the emotion we feel when confronted with an evil we feel powerless against.

What made you approach life this way?

My parents, especially my mother, my education, teachers, and of course my monastic formation. I was twenty-six or twenty-seven when I joined the monastery, and it is an ongoing formation. When I was ten, I attended a progressive Catholic boarding school run by lay people who had the kind of spirituality that nowadays would be considered very progressive in the church. That was back in 1936. I had those teachers in Austria for two years, and then the Nazis came in 1938.

I lived my teenage years under the Nazis. I continued to go to the school, although the Nazis changed the director, teachers, and administration. My classmates were the same, and we went underground. Many of them went to jail, but we met underground, we camped underground, and we went on hikes together.

I'm twenty-nine and you are sixty-three. I'm wondering, if you think back to when you were twenty-nine—what do you see as the difference? What have you learned?

Congratulations! Twenty-nine is a wonderful age. I can't honestly say that I would like to be twenty-nine again, but there are tremendous possibilities before you. The difference is that you're expanding and I'm contracting. That's a positive thing.

As you grow older, you see that you'll have to leave everything behind and that you'll have no further influence on anybody. You came naked and you go naked. Right now, I'm still encumbered with projects, relationships, books, and possessions. I'm learning to disencumber myself. Even as a monk, one has lots of stuff accumulated. It is not because we like it, not because we cling to these souvenirs, but because we feel responsible to them. But there are limitations. We can go only so far with all these different things and then we have to let go of all of them. And sooner or later, we just can't do things anymore. We just don't have the physical strength; we get forgetful.

At one time, when I was complaining about the things I was doing and the things I had to do, a very wise person said to me, "If you want to know what you really want to do, just look at what you're doing, because if you didn't really want to do it, you wouldn't be doing it."

24

THE CIRCLE IS COMPLETE

Years ago, I searched for a reason and an answer to the suffering I'd experienced and could not leave behind. This book led me back to that forgotten place where I had left myself—and my life—behind.

I always felt that if I could go back and experience my mother's death again, I would find that thing I lost. I had felt detached when she died, as if I had witnessed her death from a vantage point high up in the corner of the room. During the last few years, I've felt I left a part of myself there—at the scene of the crime. I didn't know what it was, but there was something valuable left behind, something I could find only by fully feeling what had happened.

Looking for what was lost, I sought a psychotherapist and had many sessions with him. On one occasion, I descended deeply into myself. Once again, I was a small boy, and my mother was dying. We were watching television when my mother lost consciousness. I ran to call a neighbor, but my mother regained consciousness and called me back to her. I helped her into the living room. There, she lay down on the couch under a large picture of the Last Supper and stopped breathing. I placed my hands on her head and prayed for a miracle. When it didn't come, I slumped to the floor. I felt my will to live leaving, as if I were also dying.

This time, however, instead of seeing her death from a far corner of the room, I stayed next to her, and because I stayed next to her, I experienced something I had missed before. It was a light that emanated from her body. As it expanded, it engulfed me and continued until it filled the room. It was a feeling of tremendous love and peace. I was ecstatic. My heart had never felt so open, so loved.

Then that experience of eternity turned in on itself and began to recede. Its warmth and love left me, like the rays of the sun blocked by clouds. As the light pulled away from me, I was left with the intense anguish of knowing my mother was leaving me. I felt as if I were dying.

The light contracted to a fine point and moved to the upper corner of the room. It seemed to pause there, teetering between two worlds, and then it disappeared, imploding yet somehow simultaneously exploding in my chest. I was moved in a way I couldn't understand.

That day was the most tragic, horrific experience of my life, and it was also the most loving and beautiful moment. I had never felt so loved. In this paradox was the key to my anguish. *How could life and death, joy and suffering, eternal love and tragic limitation all exist in the same moment?*

My heart was broken by that revelation, and the breaking of my heart released this book. Now it is almost done. I did not seek to find the meaning of happy, pleasant, or joyful experiences, only the meaning of unhappy experiences. Accepting the pleasant and rejecting the painful is, in part, what alienated me from life. When life is divided, each part shrivels and dies, and life no longer makes sense.

I was given a painful gift when Stephen Levine said, "Meaning slows things down and keeps us in the mind. It keeps us in that place of confusion and separation. I understand meaning to be a buffer shielding us from a painful and confusing reality."

Toni Packer said, "The one who has to ask this question feels separate from life. 'Me' and 'my life.' Because of that separation, there is the haunting question of what the purpose of life is. When there is no feeling of separation, then there is just living, just life, no one standing outside of it and worrying about the 'meaning of this.' If you see something and it is so, it is so! If you don't see, then you are afraid and you have to believe."

The people I interviewed have taught me to be a human being. Mother Teresa, in all her wonderful, unassuming simplicity, showed me that by being truly human, we touch that part of humanity that touches God.

Suzuki Roshi wrote, "When we express our true nature, we are human beings. When we do not, we do not know who we are. . . . To be a human being is to be a Buddha. Buddha nature is just another name for human nature, our true human nature.... When your practice is calm and ordinary, everyday life itself is enlightenment. Eventually you will resume your true nature. That is to say, your own true nature will resume itself."

The first time I met Jagir Singh, he wouldn't shake my hand. He said he had grease on his hands from working on his cars. After a few months, he confided in me that the real reason he doesn't shake hands with people is that the last time he shook hands with a man, the man complained that all the skin on that hand had peeled off.

One morning after ten or fifteen people had come for cures and advice, a man walked in. "Guruji," the man said to Jagir Singh in Nepalese, "I have a problem."

"Please speak in English," Jagir Singh said to the man.

The man worriedly told Jagir Singh his problem while I sat to the side listening. After the man finished, Jagir Singh closed his eyes and sat quietly. After a few moments, he opened his eyes, and turned to me. "Well, Mr. Bill, what do you think this man should do?"

I was caught by surprise but managed to give an answer I thought was quite good. Jagir Singh listened very intently to what I said, then he turned back to the man and told him something else.

I spent my last night in Nepal with Jagir Singh and his family. When it was time for me to leave, Jagir Singh rubbed his chin and looked off into the distance. His profile was that of a visionary and seemed to point to the place where the unknown becomes the known. The wind blew gently through the open window as he spoke. "You know, Mr. Bill, if you continue this search you will become..." and then his voice trailed off as the wind died down, leaving his words in the distance.

It has come full circle now, and his eyes look to me. With his elbows on his knees, Patrick, who is thirteen years old, rests his head in his hands. From time to time, he digs at the floor with the sole of his shoe as though he were trying to wipe away some unseen spot. His freshly-scrubbed hands wipe at his eyes. When he looks up at me, I see an innocence suddenly made old. He has that look on his face. His father, who is my brother, has just died.

Will it help if I tell him there's a reason for everything, but we don't always know what it is? Will it help if I tell him I was his age when my father and mother died and that as a result of those losses, I am able to be here with him and understand his pain? Will it help to tell him it was "God's will"?

I have rarely seen a face so alive as Patrick's at this moment. I see a familiar pain and anguish in his face. It is my face.

When he cries, I say, "Don't let anyone tell you a man can't cry." We cry together. If he wants to talk about his father a hundred or a million times, I'll listen, because I am listening to myself.

TYING ROCKS TO CLOUDS

I have seen cosmic beings and other worlds,
yet without seeing a flower it is nothing.

I have stopped my breath and been at one,
yet without the love of two it is nothing.

I have felt pure joy and all that it brings,
yet the greatest is to feel the pain of others.

I have predicted the future and the thoughts of others,
yet my own honesty eludes me.

I have been angelic, virtuous, and of pure heart,
yet without being human it is nothing.

Why do I crave other worlds
when the needy are here?

Why am I content with the joy of my world
when others cry?

What does this mean?

After communing with God and defeating the devil,
Jesus simply said, "I am a man."

Though he had the power to see all and everything,
the Buddha was accidentally poisoned and died.

We live side by side with paradox and illusion.
Of these things it is hard to speak.

To tie a rock to a cloud—
is this possible?

And if it is,
does the cloud descend to meet the rock
or does the rock rise to meet the cloud?